3rd Workshop on EVENTS: Definition, Detection, Coreference, and Representation 2015

Held at NAACL HLT 2015

Denver, Colorado, USA
4 June 2015

ISBN: 978-1-5108-0439-5

Printed from e-media with permission by:

Curran Associates, Inc.
57 Morehouse Lane
Red Hook, NY 12571

Some format issues inherent in the e-media version may also appear in this print version.

Printed by Curran Associates, Inc. (2015)

Association for Computational Linguistics
209 N. Eighth Street
Stroudsburg, Pennsylvania 18360

Phone: 1-570-476-8006
Fax: 1-570-476-0860

acl@aclweb.org

Additional copies of this publication are available from:

Curran Associates, Inc.
57 Morehouse Lane
Red Hook, NY 12571 USA
Phone: 845-758-0400
Fax: 845-758-2634
Email: curran@proceedings.com
Web: www.proceedings.com

Introduction

This is the third international workshop in a series devoted to ongoing interest in the computation-oriented definition, representation, and detection of events, event coreference, event structure, slot filling, and multi-event sequences (scripts).

We are very pleased to have as invited speaker Bernardo Magnini from FBK/irst, Trento, Italy. Bernardo has a long history of building superb NLP software systems that reflect a deep understanding of nature of language.

As before, the workshop is primarily structured around interactive discussions, guided by examples. We scheduled three main questions for discussion:

- Definition and categorization of events and other inter-event relations: What are events, states, and eventualities? How best to represent and organize events? What relations obtain between events? Discussions of coreference and the other relations that link them, such as cause and precondition, deepening questions left unanswered in the prior workshops. Discussion leader: Palmer.
- Event mentions: When exactly is an event mentioned? How many events occur in complex mentions such as "they shot the snake dead"? How should aspectuals and event modifiers be best treated? When are two events the same? Discussions of ongoing event mention annotation and the complexities of the annotation rules. Discussion leader: Hovy.
- Complex event structure and scripts: How can complex event structures be decomposed? How can one identify subevents of complex vents, and order them into scripts? Where do event scripts begin and end? How do they relate to participants and their goals? The manual and automated creation of event scripts, evinced by increasing interest in automated event induction in the HLT community. Discussion leader: Mitamura.

This workshop continues the previous format by including a poster session to showcase projects from around the world. We received excellent submissions, contained in this volume.

Organizers:

Eduard Hovy, Carnegie Mellon University
Teruko Mitamura, Carnegie Mellon University
Martha Palmel, University of Colorado

Program Committee:

Dan Bikel, Google Inc.
Rodolfo Delmonte, Università Ca' Foscari, Venice
Robert Frederking, Carnegie Mellon University
Marjorie Freedman, BBN
Boyan Onyshkevych, Department of Defense
James Pustejovsky , Brandeis University
Marta Recasens, Google Inc.
Tomohide Shibata, Kyoto University
Ian Soboroff, NIST
Stephanie Strassel, LDC, University of Pennsylvania
Mihai Surdeanu, University of Arizona
Lucy Vanderwende, Microsoft Inc.
Benjamin van Durme, Johns Hopkins University
Piek Vossen, Free University Amsterdam
Luke Zettlemoyer, University of Washington

Invited Speaker:

Bernardo Magnini, Fondazione Bruno Kessler / irst

Table of Contents

Workshop Program

Thursday, June 4, 2015

7:30–9:00 ***Breakfast***

9:00–9:15 ***Welcome***

9:15–10:30 ***Invited Talk: Bernardo Magnini***

10:30–10:50 ***Coffee break***

10:50–12:00 ***Session I: Subevent structure and shared task***

12:00–13:30 ***Lunch***

13:30–14:40 ***Session II: Event mention (nugget) detection***

14:40–15:30 ***Poster Session***

Translating Granularity of Event Slots into Features for Event Coreference Resolution.
Agata Cybulska and Piek Vossen

Word Sense Disambiguation via PropStore and OntoNotes for Event Mention Detection
Nicolas R Fauceglia, Yiu-Chang Lin, Xuezhe Ma and Eduard Hovy

Opposition Relations among Verb Frames
Anna Feltracco, Elisabetta Jezek and Bernardo Magnini

Encoding event structure in Urdu/Hindi VerbNet
Annette Hautli-Janisz, Tracy Holloway King and Gilian Ramchand

Using Topic Modeling and Similarity Thresholds to Detect Events
Nathan Keane, Connie Yee and Liang Zhou

Thursday, June 4, 2015 (continued)

Detecting Causally Embedded Structures Using an Evolutionary Algorithm
Chen Li and Roxana Girju

Evaluation Algorithms for Event Nugget Detection : A Pilot Study
Zhengzhong Liu, Teruko Mitamura and Eduard Hovy

Event analysis for information extraction from business-based technical documents
Bell Manrique-Losada and Carlos Mario Zapata Jaramillo

Event Nugget Annotation: Processes and Issues
Teruko Mitamura, Yukari Yamakawa, Susan Holm, Zhiyi Song, Ann Bies, Seth Kulick and Stephanie Strassel

Game-Changing Event Definition and Detection in an eSports Corpus
Emily Olshefski

Identifying Various Kinds of Event Mentions in K-Parser Output
Arpit Sharma, Nguyen Vo, Somak Aditya and Chitta Baral

From Light to Rich ERE: Annotation of Entities, Relations, and Events
Zhiyi Song, Ann Bies, Stephanie Strassel, Tom Riese, Justin Mott, Joe Ellis, Jonathan Wright, Seth Kulick, Neville Ryant and Xiaoyi Ma

Classification and Acquisition of Contradictory Event Pairs using Crowdsourcing
Yu Takabatake, Hajime Morita, Daisuke Kawahara, Sadao Kurohashi, Ryuichiro Higashinaka and Yoshihiro Matsuo

Semantic Interoperability for Cross-lingual and cross-document Event Detection
Piek Vossen, Egoitz Laparra, German Rigau and Itziar Aldabe

Modeling and Characterizing Social Media Topics Using the Gamma Distribution
Connie Yee, Nathan Keane and Liang Zhou

15:30–15:50 ***Coffee Break***

15:50–17:00 ***Session III: Inter-event relation annotation***

17:00–17:30 ***Discussion: Future event-related directions***

Thursday, June 4, 2015 (continued)

17:30 *Closing*

Translating Granularity of Event Slots into Features for Event Coreference Resolution.

Agata Cybulska
VU University Amsterdam
De Boelelaan 1105
Amsterdam, 1081HV
a.k.cybulska@vu.nl

Piek Vossen
VU University Amsterdam
De Boelelaan 1105
Amsterdam, 1081HV
piek.vossen@vu.nl

Abstract

Using clues from event semantics to solve coreference, we present an "event template" approach to cross-document event coreference resolution on news articles. The approach uses a pairwise model, in which event information is compared along five semantically motivated slots of an event template. The templates, filled in on the sentence level for every event mention from the data set, are used for supervised classification. In this study, we determine granularity of events and we use the grain size as a clue for solving event coreference. We experiment with a newly-created granularity ontology employing granularity levels of locations, times and human participants as well as event durations as features in event coreference resolution. The granularity ontology is available for research. Results show that determining granularity along semantic event slots, even on the sentence level exclusively, improves precision and solves event coreference with scores comparable to those achieved in related work.

1 Introduction

Event coreference resolution is the task of determining whether two event mentions refer to the same event instance. This paper explores cross-document resolution of coreference between events in a news corpus. We use granularity as an indication of event coreference. Our approach renders the semantic structure of event descriptions into arrangement of features for machine learning.

We use the granularity of events as a clue for event coreference resolution. The intuition behind this approach is, that an event with a longer duration, that happens on a bigger area and with multiple participants involved (for instance *a war between Russia and Ukraine*) might be related to but will probably not fully corefer with a "lower level" event of shorter duration and with single participants involved (e.g. *A Russian soldier has shot dead a Ukrainian naval officer*).

We experiment with an "event template" approach to event coreference resolution. The way in which event information can be semantically categorized is used in an event template to shape comparison of information about two event descriptions. Coreference between mentions of two events is determined through compatibility of slots of a pair of event templates. For the experiments, we use the ECB+ dataset (Cybulska and Vossen, 2014b). The five slots in our event template correspond to different elements of event information as annotated in the ECB+. The considered event slots are: 1) event action that is the event trigger (following the ACE (LDC, 2005) terminology) and four kinds of event arguments: 2) time, 3) location, 4) human and 5) non-human participant slots (for more information see Cybulska and Vossen (2014a)). An event template can be filled at different levels of information such as the entire document, a paragraph or a sentence. The approach investigated in this study operates at the sentence level which means that event templates are filled only with information available in the sentence in which an event mention occurs (for a report on experiments with a two step approach first considering document and subsequently sentence templates, see Cybulska and Vossen (2015)). Figure 1 considers an excerpt from topic one, text seven of the ECB corpus (Bejan and Harabagiu, 2010). Table 1 shows the distribution of

Proceedings of the 3rd Workshop on EVENTS at the NAACL-HLT 2015, pages 1–10,
Denver, Colorado, June 4, 2015.

Event Slot	Sentence Template 1	Sentence Template 2
Action	*entered*	*headed*
Time	*N/A*	*on Tuesday*
Location	*Promises*	*to a Malibu treatment facility*
Human Participant	*actress*	*actress*
Non-human Participant	*N/A*	*N/A*

Table 1: Sentence templates ECB topic1, text 7, sentences 1 and 2.

The "American Pie" actress has entered Promises for undisclosed reasons. The actress, 33, reportedly headed to a Malibu treatment facility on Tuesday.

Figure 1: Topic 1, text 7, ECB (Bejan and Harabagiu, 2010).

event information over the five event slots (as annotated in the ECB+) in the two example sentences. In the event template approach different kinds of event information are contrasted per slot of the template (Table 3).

We determine the grain-size within slots of the event template. The idea is to represent the grain size of the event action as well as of the entities involved with it by means of granularity features. To capture granularity we employ durations of event actions (Gusev et al., 2011) and granularity levels of event participants, time and locations. To determine granularity levels, a new granularity ontology consisting of 15 semantic classes is used. The 15 predefined semantic classes represent different granularity levels, which are defined over 434 hypernyms in WordNet, covering 11979 WordNet synsets. We make the granularity ontology available for research.

This work sheds light on the task of cross-document resolution of coreference between mentions of events in text. This study explores the actual task of resolution of coreference between two event descriptions, without letting topic classifiers first solve most of event ambiguity (following the insights of Cybulska and Vossen (2014b)). The two main contributions of this study are: (1) a new granularity ontology of event participants, times and locations and (2) a new "sentence template" approach to event coreference resolution that solves event coreference along five slots of an event template. To the best of our knowledge granularity of locations, times and human participants of events as well as durations of event actions has not been used before to solve event coreference.

We will first take a closer look at the notion of granularity and the new granularity ontology in section 2. We delineate our approach in section 3. Section 4 reports on the experiments with the new method the results of which are compared with related work in section 5. We conclude in section 6.

2 Granularity

The notion of granularity was described by (Keet, 2008) as the ability to represent and operate on different levels of detail in data, information, and knowledge. *Granularity deals with organizing data, information, and knowledge in greater or lesser detail that resides in a granular level or level of granularity and which is granulated according to certain criteria, which thereby give a* [granular] *perspective (...) on the subject domain.* (Keet, 2008). A lower granularity level captures a more detailed data representation than a more abstract higher level, which leaves out some details.

People view the world at different granularities. Humans are able to switch among different granularities of world conceptualizations (Hobbs, 1985). In a reasoning process a granularity level is distinguished, depending on what is relevant for a particular situation. Hobbs presented a framework for a theory of granularity.

Few other researchers looked at granularity in natural language. Considered the variation in the degree of specification of word meaning, Mani (1998) suggested development of a knowledge representation, which makes the notion of granularity explicit. Mani applied shifts in granularity to problems of polysemy and underspecification of nominaliza-

```
eng-30-08160276-n,gran_group,"citizenry_1,people_2"
eng-30-10638385-n,gran_person,"spokesperson_1,interpreter_3,representative_2,voice_8"
eng-30-15235126-n,gran_second,"second_1,sec_1"
eng-30-15234942-n,gran_min,"quarter_4"
eng-30-15117516-n,gran_hr,"hours_2"
eng-30-15163005-n,gran_day,"day_of_the_week_1"
eng-30-15136147-n,gran_week,"week_3,calendar_week_1"
eng-30-15209706-n,gran_month,"Gregorian_calendar_month_1"
eng-30-15239579-n,gran_season,"season_1"
eng-30-15203791-n,gran_year,"year_1"
eng-30-15231415-n,gran_thousands_years,"Bronze_Age_1"
eng-30-03449564-n,gran_street,"government_building_1"
eng-30-08537837-n,gran_city,"city_district_1"
eng-30-08898002-n,gran_country,"Upper_Egypt_1"
eng-30-08699426-n,gran_continent,"East_Africa_1"
```

Figure 2: Example entries from the granularity ontology file.

tions. Change in granularity was considered as a special case of abstraction in which elements, which are indistinguishable in a particular context, are collapsed. Mani focused on grain-size shifts amongst polysemous events.

Mulkar-Mehta et al. (2011b) describe event granularity as the concept of breaking down a higher-level event into smaller parts, fine-grained events such that each smaller granule plays a part in the higher level whole. Relation types that can exist between the objects at coarse and fine granularity are part-whole relationships amongst entities and events, and causal relationships. Based on annotation of granularity relations in text, the authors conclude that part-whole and causal relations are a good indication of shifts in granularity.

In this study we focus on the notion of granularity in event descriptions. We present a new granularity ontology, which is an attempt at capturing grain-size of events explicitly for the purpose of usage in NLP applications. We use a taxonomy based ontology to distinguish between coarse- and fine-grained granularities of different parts of event descriptions. We apply shifts in granularity to resolution of event coreference. The motivation behind this approach is an expected correlation between agreement or disagreement in grain-size levels and the notion of coreference. Agreement or small granularity differences are expected to indicate coreference. Bigger distance in granularity is expected to be a negative indicator of coreference or to indicate other event relations as scriptal or event membership. In the experiments described in this paper, we let a machine learning algorithm learn the relationships between different granularities and the notion of coreference. To capture differences in grain-size of events we employ both: (1) conceptual granularity clues being a manifestation of granularity in the form of inherent properties of word meanings, as well as (2) lexical grain-size indication expressed in number and multiplication. The intrinsic, conceptual granularity is captured by means of a number of granularity levels defined in the granularity ontology. Furthermore, we use durations of events as indication of grain size for event actions.

2.1 Granularity Ontology

We focus here on partonomic granularity relations (representing granularity through the part-of relation) between entities and events. To establish granularities of event participants, times and locations we created a new granularity ontology. Semantic classes relating to granularity levels were defined over synsets in WordNet. In the experiments we employ granularity levels to capture granularity agreement and shifts amongst event participants, times and locations. Our 15 semantic classes belong to four relationships from the taxonomy of meronymic relations by Winston et al. (1987). Granularity levels of the human participant slot are contained within Winston's et al. Member-Collection relations. Our temporal granularity levels make part of Winston's Portion-Mass relationships and our locational levels are in line with Place-Area relations in Winston's taxonomy.

Figure 2 presents a fragment of the granularity ontology with synset examples for every ontology class. The file is comma separated. In the first column synsets from WordNet 3.0 are indicated. In the second column the granularity levels are captured and the third one indicates the synset IDs as stored in the Natural Language Toolkit (NLTK, (Bird et al., 2009)). The choice of the 15 granularity classes was motivated by an analysis of event descriptions in the news. We intended to capture shifts in granularity that seemed meaningful for event coreference resolution on a news corpus such as the ECB or ECB+. We manually assigned the semantic classes to 434 hypernyms in WordNet which are linked to 11979 synsets. We recognize a number of granularity levels per event slot: nine grain levels for time expressions, four for locations and two for human participants, as presented in Table 2.

2.2 Lexical Granularity Clues

On top of granularity levels, we also account for lexical granularity clues within a level such as number indication and multiplications. At this point we only make a distinction between *single* and *multiple* "items" within a concept type (based on POS clues and occurrence of multiplications). Three kinds of parts of speech are used to determine number of a mention: (1) nominal tags: *NN, NNS, NNP, NNPS*, (2) personal pronouns tagged by the NLTK's default POS tagger as *PRP* and (3) numbers with tag *CD*. For instance the phrase *twenty soldiers* is POS-tagged as follows: *[('20', 'CD'), ('soldiers', 'NNS')]*. The nominal POS tag *NNS* is considered to indicate plural nouns. Additionally, if there is a number indication in a mention (POS-tag *CD* and lemma other than *one*), the phrase would be assigned plural number by default. If there are multiple nouns in a mention, we assign the number of the majority of nouns. If there is a tie, the number of the last noun in a mention would be decisive. For example *[('20', 'CD'), ('soldiers', 'NNS')]* would be assigned the granularity level *gran_person* and number *plural*. While *one soldier* would trigger the following analysis: *[('one', 'CD'), ('soldier', 'NN')]*, also assigned the granularity level *gran_person* but number *singular*. Since there are often multiple instances of an event slot in the sentence, there can be multiple granularity levels to consider. We calculate cosine similarity of granularity and number indications per event slot (if instantiated in the sentence) for two compared events. In the future, we will experiment with expressing the grain-size by means of numeric estimates of number of participants, duration and size of an area on which an event happened, e.g. indicating that the Boston area is ca. 125 km2 and the country of France of ca. 551500 km2.

2.3 Event Durations

To capture granularity of event actions (in Winston et al. (1987) Feature-Activity relation) we employ duration distributions from the database of event durations by Gusev et al. (2011). The lexicon of event durations (`http://cs.stanford.edu/people/agusev/durations/`) captures durations for events (with or without syntactic objects) inferred by means of web query patterns. Duration distributions were learned with an unsupervised approach. Eight duration levels are considered: *seconds, minutes, hours, days, weeks, months, years* and *decades*. The durations database covers the 1000 most frequent verbs with 10 most frequent grammatical objects of each verb from a newspaper corpus from the New York Times. For our granularity experiments we used duration distributions as determined for these 10000 events. A binary feature indicates whether there is overlap in most frequent duration levels of two events. Currently, since our approach does not consider syntactic dependencies, the duration feature is specified when disregarding the syntactic objects.

3 The Approach

We experimented with a decision-tree (hereafter also *DT*) supervised pairwise binary classifier to determine coreference of pairs of event mentions represented through templates filled in at the sentence level. We run preliminary experiments with a linear SVM and a multinomial Naive Bayes classifier

Event Slot	Granularity Class	Description	Synset Example
Human Participant	*gran_person*	individuals	spokesperson_1
	gran_group	groups or organizations	people_2
Location	*gran_street*	areas up to the size of a building	government_building_1
	gran_city	city districts and cities	city_district_1
	gran_country	size of a country	Upper_Egypt_1
	gran_continent	size of multiple countries	East_Africa_1
Time	*gran_second*	duration up to a minute	sec_1
	gran_min	from a minute to an hour	quarter_4
	gran_hr	from an hour up to 24 hours	hours_2
	gran_day	one to few days, less than a week	day_of_the_week_1
	gran_week	one to few weeks, less than a month	calendar_week_1
	gran_month	indication on the month level	Gregorian_calendar_month_1
	gran_season	few months	season_1
	gran_year	one or multiple years	year_1
	gran_thousands_years	thousands of years	Bronze_Age_1

Table 2: Granularity ontology classes.

Template Slot		Feature	Explanation
Action	Active mention coreference is solved for	Lemma overlap (L)	Numeric feature: overlap percentage.
		Duration overlap (G)	Binary: overlap in most frequent level.
		Synset overlap (S)	Numeric: overlap percentage.
		Discourse location (D)	Location within discourse. Binary:
		- document	- the same document or not
		- sentence	- the same sentence or not.
	Other sentence mentions	Lemma overlap (L)	Numeric: overlap percentage.
		Synset overlap (S)	Numeric: overlap percentage.
Location		Lemma overlap (L)	Numeric: overlap percentage.
		Granularity & num. overlap (G)	Numeric: cosine similarity.
		Synset overlap (S)	Numeric: overlap percentage.
Time		Lemma overlap (L)	Numeric: overlap percentage.
		Granularity & num. overlap (G)	Numeric: cosine similarity.
		Synset overlap (S)	Numeric: overlap percentage.
Human Participant		Lemma overlap (L)	Numeric: overlap percentage.
		Granularity & num. overlap (G)	Numeric: cosine similarity.
		Synset overlap (S)	Numeric: overlap percentage.
Non-Human Participant		Lemma overlap (L)	Numeric: overlap percentage.
		Synset overlap (S)	Numeric: overlap percentage.

Table 3: Features used in the experiments grouped into four categories: L - lemma based, G - granularity and number, D - discourse and S - synset based features.

but the decision-tree classifier outperformed both of them. We trained the DT classifier on an unbalanced training set of positive and negative samples.

In the experiments different features were assigned values per event slot. Table 3 presents all features that we experimented with. The lemma overlap feature (L) expresses a percentage of overlapping lemmas between two instances of an event slot (after removal of skip words), if instantiated in the sentence. Features indicating granularity and number compatibility of an event slot (G), are specified for every location, time and human participant mention in the sentence. Frequently, one ends up with multiple entity mentions from the same sentence for an action mention (the relation between an event and entities involved with it is not annotated in ECB+). To express the degree of overlap in grain size of mentions we used cosine similarity. For the action slot overlap in duration level of the active mentions is considered as a binary feature. For all five slots a percentage of synset overlap is calculated (S). Finally there are two features indicating mentions location within the discourse (D), specifying if mentions come from the same sentence or document.

Prior to being fed to the classifier, numeric feature vectors were normalized (missing values were imputed). We used grid search with ten fold cross-validation to optimize the depth of the decision-tree algorithm (entropy was used as the criterion).

Pairs of event templates were classified by means of the DT classifier when employing features from Table 3. To identify the final equivalence classes of corefering event mentions, mentions were grouped based on corefering pair overlap.

4 Experiments

4.1 Corpus

For the experiments we used the true mentions from the ECB+ corpus (Cybulska and Vossen, 2014b) which is an extended and re-annotated version of the ECB corpus (Bejan and Harabagiu, 2010). The ECB+ corpus contains a new corpus component, consisting of 502 texts, describing different instances of event types that were already captured by the 43 topics of the ECB.

As recommended by the authors in the release notes, for experiments on event coreference we used a subset of ECB+ annotations (based on a list of 1840 selected sentences), that were additionally reviewed with focus on coreference relations. Table 4 presents information about the data set used for the experiments. We divided the corpus into a training set (topics 1-35) and test set (topics 36 - 45).

4.2 Experimental Set Up

The ECB+ texts are available in the XML format. The texts are tokenized, hence no sentence segmentation nor tokenization needed to be done. We POS-tagged and lemmatized the corpus sentences. For the experiments we used tools from the Natural Language Toolkit (Bird et al., 2009)[1]: the NLTK's default POS tagger, and WordNet lemmatizer[2] as well as WordNet synset assignment by the NLTK[3]. For machine learning experiments we used scikit-learn (Pedregosa et al., 2011).

4.3 Singleton Baseline

As a baseline we consider event coreference evaluation scores generated taking into account all event mentions as singletons. In the singleton baseline response there are no "coreference chains" of more than one element. First row of Table 5 presents the singleton baseline results (BL) in terms of recall (R), precision (P) and F-score (F) by employing the coreference resolution evaluation metrics: MUC (Vilain et al., 1995), B3 (Bagga and Baldwin, 1998), mention-based CEAF (Luo, 2005), BLANC (Recasens and Hovy, 2011), and CoNLL F1 (Prad-

[1]NLTK version 2.0.4

[2]www.nltk.org/_modules/nltk/stem/wordnet.html

[3]http://nltk.org/_modules/nltk/corpus/reader/wordnet.html

ECB+ Corpus	#
Topics	43
Texts	982
Action mentions	6833
Location mentions	1173
Time mentions	1093
Human participant mentions	4615
Non-human participant mentions	1408
Coreference chains	1958

Table 4: ECB+ statistics.

Heuristic	Features	MUC			B3			CEAF	BLANC			CoNLL
		R	P	F	R	P	F	F	R	P	F	F
BL	-	0	0	0	45	100	62	45	50	50	50	39
DT	L	**43**	**77**	**55**	**58**	**86**	**69**	**58**	**60**	**69**	**63**	**64**
DT	LG	36	**77**	**49**	55	**90**	**68**	**56**	56	**74**	**60**	**60**
DT	LGD	28	77	42	52	93	67	55	55	77	58	57
DT	LGDS	16	76	27	49	96	65	52	52	68	54	50

Table 5: Sentence template approach to event coreference resolution evaluated on the ECB+ corpus in MUC, B3, mention-based CEAF, BLANC and CoNLL F in comparison to the singleton baseline BL.

Approach	Data	Model	MUC			B3			CEAF	BLANC			CoNLL
			R	P	F	R	P	F	F	R	P	F	F
BL	ECB+	-	0	0	0	45	100	62	54	50	50	50	39
B&H	ECB	HDp	52	90	66	69	96	80	71	NA	NA	NA	NA
Lee	ECB	LR	63	63	63	63	74	68	34	68	79	72	55
STA - L	ECB+	DT	43	77	55	58	86	69	66	60	69	63	64
STA - LG	ECB+	DT	36	77	49	55	90	68	63	56	74	60	60

Table 6: Best scoring STA approaches using feature sets L and LG evaluated in MUC, B3, entity-based CEAF, BLANC and CoNLL F; in comparison with related studies and the BL baseline. Note that the STA uses gold and related approaches system mentions.

han et al., 2011). When discussing event coreference scores must be noted that some of the commonly used metrics depend on the evaluation data set. This results in scores going up or down with the number of singleton items in the data (Recasens and Hovy, 2011). Our singleton baseline gives us zero scores in MUC, which is due to the fact that the MUC measure promotes longer chains. B3 on the other hand seems to give additional points to responses with more singletons, hence the remarkably high scores achieved by the baseline BL in B3. CEAF and BLANC as well as the CoNLL measures (the latter being an average of MUC, B3 and entity CEAF) give more realistic results.

4.4 Results

We evaluate the system output produced by the decision-tree classifier after merging pairs of event mentions with common elements into equivalence classes. The response chains generated with: (1) lemma feature set L, (2) lemma and granularity LG, (3) lemma, granularity and discourse LGD, and (4) lemma, granularity, discourse and synset features LGDS are evaluated in Table 5 in terms of R, P and F-score by employing the MUC, B3, mention-based CEAF, BLANC and CoNLL F1 metrics.

The highest F scores reached the event clusters created by the decision-tree classifier employing feature set L (marked in bold in the table). We observe a 13% improvement over the baseline BL in mention-based CEAF F and in BLANC F and a 25% gain in CoNLL F.

Addition of granularity features (LG) increases the precision scores in B3 and BLANC by 4-5%. The recall scores decrease but the F scores in most measures (except for MUC) are between 56-68%. Employing discourse with lemma and granularity features (LGD) gives us some extra precision points but costs us even more recall. Synset features lower precision and recall.

Note that these results were generated when disregarding syntactic roles and POS information. No anaphora resolution was performed and we did not group the corpus texts into topics before solving coreference between event mentions at the sentence level, which would significantly simplify the task (Cybulska and Vossen, 2014b). In the future we will run experiments aiming at improving the recall for instance through addition of semantic similarity features (in combination with the currently used features). We will also investigate the influence of syntactic features on the results.

5 Related Work

Granularity shifts and structures were recently investigated in the context of NLP applications by Mulkar-Mehta et al. (2011b). In their follow-up work (Mulkar-Mehta et al., 2011a) they describe an algorithm for extracting causal granularity structures from text and its possible applications in question answering and text summarization.
Howald and Abramson (2012) successfully used granularity types as features for prediction of rhetorical relations with a 37% performance increase.

As for event coreference resolution, Humpreys et al. (1997) performed coreference merging between event template structures. Our event template however is much more restricted (five slots only) and it is filled and compared at the level of sentence while Humpreys et al. consider discourse events and entities for event coreference resolution. No coreference evaluation scores are reported.

Considering the limitations of the event coreference resolution measures, for the sake of a meaningful comparison, it is important to consider similar data sets. The ECB and ECB+ are the only available resources annotated with both: within- and cross-document event coreference. We were unable to run our experiments on the ECB corpus, because no specific entity types are annotated in the ECB and our work depends on those for granularity estimates.[4] To the best of our knowledge, no baseline has been set yet for event coreference resolution on the ECB+ corpus. Accordingly we will look at results achieved in cross-document event coreference resolution on the ECB corpus which is a subset of ECB+, and so the closest to the data set used in our experiments. For the sake of convenience, in Table 6 we compare the best results by the sentence template approach (when using lemma features *STA - L* and a combination of lemma and granularity features *STA - LG*) with the results achieved in related studies. *B&H* stands for the approach of Bejan and Harabagiu (2010) using HDp - hierarchical Dirichlet process and *Lee* refers to the approach of Lee et al. (2012) using LR - linear regression. *BL* denotes the results by the singleton baseline.

In comparison to related studies, the best results achieved with sentence template classification (feature set L and LG) on the ECB+ are comparable to results achieved in related work on the ECB. The approach of Lee et al. (2012) reached 55.9% CoNLL-F [5] on the ECB but on a more difficult task entailing mention extraction. Another study reporting the CoNLL F score was done by Cybulska and Vossen (2013) who reached 69.8% CoNLL F1 on the ECB with a component similarity method but on a simpler - within topic task.

Note that the sentence template approach results were generated on the ECB+ corpus extended with texts capturing an additional layer of event instances from the ECB topics. Consequently, the intra-topic ambiguity in the ECB+ is higher than in the ECB. We did not perform topic clustering before comparing event mentions at the sentence level which makes it the task of the coreference resolver to solve intra- and cross-topic ambiguity between event mentions.

6 Conclusion and Future Work

This paper presents a new approach to event coreference resolution. Instead of performing topic classification before solving coreference between event mentions, as most approaches do, the event template approach compares event mentions at the sentence level. In so doing, the approach focuses on solving coreference between different slots of event descriptions, without relying on topic classification for context disambiguation. As such, this heuristic, which on itself is computationally expensive, can also be used after the primary step of topic classification. Especially in case of data sets with high within topic ambiguity where there are multiple event instances described from the same event type (for instance various instances of a *meeting* event). In the future, we will experiment with combining topic classification with the sentence template approach.

This is the only study which we are aware that employs granularity for event coreference resolution.

[4]In the future we will look into extracting the specific entity types so that they can be used for event coreference resolution, regardless of data annotation.

[5]The CoNLL F measure was used for comparison of competing coreference resolution systems in the CoNLL 2011 task.

For the purpose of this task a new granularity ontology was created. As our method does not employ POS and syntactic role information and no anaphora resolution or topic classification was performed to aid coreference resolution, the results are highly encouraging. In our future work we will look at possibilities of extending the granularity ontology learning granularity levels from corpora to overcome the low coverage limitation following from the usage of a WordNet based taxonomy. We will also augment the ontology to cover the non-human participant slot and experiment with other ways to represent event granularity with features.

Acknowledgments

This work has been carried out within the NewsReader project supported by the EC within the 7th framework programme under grant agreement nr. FP7-ICT-316404. We are grateful for the feedback from the anonymous reviewers. All mistakes are our own.

References

Amit Bagga and Breck Baldwin. 1998. Algorithms for scoring coreference chains. In *Proceedings of the International Conference on Language Resources and Evaluation (LREC)*.

Cosmin Adrian Bejan and Sanda Harabagiu. 2010. Unsupervised event coreference resolution with rich linguistic features. In *Proceedings of the 48th Annual Meeting of the Association for Computational Linguistics*, Uppsala, Sweden.

Steven Bird, Ewan Klein, and Edward Loper. 2009. *Natural Language Processing with Python*. O'Reilly Media Inc., http://nltk.org/book.

Agata Cybulska and Piek Vossen. 2013. Semantic relations between events and their time, locations and participants for event coreference resolution. In *Proceedings of recent advances in natural language processing (RANLP-2013)*.

Agata Cybulska and Piek Vossen. 2014a. Guidelines for ECB+ annotation of events and their coreference. Technical Report NWR-2014-1, VU University Amsterdam.

Agata Cybulska and Piek Vossen. 2014b. Using a sledgehammer to crack a nut? Lexical diversity and event coreference resolution. In *Proceedings of the International Conference on Language Resources and Evaluation (LREC 2014)*.

Agata Cybulska and Piek Vossen. 2015. "Bag of events" approach to event coreference resolution. Supervised classification of event templates. In *International Journal of Computational Linguistics and Applications (IJCLA)*.

Andrey Gusev, Nathanael Chambers, Pranav Khaitan, Divye Khilnani, Steven Bethard, and Dan Jurafsky. 2011. Using query patterns to learn the duration of events. In *Proceedings of the Ninth International Conference on Computational Semantics (IWCS11)*.

Jerry R. Hobbs. 1985. Granularity. In *Proceedings of the Ninth International Joint Conference on Artificial Intelligence*.

Blake Stephen Howald and Martha Abramson. 2012. The use of granularity in rhetorical prediction. In *Proceedings of the First Joint Conference on Lexi-cal and Computational Semantics (*SEM)*.

Kevin Humphreys, Robert Gaizauskas, and Saliha Azzam. 1997. Event coreference for information extraction. In *ANARESOLUTION '97 Proceedings of a Workshop on Operational Factors in Practical, Robust Anaphora Resolution for Unrestricted Texts*.

Catharina Maria Keet. 2008. A formal theory of granularity. toward enhancing biological and applied life sciences information systems with granularity. In *Ph.D. thesis, Faculty of Computer Science, Free University of Bozen-Balzano, Italy*.

LDC. 2005. ACE (Automatic Content Extraction) English Annotation Guidelines for Events ver. 5.4.3 2005.07.01. In *Linguistic Data Consortium*.

Heeyoung Lee, Marta Recasens, Angel Chang, Mihai Surdeanu, and Dan Jurafsky. 2012. Joint entity and event coreference resolution across documents. In *Proceedings of the 2012 Conference on Empirical Methods in Natural Language Processing and Natural Language Learning (EMNLP-CoNLL)*.

Xiaoqiang Luo. 2005. On coreference resolution performance metrics. In *Proceedings of the Human Language Technology Conference and Conference on Empirical Methods in Natural Language Processing (EMNLP-2005)*.

Inderjeet Mani. 1998. A theory of granularity and its application to problems of polysemy and underspecification of meaning. In *In Principles of Knowledge Representation and Reasoning: Proceedings of the Sixth International Conference (KR-98)*.

Rutu Mulkar-Mehta, Jerry R. Hobbs, and Eduard Hovy. 2011a. Applications and discovery of granularity structures in natural language discourse. In *Proceedings of The Tenth International Symposium on Logical Formalizations of Commonsense Reasoning at the AAAI Spring Symposium, Palo Alto*.

Rutu Mulkar-Mehta, Jerry R. Hobbs, and Eduard Hovy. 2011b. Granularity in natural language discourse. In

Proceedings of International Conference on Computational Semantics.

Fabian Pedregosa, Gal Varoquaux, Alexandre Gramfort, Vincent Michel, Bertrand Thirion, Olivier Grisel, Mathieu Blondel, Peter Prettenhofer, Ron Weiss, Vincent Dubourg, Jake Vanderplas, Alexandre Passos, David Cournapeau, Matthieu Brucher, Matthieu Perrot, and douard Duchesnay. 2011. Scikit-learn: Machine learning in Python. *Journal of Machine Learning Research*, 12:2825–2830.

Sameer Pradhan, Lance Ramshaw, Mitchell Marcus, Martha Palmer, Ralph Weischedel, and Nianwen Xue. 2011. CoNLL-2011 shared task: Modeling unrestricted coreference in ontonotes. In *Proceedings of CoNLL 2011: Shared Task*.

Marta Recasens and Eduard Hovy. 2011. BLANC: Implementing the rand index for coreference evaluation. *Natural Language Engineering*, 17(4):485–510.

Marc Vilain, John Burger, John Aberdeen, Dennis Connolly, and Lynette Hirschman. 1995. A model theoretic coreference scoring scheme. In *Proceedings of MUC-6*.

Morton E. Winston, Roger Chaffin, and Douglas Herrmann. 1987. A taxonomy of part-whole relations. In *Cognitive Science Volume 11, Issue 4, pages 417 - 444*.

Word Sense Disambiguation via PropStore and OntoNotes for Event Mention Detection

Nicolas Fauceglia, Yiu-Chang Lin, Xuezhe Ma, and **Eduard Hovy**
Language Technologies Institute
Carnegie Mellon University
Pittsburgh, PA 15213
USA
{fauceglia, yiuchanl, xuezhem, hovy}@cs.cmu.edu

Abstract

In this paper, we propose a novel approach for Word Sense Disambiguation (WSD) of verbs that can be applied directly in the event mention detection task to classify event types. By using the PropStore, a database of relations between words, our approach disambiguates senses of verbs by utilizing the information of verbs that appear in similar syntactic contexts. Importantly, the resource our approach requires is only a word sense dictionary, without any annotated sentences or structures and relations between different senses (as in WordNet). Our approach can be extended to disambiguate senses of words for parts of speech besides verbs.

1 Introduction

The task of Word Sense Disambiguation (WSD) is to identify the correct meaning or sense of an ambiguous word in a given context. As a fundamental task in natural language processing (NLP), WSD can benefit applications such as machine translation (Chan et al., 2007) and information retrieval (Stokoe et al., 2003). Most of the top performance WSD systems (Agirre and Soroa, 2009; Zhong and Ng, 2010), however, rely on manually annotated data or on lexical knowledge bases (e.g., WordNet), which are highly expensive to create.

In this paper, we propose a novel approach for Word Sense Disambiguation of verbs using the PropStore. With the help of PropStore, our approach can utilize information about verbs' appearance in syntactic contexts similar to the target sentence. This information significantly enriches the given contexts, and makes our approach obviate the need for annotated data and knowledge bases. The only resource our approach requires is a word sense dictionary that defines the senses and their descriptions for each word. Obviously, this dictionary is much easier to acquire than resources such as annotated data or Wordnet. Moreover, our approach can be extended to disambiguate senses of words in other types of part-of-speech. We demonstrate in this paper how our WSD method can be applied to the event mention detection task to classify event types.

1.1 Event Mention Detection Task

Event understanding has recently attracted a lot of attention[1]. A fundamental task in event understanding is to conduct Event Mention Detection (EMD). The EMD task requires a system to identify text spans in which events are mentioned, and to provide their attributes. The major attribute studied in recent EMD tasks (Li et al., 2013; Li et al., 2014) is *event mention type*, which is one of the most salient attributes relating to its semantics. In this paper, we propose a novel method on identifying event mention types. In particular, we focus on one major source of event mentions: verb-based mentions.

Given a list of possible candidates, the event mention detection task consists in identifying the type of each candidate mention (being one of the predefined event types or other). In this paper, we simply regard all verbs as mention candidates. In this setting, event mention detection can be cast as a verb sense disambiguation task, where the target senses are simply event types. We argue that our

[1]https://sites.google.com/site/wsevents2014/home

Proceedings of the 3rd Workshop on EVENTS at the NAACL-HLT 2015, pages 11–15,
Denver, Colorado, June 4, 2015.

method is especially suitable for this task because it naturally captures argument information (which is proven to be important in previous tasks) in a distributional manner.

2 The PropStore

The PropStore is a proposition knowledge base, essentially a triple store implemented as a database of relations between words, created using Wikipedia articles.

Each relation is represented in the form of a triple of two words connected by a relation:

$$< word_1, relation, word_2 >$$

Each word is an instance in the PropStore dictionary, and consists of its original form, as present in the text[2], the POS, lemma, and language. Each triple can occur one or thousands of times in the corpus. For each occurrence of a triple in a sentence, we store a new entry in the PropStore with that information.

The PropStore supports different types of relations, including dependency, semantic role, etc., and for each type, many values, including *nsubj*, *dobj*, etc. The current implementation of the PropStore uses just a single type of relation: dependency.

The source of the triples is every Wikipedia article available for each supported language. Each article is parsed and POS tagged using the Fanse Dependency Parser (Tratz and Hovy, 2011). For each triple occurrence in the corpus, we store the source article title, the sentence number, and the position of the child word in the sentence. This way, for every occurrence of a triple within a sentence, we can re-build the sentence, and also we can distinguish between two occurrences of the same triple in a sentence, allowing us to chain two or more triples in a tree configuration.

With this structure we can query the database to retrieve, for example, all sentences with a particular relation configuration; all verbs which have a particular *dobj*; all subjects of a given verb; two or more siblings of a shared head; or more complicated configurations, with their frequencies.

[2]except for normalized expressions such as numbers, punctuation and foreign words

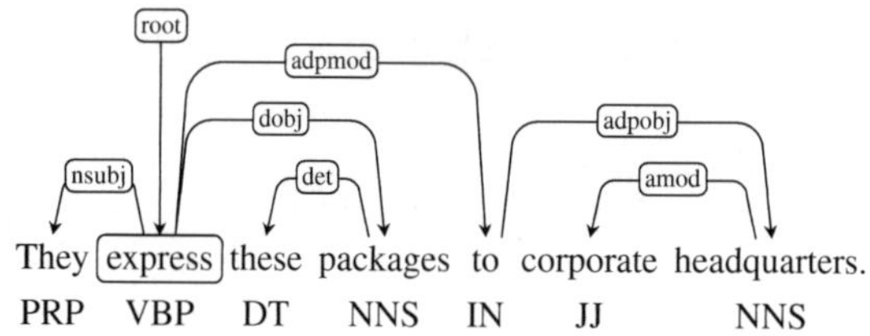

Figure 1: Dependency tree and POS tags for the example sentence.

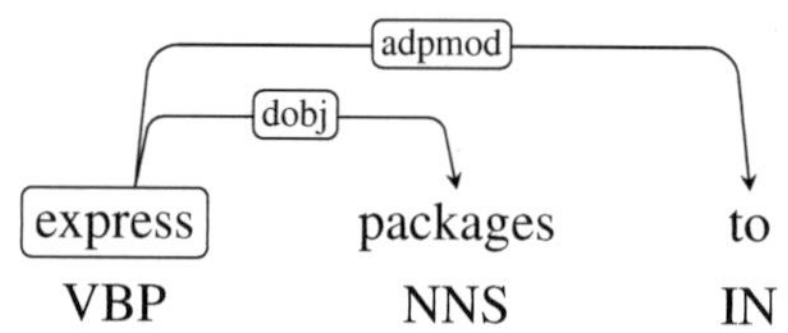

Figure 2: $Sig(express, X)$

Previous work us=ed a similar PropStore approach to build a Structured Distributional Semantics Model for event coreference (Goyal et al., 2013).

3 Our Approach for WSD

In the following, we use $X = x_1, x_2, \ldots, x_n$ to denote a generic sentence. For a given sentence X and a word $x \in X$ which we want to disambiguate, we define the signature of x in X, $Sig(x, X)$, as a "small part" of the dependency parse of X including x. For example, the sentence *They express these packages to corporate headquarters* is shown in Figure 1 along with its dependency tree, and Figure 2 gives the signature of *express*, $Sig(express, X)$, in this sentence.

Suppose x has m different senses in a dictionary (e.g., OntoNotes), $v_1, \ldots, v_m$, our task is to predict the correct sense of x in the given sentence X. This is done by selecting the sense with the highest score:

$$v^* = \operatorname*{argmax}_v score(v, x, X)$$

To simplify the model, we restrict the score function only to the signature of x:

$$score(v, x, X) = score(v, Sig(x, X))$$

which means we only use the context information within the signature of $Sig(x, X)$, ignoring other information.

3.1 WSD Algorithm via PropStore

The intuition of our approach is that verbs which appear in the same signature should have similar senses. Based on this assumption, we can define the score function $score(v, Sig(x, X))$ by two steps: first querying PropStore to collect all the verbs that appear in the same signature of $Sig(x, X)$; second defining the similarity measure for two words: $sim(x_1, x_2)$.

Specifically, to disambiguate verb $x \in X$, we first query PropStore to get the list of verb candidates:

$$W(Sig(x, X)) = \{w : Sig(w, X) \in PropStore\}$$

Here $W(Sig(x, X))$ is the set of all the verbs which appear in the same signature $Sig(x, X)$. Besides the verb list, we can also get the weight (frequency) $\theta(w)$ of each verb $w \in W(Sig(x, X))$ from PropStore.

With the list of verb candidates and their weights, we can define the score function as follows:

$$score(v, Sig(x, X)) = \sum_{w \in W} Sim(v, w)\theta(w)$$

where $Sim(v, w)$ is a function to measure the similarity between a verb w and a word sense v of x.

To define this similarity function $Sim(v, w)$, we utilize the short description of word sense v in the dictionary. We extract all the verbs in the short description of word sense v and denote it as $W(v)$. Then

$$Sim(v, w) = \frac{1}{|W(v)|} \sum_{w' \in W(v)} sim(w, w')$$

where $sim(w_1, w_2)$ is the similarity function between two verbs. To summarize, we define the similarity between a verb and a word sense as the average similarities between the verb and all the verbs which appear in the short description of this word sense.

Now, there are three remaining problems to resolve to complete the WSD algorithm:

1. How to extract signature structure $Sig(x, X)$ for the verb x in the given sentence X.

2. How to query PropStore to obtain the set of verb candidates $W(Sig(x, X))$.

3. How to measure similarity between two verbs $sim(w_1, w_2)$.

3.1.1 Extract Signature

For the first problem, the signature of a word is extracted by applying syntactic rules. Currently, we only extract the objects and prepositional modifiers (if any exist) of the verb we want to disambiguate. In the examples shown in Section 4, the signatures extracted by our simple rules perform well.

3.1.2 PropStore Query

For the second one, we query PropStore with $Sig(x, X)$ to get the lemmas of all the verbs that occur in the same signature structure as the target one. After querying PropStore, it returns a list of top k candidate words (verbs) $W = \{w_1, w_2, ..., w_k\}$ with their corresponding frequency of occurrence in descending order. For example, for the *head-and-children* template, which consists of a target head node, and two or more children, linked through a relation, we should formulate the query as follows:

```
rel1 = ('dobj', ('N', 'package'))
rel2 = ('adpmod', ('IN', 'to'))
sig = head_and_children('V', rel1, rel2)
verbs = propstore.query(sig)
```

Then we obtain a list of verbs occurring in contexts with 'package' (POS: N) as direct object and a 'adpmod' dependency relation pointing to 'to' (POS: IN) along with their frequencies.

3.1.3 Word Vectors

To measure the similarity between two words, we compute the distance between their corresponding word vectors which are trained by the word2vec continuous bag of words model (Mikolov et al., 2013). For training, we ran 15 iterations for vectors with 50 dimensions and a window size of 8, with 25 negative examples and the downsampling threshold being $1e^{-4}$. Slightly different from typical training methods, we treat the same word with different POS tags as different words so they do not share the same vector. In other words,

mail.noun and **mail.verb** are two different vectors instead of one. This is reasonable for doing WSD because distinct POS implies distinct senses. Accordingly, the distance between two words can be calculated by their Euclidean distance in the vector space:

$$dist\left(w_1, w_2\right) = \|\mathbf{v_1} - \mathbf{v_2}\|$$

and the similarity can be defined as the negative of distance:

$$sim(w_1, w_2) = -dist\left(w_1, w_2\right)$$

4 Example Results

In this section, we provide three example sentences to illustrate our WSD approach and show the corresponding result. From OntoNotes, *"express-v"* has the following three senses:

- "convey, show, state in some form"
- "press out physically"
- "to mail or post something via a rapid method"

An example sentence for the third sense is *"X = They* **express** *these packages to corporate headquarters."*. Its signature, $Sig(express, X)$, was previously shown in Fig 1 and Fig 2. The signature is composed of two *triples*, $< express, dobj, packages >$ and $< express, adpmod, to >$ with their first words anchored together. We then query the PropStore to get the set of candidate verbs $W(Sig(express, X))$ and their corresponding weight (frequency) $\theta(w)$ for each verb $w \in W(Sig(express, X))$ in descending order.

The resulting top 5 words and their weights are shown in Table 1. The most frequent word in PropStore that occurs in the same signature as $Sig(express, X)$ is *"deliver"*, which does make sense because *"deliver packages to"* is a common usage and it provides hints to disambiguate the sense of *"express"*. (*"deliver"* here is semantically closer to sense3 than the others.)

After applying the WSD algorithm mentioned in Sec 3.1, we obtain the result shown in Table 2.

word	frequency
deliver	76
offer	35
provide	28
send	25
sell	20

Table 1: Top 5 words in $W(Sig(express, X))$ and their frequency.

v_i	-Score(v_i)
sense1	9922.32
sense2	10069.5
sense3	9236.79

Table 2: $-Score(v_i)$ obtained from the WSD algorithm.

We use the value of $-Score(s_i)$ for reading convenience. Therefore, the best sense is given by the lowest score. In this example sentence, the best sense for *"express"* is sense3.

Another example sentence for the first sense of $express$ is *"X' = Picasso's Guernica vividly* **expresses** *the horrors of war."*. The signature and WSD results are shown in Fig 3, Table 3 and Table 4, respectively.

The last example is *"X" = She* **pronounced** *her first syllables at six months."*, where *"pronounce"* is the word to disambiguate. From OntoNotes, *"pronounce-v"* has two senses: "utter in a certain way"(sense1) and "pronounce judgement on"(sense2). Fig 4, Table 5 and Table 6 shows the corresponding siganture and results.

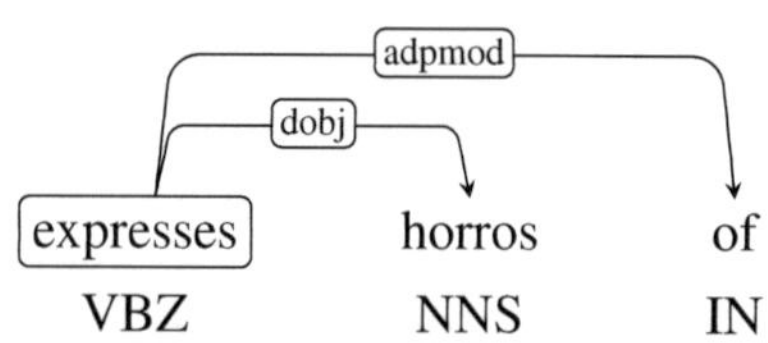

Figure 3: $Sig(express, X')$

word	frequency
know	3
demonstrate	1

Table 3: Top 5 words in $W(Sig(express, X'))$ and their frequency.

v_i	-Score(v_i)
sense1	202.49
sense2	216.91
sense3	206.43

Table 4: $-Score(v_i)$ obtained from our WSD algorithm.

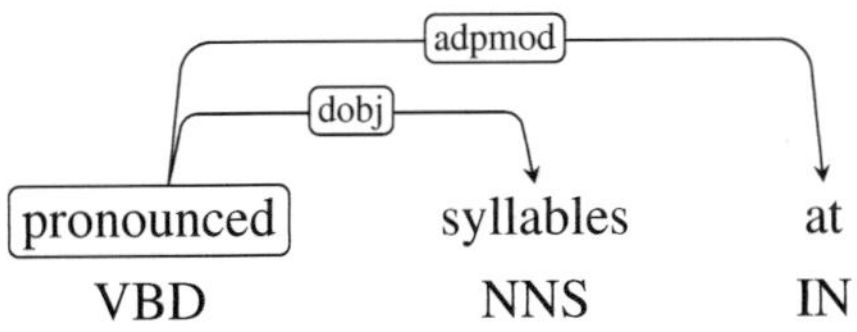

Figure 4: $Sig(pronounce, X'')$

word	frequency
have	3
leave	2
change	1
add	1
use	1

Table 5: Top 5 words in $W(Sig(pronounce, X''))$ and their frequency.

v_i	-Score(v_i)
sense1	343.36
sense2	426.71

Table 6: $-Score(v_i)$ obtained from our WSD algorithm.

5 Conclusion

In this paper, we propose a approach for Word Sense Disambiguation (WSD) of verbs using PropStore. Our approach does not require any annotated data or lexical knowledge base except an word sense dictionary. From the examples we showed in this paper, our approach can successfully disambiguate the senses of verbs *express* even when the hints from the given contexts are weak. Our approach can disambiguate senses for other POSs, too. Moreover, we described how our approach can be applied to event mention detection task to classify mention types.

There is a wide range of possible future work. First, we will build an automated system to perform all the steps together. Second, we will evaluate our approach for WSD on benchmark data sets, such as OntoNotes, and compare with current top WSD systems. At last, we will apply our approach to some really semantic tasks like event mention detection and event coreference resolution.

References

Eneko Agirre and Aitor Soroa. 2009. Personalizing PageRank for word sense disambiguation. In *Proceedings of the 12th Conference of the European Chapter of the ACL (EACL 2009)*, pages 33–41, Athens, Greece, March.

Yee Seng Chan, Hwee Tou Ng, and David Chiang. 2007. Word sense disambiguation improves statistical machine translation. In *Annual Meeting-Association for Computational Linguistics*, volume 45, page 33. Citeseer.

Kartik Goyal, Sujay Kumar Jauhar, Huiying Li, Mrinmaya Sachan, Shashank Srivastava, and Eduard Hovy. 2013. A structured distributional semantic model for event co-reference. In *Proceedings of the 51st Annual Meeting of the Association for Computational Linguistics*, pages 467–473, Sofia, Bulgaria, August.

Qi Li, Heng Ji, and Liang Huang. 2013. Joint Event Extraction via Structured Prediction with Global Features. In *Proceedings of the 51st Annual Meeting of the Association for Computational Linguistics (ACL2013)*.

Qi Li, Heng Ji, Yu Hong, and Sujian Li. 2014. Constructing Information Networks Using One Single Model. In *Proceedings the 2014 Conference on Empirical Methods on Natural Language Processing (EMNLP2014)*.

Tomas Mikolov, Kai Chen, Greg Corrado, and Jeffrey Dean. 2013. Efficient estimation of word representations in vector space. *arXiv preprint arXiv:1301.3781*.

Christopher Stokoe, Michael P. Oakes, and John Tait. 2003. Word sense disambiguation in information retrieval revisited. In *Proceedings of the 26th Annual International ACM SIGIR Conference on Research and Development in Informaion Retrieval, SIGIR 03*, pages 159–166, New York, NY, USA. ACM.

Stephen Tratz and Eduard Hovy. 2011. A fast, accurate, non-projective, semantically-enriched parser. In *Proceedings of the Conference on Empirical Methods in Natural Language Processing*, pages 1257–1268.

Zhi Zhong and Hwee Tou Ng. 2010. It makes sense: A wide-coverage word sense disambiguation system for free text. In *Proceedings of the ACL 2010 System Demonstrations*, pages 78–83, Uppsala, Sweden, July.

Opposition Relations among Verb Frames

Anna Feltracco
Fondazione Bruno Kessler
University of Pavia
feltracco@fbk.eu

Elisabetta Jezek
University of Pavia
Pavia, Italy
jezek@unipv.it

Bernardo Magnini
Fondazione Bruno Kessler
Povo-Trento, Italy
magnini@fbk.eu

Abstract

In this paper we propose a scheme for annotating opposition relations among verb frames in lexical resources. The scheme is tested on the T-PAS resource, an inventory of typed predicate argument structures for Italian, conceived for both linguistic research and computational tasks. After discussing opposition relations from a linguistic point of view and listing the tags we decided to use, we report the results of the experiment we performed to test the annotation scheme, in terms of interannotation agreement and linguistic analysis of annotated data.

1 Introduction

Several studies have been carried out on the definition and classification of oppositions in linguistics, philosophy, cognitive science and psychology. Our notion of opposition is based on lexical semantic studies by Lyons (1977), Cruse (1986; 2002; 2011), and Pustejovsky (2000). In the presentation that follows, we draw from the synthesis of these studies reported in Jezek (2015), and focus on oppositions among verb frames.

Traditionally, the study of semantic relations among verbs or verb frames has focused on the manner relation, the cause relation, and the relation of lexical entailment (see, for example, the classification in Fellbaum (1998)). In the computational field, several initiatives have proposed annotation schemas both for the annotation of the internal structure of events (see, for instance, Aguilar et al. (2014), Fokkens et al. (2013)) and for relations among events, including for instance temporal relations as proposed in the TimeML scheme (Pustejovsky et al., 2003). However, less works have systematically addressed the relation of opposition for verbs.

From a general point of view, the category of opposites can be said to include pairs of terms that contrast each other with respect to one key aspect of their meaning, such that together they exhaust this aspect completely. Examples include the following pairs: *to open* / *to close*, *to rise* / *to fall*. Paradoxically, the first step in the process of identifying a relationship of opposition often consists in identifying something that the meanings of the words under examination have in common. A second step is to identify a key aspect in which the two meanings oppose each other.[1]

Opposites cannot be true simultaneously of the same entity at the same time, for example a *price* cannot be said *to rise* and *fall* at exactly the same point in time. A basic test to identify an opposition is *It is both X and Y*. Based on this test, "*The price is both rising and falling" is ruled out as odd because to rise and to fall are opposites in the sense of being mutually exclusive. The test, however, does not tell us what kind of opposition it is.

Among the various types of oppositions that can be said to exist among verbs, we focus here on

[1] According to Cruse, opposites indicate the relation in which two terms typically differ along only one dimension of meaning: in respect of all other features they are identical (Cruse, 1986, p.197). For example, given two terms such as Engl. *to rise* and *to fall*, starting from the identification of a shared element (movement along an axis) we may identify a key point of differentiation (directionality), on which base we finally identify a relation of opposition.

Proceedings of the 3rd Workshop on EVENTS at the NAACL-HLT 2015, pages 16–24,
Denver, Colorado, June 4, 2015.

antonymy, complementarity, converseness and reversiveness, which appear to recur frequently across the vocabulary and have been discussed at length in the literature, with some points of divergence.

Two verbs are antonyms when they denote a change in property (*to increase / to decrease*) that has the characteristic of being gradual from a conceptual point of view. Two antonyms, therefore, oppose each other in relation to a scale of values for a given property, of which they may specify the two poles (or bounds). For this reason in the case of antonyms one may also speak of *polar* (Pustejovsky, 2000) or *scalar opposition*. From a logical point of view, antonyms are contraries, not contradictories; the negation of one term is not equivalent to the opposite term. For example, *not increased* does not necessarily mean *decreased*.

In the world's languages it is easy to find series of terms that identify very refined gradations of a specific property, for example with temperature: *freeze, cool, warm up, boil*. Potentially, along a scale of this type we could have very many terms lexicalizing different degrees along the scale. In reality, as a rule, we have a few, and use degree modifiers (such as *a bit* or *slightly*) to refine the concept; for example, we say "The weather warmed slightly".

Two verbs are complementary (*to accept / to reject*; *to succeed / to fail*) when they oppose each other with regards to a distinction that is not polar but binary; in other words, complementaries partition a conceptual domain into mutually exclusive compartments. For this reason, this opposition can also be called binary opposition (Pustejovsky, 2000). Complementary terms exclude each other and there is never an intermediate term. Therefore, a binary opposition corresponds to the relationship "X is equivalent to non-Y": *accept* is equivalent to *non-reject*, *fail* is equivalent to *non-succeed*, and so on. There is no underlying scale of values.

Converses (*to lend / to borrow*) are terms whose meaning involves necessarily a relation between at least two elements. That is, a person can lend something only if there is a borrower, and so forth. Therefore, converse terms are inherently relational. The underlying relation is asymmetrical that is, it is seen from the point of view of one of the two participants:

(1) *x* lends something to *y*

y borrows something from *x*

The characteristic of two converse terms is that each expresses the underlying relation in the opposite way from the other. Therefore, not all relational terms are converses, but only those with reversed or converted roles.

Finally, terms which denote reversive actions or events, such as *build / destroy*, *assemble / disperse*, *wrap / unwrap*, are reversives. It has been proposed (Cruse 2011) that reversives include two main subtypes: directional opposites, defined as verbs denoting movement in opposite directions between two terminal states (such as *rise / fall* or *enter / leave*), and "more abstract examples" denoting change in opposite directions between two states (such as all the examples above). According to Cruse (2011), in the case of reversives, the manner of the process and details of the path do not count, it is the effective direction from origin to goal which matters. Compare *tie* and *untie*: both are different actions, but the states in the beginning and the ends of both are the same. Fellbaum (1998) has noted that the relation between the verbs in these pairs seems less one of contrast than one of lexical entailment (Fellbaum, 1998, p. 75); for example one can only *unwrap* something which has been previously wrapped. We will consider them as opposites with a temporal entailment.

It is an open discussion whether opposition is a semantic relation or a lexical relation (Murphy, 2010; Fellbaum, 1998); what is clear is that that the predicate that is considered opposite of another predicate, does not activate this relation for all its senses. Our schema, as referenced above, will anyway apply to patterns and not to verbs.

Finally, let us look how opposition relations are encoded in lexical resources. WordNet 3.1 (Miller et al., 1990) has one single label, *antonymy* to identify opposition relations among senses for verbs; for example, increase#1 is in antonymy relation with decrease#1, diminish#1, lessen#1, fall#11. Antonymy in WordNet subsumes all the categories discussed above: complementaries (as in succeed#1 / fail#1), converses (as in buy#1 / sell#1) and reversives (as in tie#1 / untie#1). In FrameNet (Ruppenhofer et al., 2010), on the other hand, despite the attention given to relations among frames in the resource, no relation of opposition is considered, not even converseness, as we can see from Figure 1 where *commerce_buy* and *commerce_sell*, both specializations of the *commerce_good-transfer* frame, are indirectly related by the *"perspective on"* relation, but they are not related to each other by a direct converse relation.

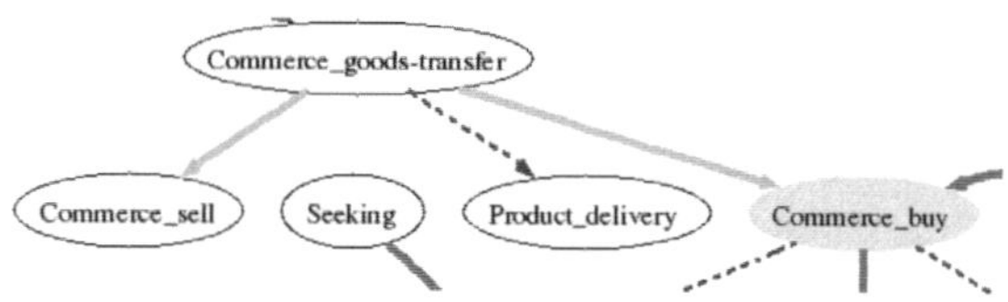

Figure 1: Frame relations in FrameNet.

After presenting the main categories introduced in the literature for opposites, and inspecting whether and how they are implemented in lexical resources such as WordNet e FrameNet, before illustrating our annotation scheme of opposition relations among frames, in the next Section we introduce the resource on which the annotation is being performed.

2 The T-PAS Resource and Oppositions among Patterns

The T-PAS resource (Jezek et al., 2014) is a repository of Typed Predicate Argument Structures for Italian acquired from corpora by manual clustering of distributional information about Italian verbs, freely available under a Creative Common Attribution 3.0 license[2]. T-PAS are corpus-derived verb patterns with specification of the expected semantic type (ST) for each argument slot, such as [Human]] guida [[Vehicle]]. T-PAS is the first resource for Italian in which semantic selection properties and sense-in context distinctions of verbal predicates are characterized fully on empirical ground. In the resource, the acquisition of T-PAS is totally corpus-driven. We discover the most salient verbal patterns using a lexicographic procedure called Corpus Pattern Analysis (CPA) (Hanks, 2004), which relies on the analysis of co-occurrence statistics of syntactic slots in concrete examples found in corpora.[3]

The first release contains 1000 analyzed average polysemy verbs, selected on the basis of random extraction of 1000 lemmas out of the total set of fundamental lemmas of Sabatini Coletti 2008 (Sabatini and Coletti, 2007), according to the following proportions: 10% 2-sense verbs, 60% 3-5-sense verbs, 30% 6-11-sense verbs.

The resource consists of three components:

1. a repository of corpus-derived T-PAS linked to lexical units (verbs);

2. an inventory of about 230 corpus-derived semantic types (STs) for nouns (HUMAN, ARTIFACT, EVENT, etc.), relevant for disambiguation of the verb in context, which was obtained by applying the CPA procedure to the analysis of concordances for ca 1500 English and Italian verbs;

3. a corpus of sentences that instantiate T-PAS, tagged with lexical unit (verb) and pattern number.

The reference corpus is a reduced version of ItWAC (Baroni and Kilgarriff, 2006).

Pattern acquisition and ST tagging involves the following steps:

1) choose a target verb and create a sample of 250 concordances in the corpus;

2) while browsing the corpus lines, identify the variety of relevant syntagmatic structures corresponding to the minimal contexts where all words are disambiguated;

3) identify the typing constraint of each argument slot of the structure by inspecting the lexical set of fillers: such constraints are crucial to distinguish

[2]tpas.fbk.eu

[3]Important reference points for the T-PAS project are FrameNet (Ruppenhofer et al., 2010) and VerbNet (Schuler, 2005). They differ from T-PAS because the structures they identify are not acquired from corpora following a systematic procedure. Another important resource is PDEV (Hanks and Pustejovsky, 2005), a pattern dictionary of English verbs which is the main product of the CPA procedure applied to English. As for Italian, a complementary project is LexIt (Lenci et al., 2012), a resource providing automatically acquired distributional information about verbs, adjectives and nouns. Differently from T-PAS, LexIt does not convey an inventory of patterns and the categories used for classifying the semantics of arguments are not corpus-driven. Inventory of senses such as MultiWordNet (Pianta et al., 2002) and Senso Comune (Oltramari et al., 2013) are resources to which T-PAS can be successfully linked with the goal of populating the former with corpus-driven pattern-based sense distinctions for verbs.

Figure 2: Selected pattern for the verb *divorare*.

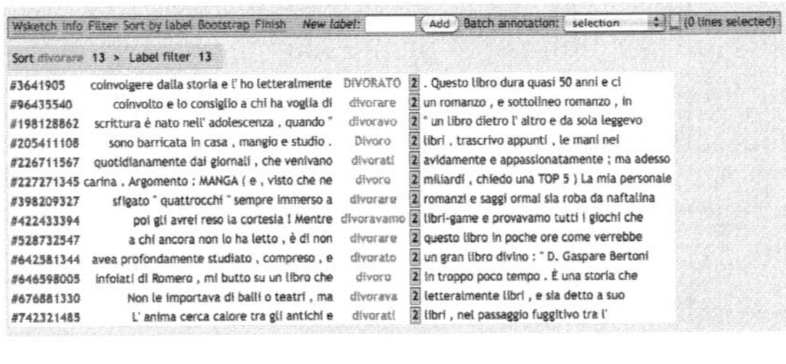

Figure 3: Example of sample annotation for pattern 2 of *divorare*.

among the different senses of the target verb in context. Each semantic class of fillers corresponds to a category from the inventory the analyst is provided with. If none of the existing ones captures the selectional properties of the predicate, the analyst can propose a new ST or list a lexical set, in case no generalization can be done;

4) when the structures and the typing constraints are identified, registration of the patterns in the Resource using the Pattern Editor. Each pattern has a unique identification number, and a description of its sense, expressed in the form of an implicature linked to the typing constrains of the pattern, for example the T-PAS in Figure 2 has the implicature [[Human]] *legge* [[Document]] *con grande interesse*:

5) assignment of the instances of the sample to the corresponding patterns, as shown in Figure 3.

In this phase, the analyst annotates the corpus line by assigning it the same number associated with the pattern. Concordances containing tagging errors are annotated as x and verb uses that do not come close to matching any of the normal patterns are tagged u (unclassifiable). All above mentioned steps are explained in details in Guidelines, which are provided to the analysts before starting the annotation.

At present, patterns are stored in the resource as a flat list, in the sense that they are not linked by any semantic relation. In the following Section, we describe the motivation for extending the resource by adding opposition relations among patterns, then illustrate the annotation scheme we elaborated for this task and its evaluation.

3 Motivation and Background

Detecting oppositions, both among words and among portions of text, is a fundamental requirement for any approach in Computational Linguistics aiming to deep language understanding. Indeed, textual opposition plays a crucial role in applications such as machine translation, discourse understanding, summarization and information retrieval.

On the lexical side, most of the computational work focused on approaches for the automatic acquisition of oppositions from corpora. Saif et al. (2013) propose an automatic method to identify contrasting word pairs that is based on the *contrast hypothesis*, i.e. that if a pair of words, A and B, are contrasting, then there is a pair of opposites, C and D, such that A and C are strongly related and B and D are strongly related. For example, there exists the pair of opposites *hot* and *cold* such that *tropical* is related to *hot*, and *freezing* is related to *cold*.

With a similar goal, Santus et al. (2014) apply Distributional Semantic Models to detect pairs of antonyms from corpora in an unsupervised manner. Under the hypothesis that antonym words share a salient contrasting dimension of meaning, this dimension can be used to discriminate antonyms from synonyms. For example, size is the salient dimension of meaning for the words *giant* and *dwarf* and it is expected that while *giant* occurs more often with words such as *big*, *huge*, etc., *dwarf* is more likely to occur in contexts such as *small* and *hide*. Accordingly, this work predicts that synonyms share a number of salient contexts that is significantly higher than the one shared by antonyms.

At the textual level, i.e. oppositions between portions of text, de Marneffe (2012) has investigated automatic methods for detecting contradictions in text pairs, based on the pragmatic definition that contradiction occurs when two sentences are extremely unlikely to be true simultaneously. It is worth to note that one the outcome of this work is that event coreference plays a crucial role in detecting textual oppositions, very much as similarity features are relevant to establish opposition at the lexical level.

The Recognizing Textual Entailment initiative (Dagan et al., 2009) addressed contradiction under the so called "three-way" evaluation schema (i.e. entailment, contradiction, unknown). Specific techniques for detecting contradiction include the use of "negative alignments" among portions of text (Magnini et al., 2014) and methods for detecting the polarity of predicates (Lotan et al., 2013).

As far as applications are concerned, there is an increasing interest in detecting various kinds of oppositions in large document repositories. Few examples include recent approaches that address inconsistencies in Wikipedia (Cabrio et al., 2014), approaches to estimate the truth of a certain fact (Martinez-Gomez et al., 2014), and the automatic reconstruction of consistent story-lines on a certain topic of interest.

4 Annotation Schema for Opposite Relations

For Italian, to the best of our knowledge, there are no annotation schemas that identify different types of opposition applied to verbal frames. In general, lexical resources, such as synonyms and antonyms dictionaries, list semantic opposition using the cover term *antonymy* or *contraries*. Differently, we want to develop an annotation schema that specifies the type of opposition between frames, maintaining all the semantic and syntactic information that frames may contain.

Following the classification we described in the Introduction, we propose guidelines for the annotation of oppositions among frame structures where we distinguish:

- Antonymy (tag: ANT)
- Complementarity (tag: COMPL)
- Converseness (tag: CONV)
- Reversiveness (tag: REV)

The standard tests to determine whether two words are antonyms are the following: "neither X nor Y"; "It X moderately / lightly / a bit". For example: "The water did not cool nor warm (up)"; "The weather has warmed moderately". The "neither X nor Y" test verifies whether it is possible to negate both terms simultaneously, and whether there is a neutral interval with respect to the two terms. The second test verifies whether the terms of the opposition express a scalable dimension.

The same test can be used for complementaries ("*he was neither accepted nor rejected"; "*He neither failed nor succeeded"). Complementary terms fail the test because the opposition they encode is exclusive, in the sense that the assertion of one term entails the negation of the other (and vice versa); there are no intermediate cases. It is not possible to negate both terms simultaneously.

Converses describe the same action from an opposite perspective with regard to the participant roles. If syntactical changes are adopted, converses can be substituted without affecting the meaning of the sentence (see (1) in Section 1). Converses can be two-place predicates, where two elements are involved or three-place predicates, where more than two elements are involved. In three-place converses, one of the arguments can be omitted.

As for reversives, a test which permits the delimitation of a coherent set of reversible verbs is the "again-test", which verifies the possibility of using unstressed *again* without the process denoted by the verb having happened before (Cruse, 2002). For example, the following sentences are taken as evidence that *enter* and *leave* are a reversive pair:

(2) a. The spacecraft left the earth's atmosphere.
b. Five days later, the spacecraft entered the atmosphere again.
c. The alien spacecraft entered the earth's atmosphere.
d. Five days later, the spacecraft left the atmosphere again.

5 Pilot Experiment on T-PAS

In order to determine the reliability of the opposition schema, we conducted a pilot experiment on the T-PAS resource described in Section 2. In particular, we calculated the degree of agreement between two annotators on the application of the scheme among the verbal patterns of T-PAS.

In the next Sections, we first describe the setting of the pilot experiment (Section 5.1), then the inter annotator agreement results (Section 5.2), and finally we discuss the obtained results (Section 5.3).

5.1 Experimental Setting

We designed and ran a pilot annotation over a selected set of verbs defined in T-PAS. Specifically, a set of 25 pairs of verbs (for a total of 216 patterns) have been identified, which, according to human judgment, display a relation of opposition for at least one of their pattern. Consequently, such verb pairs are expected to present a high frequency of the phenomena the schema is designed for. We provided the annotators with the list of verbs and their respective patterns and implicatures. Moreover, annotated corpus-derived examples in T-PAS could be consulted.

The two annotators, both familiar with verbal pattern structures and pattern acquisition, were asked to identify and classify opposition relations between patterns following the annotation schema proposed in Section 4. For each given pair of verbs, the annotation task consists in two main steps: (i) for each pair of patterns, to identify the presence or absence of an opposition relation and (ii), if the opposition relation is present, to recognize which type of opposition occurs.

In both steps of the task, annotators make use of the semantic types expressed in the verb pattern. In particular, STs help annotators in interpreting the sense of the pattern and consequently in identifying which are the senses of the verbs in an opposition relation (if an opposition relation is realized). As an example, consider patterns 2 and 3 of the verb *abbattere* (in (3) and (4)) and pattern 1 of the verb *costruire* (in (5)) and their implicatures.

Pattern 2 of the verb *abbattere (to demolish, to destroy)* with its implicature:

(3) pattern: [[Human | Event]] *abbattere* [[Building]]
implicature: [[Human | Event]] demolisce, distrugge [[Building]]

(eng.[4]: [[Human | Event]] demolishes, destroys [[Building]])

Pattern 3 of the verb *abbattere (to kill, to suppress)* with its implicature:

(4) pattern: [[Human]] *abbattere* [[Animate]]
implicature:[[Human]] uccide, ammazza [[Animate]]

(eng.: [[Human]] kills, suppresses [[Animate]])

Pattern 1 of the verb *costruire (to build, to erect)* with its implicature:

(5) pattern: [[Human | Institution]] *costruire* ([[Building | Route]])
implicature: [[Human | Institution]] erige, innalza ([[Building | Route]])

(eng.: [[Human | Institution]] builds, erects ([[Building | Route]]))

In this example, STs (in particular [[Human]], [[Building]] and [[Animate]]), help the annotator in understanding which senses of the two verbs s/he is comparing, and, possibly, to establish an opposition relation between (3) and (5), but not between (4) and (5).

In case of multiple semantic types for the same argument slot, annotators are allowed to mark opposition relations between patterns even if they are realized only by a subset of such STs. For instance, (3) and (5) are opposites only as far as [[Human]] is considered as the subject of the two predicates (i.e. pattern 1 of the verb *costruire* shows multiple semantic types, and does not select [[Event]] as subject).

Finally, annotators can match the same pattern of a verb to more than one patterns of the other verb: this is mainly due to the fact that in T-PAS lexicographers can possibly have adopted a different degree of specification for pattern acquisition (Jezek et al., 2014). In total each annotator had to judge 595 pattern pairs. To complete the task annotators took approximately two days, including corpus examples consultation.

5.2 Inter Annotator Agreement

To calculate the agreement between the two annotators, we have adopted the Dice's coefficient (Rijsbergen, 1997), which measures how similar two sets

[4]The English version is intended only for readability purposes and it is not meant to represent a corresponding English pattern of the Italian pattern.

are by dividing the number of shared elements of the two sets by the total number of elements they are composed by. This produces a value from 1, if both sets share all elements, to 0, if they have no element in common.

We calculate the Dice's coefficient for two configurations. In the first configuration, *opposition recognition*, we consider one agreement if both annotators agree on recognizing opposition or non-opposition between two patterns, 0 if they do not agree. In the second configuration, we calculate the agreement considering *opposition category*, i.e. we consider as agreement if both annotators identify exactly the same opposition relation.

Finally, for each category, we calculate the *per category disagreement* as the proportion of pairs where the two annotators disagree over the total pairs in which the category has been recognized.

Out of 595 pairs of patterns used in the experiment, the two annotators agreed in recognizing a pair as displaying or not an opposition relation in 588 cases (44 are marked as opposites by both annotators, 544 as non-opposites): the Dice value for opposition recognition is 0,98. This result suggests that identifying opposition relations between patterns is not to a controversial decision among annotators. Moreover, annotators identified the same type of opposition or agreed in recognizing non-opposition in 582 cases, thus Dice value for type of opposition is 0,97 showing that the agreement between the two annotators has a very high degree of overlap.

On the other hand, considering disagreement for each opposition category (see Table 1), results show that most cases stem from annotating the COMPL category (annotators identified this category in 16 pairs but disagreed on 6 of them) and the REV category (disagreement on 9/21 pairs); by contrast, annotators agreed more consistently on recognizing CONV pairs (just one case of disagreement).

In order to understand the motivations of these discrepancies, we have adopted a reconciliation strategy among annotators. In particular, we asked annotators to motivate their choices with the possibility to revise their selections. After the reconciliation discussion, Dice values increased to 0,99 (considering only opposition recognition) and to 0,98 (considering opposition category) and the per category disagreement decreased for every category (see Table 2).

Category	**#disagreement / #total**	%
COMPL	6 / 16	37,5
ANT	3 / 13	23
CONV	1 / 9	11,1
REV	9 / 21	42,8
NON-OPP	7 / 551	1,2

Table 1: Per category disagreement (pre-reconciliation).

Category	**#disagreement / #total**	%
COMPL	3 / 15	20
ANT	2 / 12	16,6
CONV	0 / 9	0
REV	5 / 18	27,7
NON-OPP	5 / 550	0,9

Table 2: Per category disagreement (post-reconciliation).

5.3 Discussion

In this Section we discuss three cases of disagreement among annotators.

A first case concerns disagreement when the semantic types specified in the pattern include elements with different characteristics. This, in some cases, has induced annotators to consider the pattern as opposite (or not) of another pattern. As an example, consider *mettere*, pattern 1 in (6) - *togliere*, pattern 2 in (7).

Pattern 1 of the verb *mettere (to place)*:

(6) pattern: [[Human]] mettere [[Artifact | Body Part]] {in [[Location]] | in [[Container]]}

(eng.: [[Human]] place [[Artifact | Body Part]] {in [[Location]] | in [[Container]]})

Pattern 2 of the verb *togliere (to remove)*:

(7) pattern: [[Human]] togliere [[Inanimate]]

(*eng.: [[Human]] removes [[Inanimate]]*)

In this example, one annotator recognized the two patterns as REV (you first *place*, then you *remove*, then you can *place* again). On the contrary, the other annotator, referring to examples in the corpus for *togliere*, pattern 2, decided not to mark the opposition, as most of the lexical items over which the ST [[Inanimate]] generalises identify elements that cannot be placed or re-placed in a certain [[Location]] or [[Container]] (e.g. to remove a tooth).

The second case we discuss concerns disagreement between opposition category selection, as observable in *caricare*, pattern 1, in (8) - *scaricare*, pattern 3, in (9).

Pattern 1 of the verb *caricare (to load)*:

(8) pattern: [[Human]] caricare [[Animate | Inanimate]] (su | in [[Vehicle]] | su | in {spalle|schiena})

(eng.: [[Human]] load [[Animate | Inanimate]] (into [[Vehicle]]) or carry [[Animate | Inanimate]] on {his | her shoulders})

Pattern 3 of the verb *scaricare (to unload)*:

(9) pattern: [[Human | Machine]] *scaricare* [[Inanimate]]

(eng.: [[Human | Machine]] unload [[Inanimate]])

In this pair, one annotator recognized the two patterns as REV, as the two events describe a change in opposite direction, and display a temporal relation; in contrast, the other annotator selected ANT, considering that, for both predicates, the objects of *caricare* - *scaricare* observed in the corpus samples are quantifiable, and thus the actions are in a certain way measurable.

The third case we discuss highlights disagreement due to the semantic interpretation of the verbal patterns. In these cases, it seems that while one annotator focuses on the temporal entailment relation among patterns, thus marking the pair as REV; the other mainly recognizes that the two patterns divide in two a conceptual domain (see Introduction), thus selecting COMPL. This reason for disagreement lead to an interesting possible interpretation. As detailed in our schema, reversives hold also a temporal relation: a dimension that is not captured by the other opposition relations of the schema. In that sense the category of reversives seems not to be exclusive, but in some cases it appears to be a cross relation that co-exists with other types of oppositions.

6 Conclusions

In this paper we have presented an annotation schema of oppositions among verbal frames. In our schema, opposition relations have been classified in four categories: complementaries, antonyms, converses, reversives. We have conducted a pilot annotation experiment selecting 25 verb pairs from the T-PAS resource to access the reliability of the scheme. Results show that the IA agreement is very high in the identification of opposite pattern pairs, and fair in distinguishing among categories. We also found that several pattern pairs appear to have properties pertaining to more than one kind of opposites. The experiment confirms that the annotation is doable and can be extended to all verbs in the resource, thus enriching it with opposition relations among frames. For extending the annotation to the whole T-PAS resource, we plan to adopt crowdsourcing, with a more systematic use of the corpus samples associated to each pattern in T-PAS (see Section 2). This will make T-PAS the first resource systematically enriched with opposition relations, which can potentially be exploited to investigate opposition at textual level.

References

Jacqueline Aguilar, Charley Beller, Paul McNamee, Benjamin Van Durme, Stephanie Strassel, Zhiyi Song, and Joe Ellis. 2014. A comparison of the events and relations across ace, ere, tac-kbp, and framenet annotation standards. In *Proceedings of the Second Workshop on EVENTS: Definition, Detection, Coreference, and Representation*, pages 45–53, Baltimore, Maryland, USA, June. Association for Computational Linguistics.

Marco Baroni and Adam Kilgarriff. 2006. Large linguistically-processed web corpora for multiple languages. In *Proceedings of the Eleventh Conference of the European Chapter of the Association for Computational Linguistics: Posters & Demonstrations*, pages 87–90. Association for Computational Linguistics.

Elena Cabrio, Serena Villata, Julien Cojan, and Fabien Gandon. 2014. Classifying inconsistencies in dbpedia multilingual chapters. In *Proceedings of the Language Resources and Evaluation Conference (LREC-2014)*.

D Alan Cruse. 1986. *Lexical semantics*. Cambridge University Press.

D Alan Cruse. 2002. Paradigmatic relations of exclusion and opposition ii: Reversivity. *Lexikologie: Ein internationales Handbuch zur Natur und Struktur von Wörtern und Wortschätzen: Lexicology: An international handbook on the nature and structure of words and vocabularies*, 1:507–510.

D Alan Cruse. 2011. *Meaning In Language: An Introduction To Semantics And Pragmatics*. Oxford University Press, USA.

Ido Dagan, Bill Dolan, Bernardo Magnini, and Dan Roth. 2009. Recognizing textual entailment: Rational, evaluation and approaches. *Journal of Natural Language Engineering*, 15(4):i–xvii.

Marie-Catherine de Marneffe. 2012. *What's that supposed to mean?* Ph.D. thesis, Stanford Univeristy.

Christiane Fellbaum. 1998. *WordNet*. Wiley Online Library.

Antske Fokkens, Marieke Van Erp, Piek Vossen, Sara Tonelli, Willem Robert Van Hage, BV SynerScope, Luciano Serafini, Rachele Sprugnoli, and Jesper Hoeksema. 2013. Gaf: A grounded annotation framework for events. In *Proceedings of the The 1st Workshop on EVENTS: Definition, Detection, Coreference, and Representation*, pages 11–20, Atlanta, Georgia, June. Association for Computational Linguistics.

Patrick Hanks and James Pustejovsky. 2005. A pattern dictionary for natural language processing. *Revue française de linguistique appliquée*, 10(2):63–82.

Patrick Hanks. 2004. Corpus pattern analysis. In *Proceedings of the Eleventh EURALEX International Congress, Lorient, France, Universite de Bretagne-Sud*.

Elisabetta Jezek, Bernardo Magnini, Anna Feltracco, Alessia Bianchini, and Octavian Popescu. 2014. T-pas: A resource of corpus-derived types predicate-argument structures for linguistic analysis and semantic processing. In *Proceedings of LREC*.

Elisabetta Jezek. 2015. *The Lexicon. An Introduction.* Oxford: Oxford University Press.

Alessandro Lenci, Gabriella Lapesa, and Giulia Bonansinga. 2012. Lexit: A computational resource on italian argument structure. In *LREC*, pages 3712–3718.

Amnon Lotan, Asher Stern, and Ido Dagan. 2013. TruthTeller: Annotating predicate truth. In *Proceedings of the Annual Meeting of the North American Chapter of the ACL*, pages 752–757, Atlanta, Georgia.

John Lyons. 1977. Semantics, vol. i. *Cambridge: Cambridge*.

Bernardo Magnini, Roberto Zanoli, Ido Dagan, Kathrin Eichler, Günter Neumann, Tae-Gil Noh, Sebastian Padó, Asher Stern, and Omer Levy. 2014. The excitement open platform for textual inferences. In *Proceedings of the 52nd Meeting of the Association for Computational Linguistics, Demo papers*.

Pascual Martinez-Gomez, Ran Tian, and Yusuke Miyao. 2014. Bno at the ntcir-11 english fact validation task. In *Proceedings of NTCIR-11*.

George A Miller, Richard Beckwith, Christiane Fellbaum, Derek Gross, and Katherine J Miller. 1990. Introduction to wordnet: An on-line lexical database*. *International journal of lexicography*, 3(4):235–244.

M Lynne Murphy. 2010. *Lexical meaning*. Cambridge University Press.

Alessandro Oltramari, Guido Vetere, Isabella Chiari, Elisabetta Jezek, Fabio Massimo Zanzotto, Malvina Nissim, and Aldo Gangemi. 2013. Senso comune: A collaborative knowledge resource for italian. In *The Peoples Web Meets NLP*, pages 45–67. Springer.

Emanuele Pianta, Luisa Bentivogli, and Christian Girardi. 2002. Developing an aligned multilingual database. In *Proc. 1st Intl Conference on Global WordNet*.

James Pustejovsky, José Castaño, Robert Ingria, Roser Saurí, Rob Gaizauskas, Andrea Setzer, Graham Katz, and D Radev. 2003. Timeml: A specification language for temporal and event expressions. In *Proceedings of the International Workshop of Computational Semantics*, page 193.

James Pustejovsky. 2000. Events and the semantics of opposition. *Events as grammatical objects*, pages 445–482.

CJ van Rijsbergen. 1997. Information retrieval. 1979.

J Ruppenhofer, M Ellsworth, MRL Petruck, C Johnson, and J Scheffczyk. 2010. Framenet ii: Extended theory and practice. retrieved november 12, 2013.

Francesco Sabatini and Vittorio Coletti. 2007. Dizionario della lingua italiana 2008 (2007). *Milano: Rizzoli Larousse*.

Mohammad Saif, Bonnie Dorr, Graeme Hirst, and Peter D. Turney. 2013. Computing lexical contrast. *Computational Linguistics*, 39(3):555590.

Enrico Santus, Qin Lu, Alessandro Lenci, and Chu-Ren Huang. 2014. Unsupervised antonym-synonym discrimination in vector space. In *Proceedings of the First Italian Conference on Computational Linguistics (CLIC-it 2014)*.

Karin Kipper Schuler. 2005. Verbnet: A broad-coverage, comprehensive verb lexicon.

Encoding event structure in Urdu/Hindi VerbNet

Annette Hautli-Janisz
Department of Linguistics
University of Konstanz
annette.hautli@uni-konstanz.de

Tracy Holloway King
Search Science
eBay Inc.
tracyhollowayking@gmail.com

Gillian Ramchand
Institute for Linguistics
University of Tromsø
gillian.ramchand@uit.no

Abstract

We propose a new kind of event structure representation for computational linguistics, based on the theoretical framework of First-Phase Syntax (Ramchand, 2008). We show that the approach not only gives a theoretically well-motivated set of subevents and related semantic roles, it also posits the levels of representation needed for analyzing a linguistic phenomenon that has repeatedly caused problems in computational systems, namely the treatment of complex predication. In particular, we look at V+V complex predicates in Urdu/Hindi and show that Ramchand's subevent decomposition implemented in a VerbNet-style resource allows for a consistent semantic analysis of these complex events. We also show how the proposed event representation can be added to existing resources in the language, in particular the Hindi-Urdu Treebank and Hindi PropBank.

1 Introduction

With the advent of large-scale computational semantic analyses, an issue that repeatedly crops up is how verbal event structure can be represented. In this paper we propose a new way of representing events and semantic roles in computational linguistics, based on the theoretical linguistic framework of First-Phase Syntax (Ramchand, 2008). The approach makes predictions as to how events should be encoded across languages; moreover it provides a computationally attractive way of encoding them in a lexical resource. We demonstrate this by tackling a notoriously difficult phenomenon, namely the analysis of complex predicates (CPs) in Urdu/Hindi, and show that First-Phase Syntax not only provides a well-motivated analysis for simplex verbs, but also posits the levels of representation needed for providing a consistent and computational analysis for CPs. We encode the representation in a VerbNet-style resource for Urdu/Hindi and show that it can also be incorporated into existing lexical resources, namely the Hindi-Urdu Treebank (Bhatt et al., 2009) and Hindi PropBank (Hwang et al., 2010; Vaidya et al., 2012).

The paper proceeds as follows: After providing a brief overview of related work in Section 2, we introduce First-Phase Syntax and its application in computational linguistics and also provide a linguistic background to Urdu/Hindi CPs (Section 3). We then show how these complex predicates are handled in First-Phase Syntax and how the information is incorporated in the VerbNet-style lexical resource for Urdu/Hindi (Section 4). This is followed by a discussion on how the information can be incorporated into other resources for the language (Section 5). Section 6 concludes the paper.

2 Related work

For English, one of the central resources for encoding the syntactic and semantic information on verbs is VerbNet (Kipper-Schuler, 2005). VerbNet uses the temporal ontology proposed by Moens and Steedman (1988), an approach that has proven highly useful in the past and is still employed in many computational applications. However, with the substantial progress of theoretical linguistic work in the area of formalizing event structure, the

Proceedings of the 3rd Workshop on EVENTS at the NAACL-HLT 2015, pages 25–33,
Denver, Colorado, June 4, 2015.

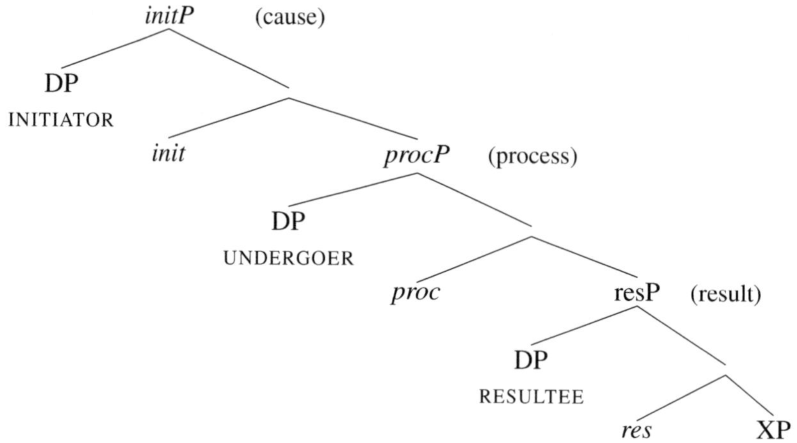

Figure 1: Event decomposition and projection by Ramchand (2008)

field has gained a deeper understanding of the underlying structure of events.

One key aspect of the automatic meaning representation of verbs is the assignment of semantic roles to the participants of the event. Here, VerbNet uses thematic roles (e.g. Agent, Patient, Theme) based on work of Gruber (1965), Fillmore (1968) and Jackendoff (1972). In contrast, FrameNet (Baker et al., 1998) is based on a cognitive approach to event structure and defines frames which are characterized by frame-specific roles, yielding a large number of distinct roles. Finally, in PropBank (Palmer et al., 2005), verb arguments are given numerical values: Arg0 has agentive or causer-like properties, whereas Arg1 is more patient-like.

For Urdu/Hindi, only a few lexical resources exist to date. In the spirit of English PropBank, Hindi-Urdu PropBank (Vaidya et al., 2011; Vaidya et al., 2012) uses PropBank-style thematic roles, accounting for CPs by merging the roles of main verbs and light verbs. In the Hindi/Urdu Treebank (Bhatt et al., 2009), these PropBank-style roles are combined with the kaṛaka roles assumed by Pāṇini (see Butt (2006) for a discussion of Pāṇini's system).

In general, the issue with thematic roles is that they are difficult to define and hard to consistently apply across verb classes (let alone across languages). As we will show in the following, the semantic roles assumed in First-Phase Syntax are language-independent and can be motivated by language-internal entailments based on event structure. Moreover, the complex predicates found in Urdu/Hindi call for an analysis that is theoretically well-motivated and can be consistently and productively applied across the verbal inventory.

In the following we introduce the framework of First-Phase Syntax (§3.1) and provide an overview of the phenomenon of complex predication in Urdu/Hindi (§3.2).

3 Background

3.1 First-Phase Syntax

First-Phase Syntax (Ramchand, 2008) is an approach which proposes hierarchical linguistic representations that directly encode structural semantic interpretational properties in the domain of event structure. In the framework, an event maximally decomposes into three subevents: an initiation subevent, a process subevent and a subevent denoting a result state. Each subevent licenses a semantic role and has its own projection in the tree. Figure 1 shows the general architecture: The [init] projection is responsible for introducing the external argument, i.e. the causer of the event ('subject' of cause = INITIATOR), the specifier of the process subevent undergoes the action denoted by the verb ('subject' of process = UNDERGOER) and the result state of the event is licensed by *resP* ('subject' of result = RESULTEE). The initiating as well as the resultative subevent are stative, whereas the process subevent has a dynamic interpretation. The "glue" between subevents is one of causation: The [init] subevent

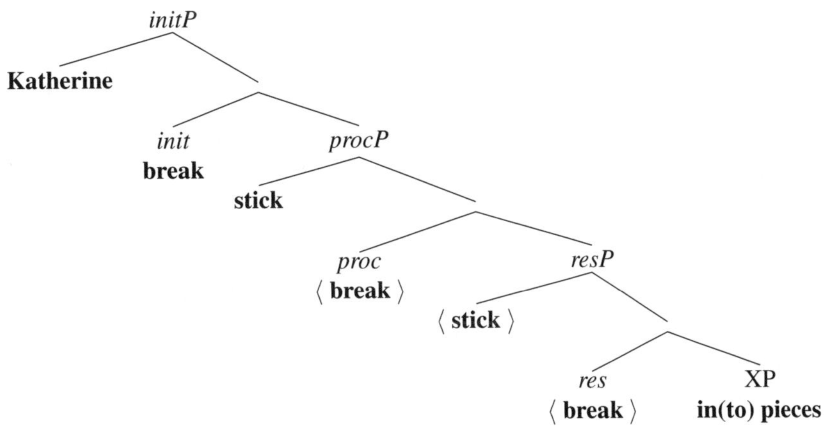

Figure 2: First-phase representation of (1)

causes the [proc] subevent to happen which brings about a change of state, which in turn leads to a result state under [res]. The reason for this decomposition is that across languages, the system allows for the identification of the general parts of verb meaning and therefore provides a set of principles that languages adhere to.

For example, the English verb 'to break', as shown in example (1) with the analysis in Figure 2[1], licenses three subevents, namely [init], [proc] and [res]. Here, Katherine is the INITIATOR of the event, with the stick being the UNDERGOER as well as the RESULTEE of the breaking event. The optional phrase 'in(to) pieces' is a RHEME, a semantic role which contributes the predicational/rhematic content to the state described by the result projection. The syntactic diagnostics for the subevent decomposition in English are the following: The [init] subevent is licensed by the ungrammaticality of the causative form of the verb, with [proc] being licensed by the grammaticality of a durative event modification like 'for hours'. The result subevent is licensed by the ungrammaticality of the latter.

(1) Katherine broke the stick in(to) pieces.

In order to make the approach compatible with computational lexical resources, we assume that each verb corresponds to a lexical entry which contains the subevental structure of the verb and the semantic roles that it licenses.[2] Since one argument can carry more than one semantic role, e.g. the stick in Figure 2 is both the UNDERGOER and the RESULTEE of the breaking event, the subevental structure is indexed as shown in (2). The subscripts $_i$ and $_j$ indicate that the semantic role of the INITIATOR in [init$_i$] is filled by a different argument than the roles licensed by the [proc] and the [res] subevent ([proc$_j$, res$_j$]). As will be shown in Section 4, this information can be encoded in a VerbNet-style resource.

(2) break: [init$_i$, proc$_j$, res$_j$]

First-Phase Syntax has a number of properties that set it apart from other approaches to event structure and semantic role representation and make it attractive to use in computational linguistics. First of all, it preempts the problem that thematic roles are hard to delimit and to define. In First-Phase Syntax, each semantic role is licensed by a subevent which in turn is tied to a syntactic diagnostic that identifies it. These diagnostics can vary from language to language, but have to be consistent within a language. Defining these syntactic criteria does away with the recurring

[1]The terminals in angle brackets represent the Minimalist assumptions of insertion and movement of lexical items in the tree.

[2]Unlike some explicitly syntactic decompositional accounts of argument structure (e.g. Distributed Morphology), Ramchand assumes that the syntactically relevant part of the verb entries containa information on the event structures licensed as well as the relevant coindexation relations among subevents. Thus, her lexical entries are similar to what we assume here. Unlike lexical decompositional accounts, Ramchand does not assume that lexical entries contain richer argument role information independent of the relationship to event structure.

problem of thematic role assignment, which generally lacks an explicit demarcation. Moreover, in the light of lexical resource development, these criteria greatly facilitate the annotation process.

Another property of First-Phase Syntax is that composite semantic roles are explicitly allowed, i.e. an entity can be both the INITIATOR and the UNDERGOER of an event. This feature is not accounted for in other semantic role encodings, but it adds considerable expressive power to the system without extending the set of roles. Moreover, the roles proposed by Ramchand (2008) have the benefit that they are abstract enough to allow for a consistent semantic analysis and are valid across languages. The set of roles bears a striking resemblance to the topmost level of the role hierarchy introduced by Bonial et al. (2011), an attempt to find a more coarse-grained and language-independent set of semantic roles for the mapping between different resources. A direct comparison of the two sets is difficult, because the role set of Bonial et al. is motivated by a conceptual view of semantics. Nevertheless, Ramchand's roles are in the spirit of other approaches that aim at establishing a more general set of semantic roles in theoretical and computational linguistics, with the First-Phase roles having the additional benefit of being tied to concrete syntactic diagnostics.

3.2 Urdu/Hindi complex predicates

A central characteristic of the verbal system of Urdu/Hindi is the heavy usage of complex predicates (CPs) that can appear in V+V, N+V, A+V and P+V combinations (Hook (1974), Masica (1976), Mohanan (1994), Butt (1995), Raza (2011), inter alia). The formation of CPs is a highly productive process with around 20 light verbs participating. As a consequence of the expressive power of CPs, the number of simple verbs in Urdu/Hindi ($\sim$700 verb roots (Raza, 2011)) is comparatively fewer than in many other languages.

In general, Urdu/Hindi CPs comprise two verbs: The first verb is the main verb and contributes the main propositional content of the clause. The second verb is finite and serves as the light verb of the CP, contributing a bleached-out version of its full verb meaning to the event denoted by the main verb of the CP. In Urdu/Hindi, different types of CPs exist: One type of CP are *aspectual complex predicates* (Butt, 1995) where the light verbs contribute a sense of "completion, suddenness, directionality, benefaction, etc." (Masica, 1976, p. 143): The example in (3) (Butt, 1995, p. 91) shows a construction with *gɪr-na* 'to fall' as the main verb of the clause and the light verb *ja-na* 'to go', which adds completeness to the falling event. Example (4) (Butt, 1995, p. 34) shows a *permissive complex predicate* with the main verb *ja-na* 'to go' and the permissive light verb *de-na* 'to give'. Here, the light verb adds an argument to the clause which is not licensed by the main verb, namely the 'lettee', *Anjum*. A third type of complex predicate, the *complex predicate of motion* (Hautli-Janisz, 2013), is illustrated in example (5): Here, the main verb *kud-na* 'to jump' is complemented by the light verb *nɪkal-na* 'to emerge', which adds the source argument *makan=se* 'from the house' to the clause and adds a general telic path reading.

CPs in Urdu/Hindi are problematic for shallow as well as deep parsing approaches. Their frequency and productivity means that a static list is insufficient, but a dynamic resource has to account for the fact that the syntactic structures, semantic roles and event structures of two verbs need to be merged to form a single predicational head. This, we claim, can be done with the First-Phase Syntax approach presented above and we implement it using a class-based approach like VerbNet. The methodology is described in the remainder of the paper.

4 Encoding event structure

The two levels of representation that are generally assumed in VerbNet are the syntactic and the semantic/conceptual representation. Each verb is characterized by a set of syntactic frames or alternations that it participates in. From the viewpoint of syntax, a frame is characterized by the obligatory syntactic constituents and the semantic roles that these constituents play in the event.

One difference in the syntactic representation between English and Urdu/Hindi VerbNet (henceforth UHVN) is due to a structural difference between the two languages. English has a fixed word order and the order of constituents in the description and the order of elements in the syntactic frame indicate which constituent occupies which thematic role in the frame. This way of relating syntactic to seman-

(3) ɑnjʊm **gɪr gɑ-yi**
Anjum.F=Erg **fall go-Perf.F.Sg**
'Anjum fell (completely).'

(4) ɑnjʊm=ne sɑddɑf=ko **ja-ne dɪ-ya**
Anjum.F=Erg Saddaf.F=Dat **go-Inf.Obl give-Perf.M.Sg**
'Anjum let Saddaf go.'

(5) cor mɑkan=se bahɑr **kud nɪkl-a**
thief.M.Sg.Nom house.M.Sg=Source outside **jump emerge-Perf.M.Sg**
'The thief jumped out of the house.' (Hook 1974, p. 69)

tic information cannot be directly transferred to languages with a free word order such as Urdu/Hindi, which require the resource to be more explicit about the way the syntactic and semantic role information is connected. To account for this, case information is recorded in the syntactic frames to capture the mapping of semantic roles to syntactic constituents.

Another difference between English and Urdu/Hindi is the existence of several classes of light verbs, in addition to the standard VerbNet classes representing main verbs. Extending the VerbNet system, we posit a special class for light verbs in Urdu/Hindi and within this class are several subclasses. The syntactic and semantic structures of the light verbs and main verbs constrain the possible CPs in the language and their interpretation.

4.1 Simple verbs

The main verb component of a CP has an underlying semantics which includes the First-Phase subevents and the roles of its arguments. A basic intransitive motion verb like *gɪr-na* 'to fall' has a VerbNet entry as shown in Figure 3: The verb licenses a [proc] subevent, with the nominative argument in the clause occupying the UNDERGOER role. The semantic representation employs the 'motion' predicate also used in English VerbNet, showing that the UNDERGOER undergoes motion in the process subevent (motion(proc, UNDERGOER)).

Paths and locations of motion are also encoded as in English VerbNet, in particular following the proposal made by Hwang et al. (2013). For that, the rhematic position of the [res] subevent, interpreted as the LOCATION role in motion events, is split into INITIAL_LOCATION and DESTINATION.

Main verb *gɪr-na* **'to fall'**	
Frame:	1.2.1
Description:	NP.UNDERGOER V
Syntax:	NP (nom) = UNDERGOER V
Semantics:	motion(proc, UNDERGOER)
Example:	*anjʊm gɪri.* 'Anjum fell.'

Figure 3: Example of [proc] event structure in UHVN

The representation in UHVN is illustrated in Figure 4: The verb *nɪkal-na* 'to emerge' licenses two subevents, namely [proc, res], with the semantic roles of the UNDERGOER and the RESULTEE combined on the nominative argument (the subject). The INITIAL_LOCATION is characterized by an NP with locative case marking. The semantic representation of *nɪkal-na* 'to emerge' is similar to the one in Figure 3: The UNDERGOER performs a motion in the process subevent, but with the additional information on the path of motion that is defined by the INITIAL_LOCATION, with DESTINATION and TRAJECTORY left unspecified in the frame. In the result subevent, the RESULTEE is not at the INITIAL_LOCATION anymore (!at(INITIAL_LOCATION)).

4.2 Light verbs

In CPs, the light verb only contributes a bleached version of its full verb counterpart to the event. In CP formation, the VerbNet lexical entry of the main verb combines with that of the light verb. The same main verb may combine with different light verbs, and it is the VerbNet syntax of the light verb

Main verb *nɪkal-na* 'to emerge'	
Frame:	1.2.4
Description:	NP.UNDERGOER+RESULTEE NP.INITIAL_LOCATION V
Syntax:	NP (nom) = UNDERGOER + RESULTEE
	NP (loc) = INITIAL_LOCATION
	V
Semantics:	motion(proc, UNDERGOER)
	path(proc, INITIAL_LOCATION, ?TRAJECTORY, ?DESTINATION)
	result_state(res, RESULTEE, !at(INITIAL_LOCATION))
Example:	*amra kamre=se nɪkli.*
	'Amra emerged from the room.'

Figure 4: Semantic representation of location and path in UHVN

Permissive light verb *de-na* 'to give'	
Frame:	0.1
Description:	NPINITIATOR XP* V Vlight
Syntax:	NP (erg/nom) = INITIATOR
	XP*
	Vn
	Vlight
Semantics:	permission(init, INITIATOR, UNDERGOER)
Example:	*anjʊm=ne saddaf=ko gaṛi calane di.*
	'Anjum let Saddaf drive the car.'

Figure 5: Syntactic frame for the permissive light verb *de-na* 'to give' in UHVN

which governs the surface realization of the arguments. The light verb may introduce new semantic arguments and the structure of the First-Phrase roles (Figure 1) governs which light verbs can combine with which main verbs.

Figure 5 shows the lexical entry for the permissive light verb *de-na* 'to give' (as exemplified in (4)), which adds a permission-giving argument to the event denoted by the main verb. On the syntactic level, the light verb contributes an argument which can alternate between nominative and ergative case marking (Mohanan (1994), Butt and King (2005), inter alia). This is the INITIATOR of the event. Otherwise, no restriction on the number and role of the other arguments in the clause is assumed, represented by XP* for any kind of phrase appearing zero or more times. For the CP, the light verb *de-na* 'to give' expects the main verb in the nominal form (Vn). For the semantic representation, we introduce the predicate 'permission', showing that in the initiation subevent, the INITIATOR gives permission to the UNDERGOER (permission(init, INITIATOR, UNDERGOER)). The remaining semantic information of the event, e.g. the aspect of motion as in (4), is contributed by the main verb *ja-na* 'to go'.

As shown in example (5), *nɪkal-na* 'to emerge' can, in addition to its full-verb counterpart, also serve as a light verb in CPs of motion. Figure 6 shows the light verb entry in UHVN: Similar to the permissive light verb, the syntactic frame comprises the arguments that are required by the light verb, here a nominative-marked argument which is the RESULTEE and a locative-marked argument which denotes the INITIAL_LOCATION. As the light verb can only combine with main motion verbs of the class 'iTHlAnA-1.1', a syntactic restriction needs to be encoded in the VerbNet entry: In UHVN, this information is attached to the main verb entry in the syntactic frame (V: synres=iTHlAnA-1.1), facilitating an automatic lookup and analysis of valid CP constructions. If no constraint is encoded, as is the case for the permissive light verb *de-na* 'to give' in

Light verb of motion *nɪkal-na* 'to emerge'	
Frame:	1.4.2.1
Description:	NP (nom) NP (loc) XP* V Vlight
Syntax:	NP (nom) = RESULTEE
	NP (loc) = INITIAL_LOCATION
	XP*
	V: synres = iTHIAnA-1.1
	Vlight
Semantics:	path(proc, INITIAL_LOCATION, ?TRAJECTORY, ?DESTINATION)
	result_state(res, RESULTEE, !at(INITIAL_LOCATION))
Example:	*cor makan=sE kud nɪkla*
	'The thief jumped out of the house.'

Figure 6: Syntactic frames for light verbs of motion in UHVN

Figure 5, the light verb forms CPs with verbs from across the verbal inventory.

The semantic representation of the light verb does not contribute motion information, but solely contributes the 'path' and 'result_state' predicates, in parallel to the encoding of these notions for main verbs. This reduced information in the VerbNet entry of the light verb reflects the view in theoretical linguistics that light verbs only contribute a bleached version of their full verb meaning.

4.3 Representing CPs

As shown above, light verbs comprise a separate class in UHVN. Many light verbs in Urdu/Hindi have full verb counterparts and hence have multiple entries in UHVN: one for the light verb meaning and one (or more) for their full, main verb meaning. For a semantic representation of CPs, the VerbNet information of the main and the light verb is merged: The syntactic constraints of the light verb are checked against the information contained in the main verb entry; if they are fulfilled, the information regarding event structure, semantic roles and semantic predicates is combined.[3] In the following we illustrate the resulting CP analysis using example (5) with the CP of motion *kud nɪkal-na* 'to jump out of (lit. to jump emerge)'. The representation looks as in (6): The motion information in the first line is contributed by the main verb *kud-na* 'to jump', which licenses a [proc] subevent in which an UNDERGOER undergoes motion. The path and the resultative information (second and third line) come from the light verb *nɪkal-na* 'to emerge', which licenses a [res] subevent and, in its light verb usage, only contributes the 'path' and 'result' information.

Similarly, the analysis of the permissive CP *ja-ne de-na* 'to let go (lit. to go give)' exemplified in (4) is a combined version of the representations of the main and light verbs: The 'permission' information and the INITIATOR in (7) is contributed by the light verb *de-na* 'to give', with the motion information coming from the main verb *ja-na* 'to go'.

This treatment of CPs in UHVN reflects the theoretical linguistic approach to analyzing these constructions: The light verb only contributes a bleached version of its full-verb-information to the CP and constrains the types of arguments and the combinatorial possibilities of the verbs. Both of these aspects are accounted for in the resource.

4.4 Interim summary

Overall, the UHVN approach to encoding event structure makes use of three subevents, namely initiation, process and result. In order to represent motion events and CPs, we use the semantic roles of INITIATOR, UNDERGOER and RESULTEE. For the VerbNet-encoding of the path, the First-Phase roles of LOCATION and RHEME are further split into INITIAL_LOCATION, TRAJECTORY and DESTINATION.

[3] Ramchand explicitly assumes the merging of information in First-Phase Syntax by way of the *underassociation* principle, whereby semantic roles that can be identified based on their encyclopedic content can be unified.

(6) motion(proc, UNDERGOER)
path(proc, INITIAL_LOCATION, ?TRAJECTORY, ?DESTINATION)
result_state(res, RESULTEE, !at(INITIAL_LOCATION))

(7) permission(init, INITIATOR)
motion(proc, UNDERGOER)

5 Implementation in other resources

The subevents and semantic roles of UHVN are compatible with information contained in other lexical resources for Urdu/Hindi, in particular Hindi/Urdu PropBank (Palmer et al., 2005; Hwang et al., 2010) and the Hindi/Urdu Treebank (Bhatt et al., 2009). In Hindi/Urdu PropBank, the semantic role information of each verb is stored in a frame, which can, with the semantic role encoding assumed in First-Phase Syntax, be extended to encode two different layers of semantic role assignment. Figure 7 shows the annotation for *nıkal-na* 'to emerge': Whereas the PropBank entry assigns Arg0 (actor) and Arg2-sou (source attribute) to the arguments of the frame, the UHVN representation assigns the UNDERGOER as well as the RESULTEE role to the moving entity, with the source location complemented by the INITIAL_LOCATION role.

Main verb *nıkal-na* 'to emerge'	
Hindi/Urdu PropBank	**Urdu/Hindi VerbNet**
Arg0	UNDERGOER
	RESULTEE
Arg2-sou	INITIAL_LOCATION

Figure 7: Hindi/Urdu PropBank and UHVN roles

The light verb entry of *nıkal-na* 'to emerge' in Hindi/Urdu PropBank contains an Argm, an argument modifier role, which combines with nouns in N+V CPs (Vaidya et al., 2013). This entry, as shown for complex predicates of motion, can be extended, adding the semantic roles of RESULTEE and INITIAL_LOCATION shown in Figure 6.

The semantic roles can also be added to the Hindi/Urdu Treebank, where the dependencies between verbs and arguments are encoded using the kaṛaka roles of Pāṇini. Here, *nıkal-na* 'to emerge' receives the roles k1 'karta' (most independent participant in an event) and k2 'karma' (locus of the result implied by the verb root). Extending the layer of annotation with the semantic roles established here would provide an interesting comparison of different principles of annotating participants of an event.

6 Discussion and conclusion

Overall, for its use in computational linguistics, First-Phase Syntax has a number of attractive properties: First of all, participants in an event can have more than one semantic role, enhancing the expressiveness of the system without increasing the number of roles. Secondly, having a set of syntactic criteria that govern the assignment of the semantic roles facilitates the process of extending the resource, as annotators can more easily decide what the correct semantic role of an argument is. Moreover, the assumptions made in First-Phase Syntax provides a framework for analyzing a notoriously difficult construction in Urdu/Hindi, namely CP formation.

Another benefit of First-Phase Syntax is its crosslinguistic validity. As shown in Ramchand (2008), the framework can be applied across languages and linguistic phenomena. Instead of having different annotation schemes emerge to accommodate constructions in languages other than English, the framework can serve as a guiding principle to encode event structure consistently across languages.

Using the class-based approach of VerbNet to analyzing CPs of different types has been shown to be a clean and theoretically well-motivated way of dealing with CPs in this kind of resource. The bleached content of the light verbs is reflected at the syntactic as well as semantic level of the VerbNet entries. The syntactic constraints as to their combinatorial possibilities with main verbs allow for a consistent and efficient computational treatment. This, together with the event decomposition and semantic roles assumed in First-Phase Syntax, paves the way for a cross-linguistic, theoretically well-motivated computational analysis of event structure.

References

Collin F. Baker, Charles J. Filmore, and John B. Lowe. 1998. The Berkeley FrameNet Project. In *Proceedings of the 17th International Conference on Computational Linguistics (Coling-ACL'98)*, pages 86–90.

Rajesh Bhatt, Bhuvana Narasimhan, Martha Palmer, Owen Rambow, Dipti Sharma, and Fei Xia. 2009. A Multi-Representational and Multi-Layered Treebank for Hindi/Urdu. In *Proceedings of the Third Linguistic Annotation Workshop, ACL-IJCNLP 2009*, pages 186–189.

Claire Bonial, William Corvey, Martha Palmer, Volha Petukhova, and Harry Bunt. 2011. A Hierarchical Unification of LIRICS and VerbNet Semantic Roles. In *Proceedings of the ICSC Workshop on Semantic Annotation for Computational Linguistic Resources (SACL-ICSC 2011)*, pages 483–489.

Miriam Butt and Tracy Holloway King. 2005. The status of case. In V. Dayal and A. Mahajan, editors, *Clause Structure in South Asian Languages*, pages 153–198. Berlin: Springer Verlag.

Miriam Butt. 1995. *The Structure of Complex Predicates in Urdu*. Stanford: CSLI Publications.

Miriam Butt. 2006. *Theories of Case*. Cambridge: Cambridge University Press.

Charles J. Fillmore. 1968. Lexical entries for verbs. *Foundations of Language*, 4(4):373–393.

Jeffrey Gruber. 1965. *Studies in Lexical Relations*. Ph.D. thesis, MIT, (reprinted in Lexical Strutures in Syntax and Semantics. Amsterdam, North-Holland, 1976).

Annette Hautli-Janisz. 2013. Moving Right Along: Motion verb sequences in Urdu. In M. Butt and T. Holloway King, editors, *In Proceedings of the LFG13 Conference*, pages 295–215.

Peter Edwin Hook. 1974. *The Compound Verb in Hindi*. The University of Michigan: Center for South and Southeast Asian Studies.

Jena D. Hwang, Archna Bhatia, Claire Bonial, Aous Mansouri, Ashwini Vaidya, Nianwen Xue, and Martha Palmer. 2010. Propbank annotation of multilingual light verb constructions. In *Proceedings of ACL 2010: The Fourth Linguistic Annotation Workshop*, pages 82–90.

Jena D. Hwang, Martha Palmer, and Annie Zaenen. 2013. Representing paths of motion in verbnet. In T. Holloway King and V. de Paiva, editors, *From Quirky Case to Representing Space: Papers in Honour of Annie Zaenen*, pages 155–166. Stanford: CSLI Publications online.

Ray Jackendoff. 1972. *Semantic Interpretation in Generative Grammar*. Cambridge, MA: MIT Press.

Karin Kipper-Schuler. 2005. *VerbNet: A Broad-Coverage, Comprehensive Verb Lexicon*. Ph.D. thesis, University of Pennsylvania.

Colin P. Masica. 1976. *Defining a Linguistic Area*. Chicago and London: The University of Chicago Press.

Marc Moens and Mark Steedman. 1988. Temporal ontology and temporal reference. *Computational Linguistics*, 14:15–38.

Tara Mohanan. 1994. *Argument Structure in Hindi*. Dissertations in Linguistics. Stanford: CSLI Publications.

Martha Palmer, Daniel Gildea, and Paul Kingsbury. 2005. The Proposition Bank: An Annotated Corpus of Semantic Roles. *Computational Linguistics*, 31(1):71–106.

Gillian Ramchand. 2008. *Verb Meaning and the Lexicon: A First-Phase Syntax*. Cambridge: Cambridge University Press.

Ghulam Raza. 2011. *Subcategorization Acquisition and Classes of Predication in Urdu*. Ph.D. thesis, Universität Konstanz.

Ashwini Vaidya, Jinho Choi, Martha Palmer, and Bhuvana Narasimhan. 2011. Analysis of the hindi proposition bank using dependency structure. In *Proceedings of the Fifth Linguistic Annotation Workshop (ACL'11)*, pages 21–29.

Ashwini Vaidya, Jinho Choi, Martha Palmer, and Bhuvana Narasimhan. 2012. Empty Argument Insertion in Hindi PropBank. In *Proceedings of the Eighth International Conference on Language Resources and Evaluation (LREC 2012)*, pages 1522–1526.

Ashwini Vaidya, Martha Palmer, and Bhuvana Narasimhan. 2013. Semantic roles for nominal predicates: Building a lexical resource. In *Proceedings of the 9th Workshop on Multiword Expressions (MWE 2013)*, pages 126–131.

Using Topic Modeling and Similarity Thresholds to Detect Events

Nathan Keane, Connie Yee, Liang Zhou
Text Analytics and Machine Learning
Thomson Reuters
New York, NY 10036, USA
{nathan.keane,connie.yee,l.zhou}@thomsonreuters.com

Abstract

This paper presents a Retrospective Event Detection algorithm, called Eventy-Topic Detection (ETD), which automatically generates topics that describe events in a large, temporal text corpus. Our approach leverages the structure of the topic modeling framework, specifically the Latent Dirichlet Allocation (LDA), to generate topics which are then later labeled as Eventy-Topics or non-Eventy-Topics. The system first runs daily LDA topic models, then calculates the cosine similarity between the topics of the daily topic models, and then runs our novel Bump-Detection algorithm. Similar topics labeled as an Eventy-Topic are then grouped together. The algorithm is demonstrated on two Terabyte sized corpuses - a Reuters News corpus and a Twitter corpus. Our method is evaluated on a human annotated test set. Our algorithm demonstrates its ability to accurately describe and label events in a temporal text corpus.

1 Introduction

Vast amounts of research has been developed to help organize, search, index, browse and understand the immense number of electronic documents. Topic models have emerged as a powerful technique to discover patterns of words that reflect the underlying topics that are combined to form documents. Latent Dirichlet Allocation (Blei et al., 2003) defines topics as multinomial distributions over words, and documents as multinomial distributions over these topics. LDA uses Dirichlet priors for both the document-topic and topic-word distributions.

Topic Detection and Tracking(TDT) is an area of research that was prominent in the 1990's (Allan et al., 1998). The goal of TDT is to detect the appearance of new topics and track their evolution over time. Specifically relevant to our paper is the task of Retrospective Event Detection. It is defined as the task of identifying all events in a corpus of stories.

In our Eventy-Topic Detection (ETD) algorithm we wish to leverage the powerful structure of topic models in the Retrospective Event Detection task. In particular, we develop an algorithm that is capable of identifying Eventy-Topics in a sequentially ordered, massive 'Big Data' sized corpus. We define an Eventy-Topic to be a topic that solely describes a specific, time sensitive news event. A topic that is consistently and persistently in the news is not an Eventy-Topic.

We run daily LDA topic models, then calculate the cosine similarities between the topics in all the models. Eventy-Topics contain a noticeable spike around the date of the event in these cosine similarity graphs. To detect these spikes, we smooth the cosine similarity values so that the bump has a monotonically increasing section, followed by a plateau, followed by a monotonically decreasing section. We then then run a novel algorithm called Bump Detection that searches for these properties.

Given a time-stamped corpus, our goal is to automatically detect and describe all of these Eventy-Topics. Our algorithm is capable of detecting one-time (uni-modal) Eventy-Topics, such as "Robin Williams Death", as well as multi-time (multi-modal) related Eventy-Topics, such as "The Masters Golf Tournament".

Proceedings of the 3rd Workshop on EVENTS at the NAACL-HLT 2015, pages 34–42,
Denver, Colorado, June 4, 2015.

2 Related Work

There have been multiple works that studied the topics of temporal corpora. Topics over Time (Wang and McCallum, 2006) incorporates time directly into the generative topic model. A timestamp is drawn from a beta distribution for every word in the corpus. One limitation of this method is the restrictiveness of the beta distribution. The presence of a topic in a corpus can be multi-modal, which conflicts with the beta distribution. In contrast, our work does not assume that the presence of an event in a corpus is unimodal.

Dynamic topic models (Blei and Lafferty, 2006) capture the evolution of topics in a time stamped corpus. It involves multiple static topic models in each time slice and models how the prior parameters change over time, given a logistic normal prior. The motivation for dynamic topic models is to track the evolution of topics, not to detect emerging topics that correspond to events.

Retrospective New Event Detection research utilizes metrics such as cosine similarity, Hellinger similarity, and KL Divergence to determine how similar documents are (Dou et al., 2012). On-line LDA (AlSumait et al., 2008) incorporates topic detection into its algorithm by calculating the KL divergence of evolving topics at adjacent time periods. If the calculated KL divergence exceeds an historic percentiled threshold, then the topic is flagged as an emerging, new topic. Our work is similar in spirit, but we use difference measures against all previous topics as opposed to just adjacent ones.

There has been success modeling the burstiness of phrases in the news cycle (Leskovec et al., 2008). Static LDA topic models have had their topics labeled as hot and cold based on the mean document-topic mixtures in different time segments (Griffiths and Steyvers, 2004).

TimeMines (Swan and Jensen, 200) is a TDT, 3 step system that first creates noun phrases for features, then finds significant features using a 2x2 contingency table and χ^2 test, then groups significant features together by testing for dependence. These groups of noun phrases for the topic description form the emerging topic.

The Group-Topic model (Wang et al., 2005) slices a 15 year U.N. text corpus into year slices, then runs a topic-relation model and later compares the trends of topics.

Multiscale Topic Tomography (Nallapati et al., 2007) uses a conjugative priors on the topic parameters to model the evolution of topics (simliar to DTM, but with conjugative priors). They present a tree-like hierarchy of topics, where topics can be zoomed in on different time periods, and topic trends can be analyzed.

Multi-Modal Retrospective News Event Detection (Li et al., 2005) is an extensive generative model that incorporates content, time, persons, and location. One challenge of this model is one needs to input the number of events to generate, just like a clustering application.

3 Eventy-Topic Detection

3.1 Training Corpus

Our Eventy-Topic Detection algorithm is demonstrated on a 525 day, 350,000 story Reuters News corpus and a 200 day, 2 billion tweet Twitter corpus. This comes out to average about 6200 stories per 10 day stretch and 10 million tweets a day, respectively. The computation is run over a 30 node Hadoop cluster.

3.2 Daily Topic Modeling

LDA Topic Modeling is run daily on the sequential text corpus. Topic modeling is done with our implementation of LDA topic modeling algorithm that uses efficient gibbs sampling (Yao et al., 2009) and is similar to the algorithm used in Mallet (McCallum, 2002). The text input for each LDA model training is the text that occurs between a fixed amount, N, of days before the date of interest. For the Reuters news corpus $N = 9$ so a total of 10 days is used in the training of each topic model. For the Twitter corpus $N = 0$ is used so only that exact day is inputed. N is chosen based off a couple of factors including having a max input of 6GB for each training model as well as having enough text to derive meaningful, consistent topics. Character unigrams are used as features for the Reuters news corpus and Alphabetic unigrams as well as hashtags are used as features for the Twitter Corpus. The models for each of the daily training runs are then serialized.

Topic Pair	Cosine Similarity
20130101:000_20130302:032	.423
20130101:000_20130303:021	.520
...	
20130101:000_20140630:003	.662
20130101:001_20130302:017	.852
...	
20130101:079_20130630:065	.191
20130102:000_20130301:048	.232
...	
20130630:079_20130629:050	.924

Table 1: Cosine similarity pair mapping table. $date1{:}topic1\_date2{:}topic2 \rightarrow cosineSimilarity$

3.3 Similarity Measures

There are D serialized topic models (one for each day), with each topic model having K topics. Thus there are $D \times K$ total serialized topics, where each topic is represented as a multinomial distribution over words. For each of these topics, the cosine similarity is calculated between that topic and every other $(D-1) \times K$ topics not in that day. Thus, there are a total of $D \times K \times (D-1) \times K$ cosine similarity calculations. The symmetric KL divergence value can also be calculated for these pairs. The rest of the methodology only describes using cosine similarity; however it can be easily modified to use the symmetric KL-Divergence.

For each topic ($date1{:}topic1$), the topic with the highest cosine similarity score from each of the other D-1 daily topic models is saved ($date2{:}topic2$). This creates a mapping table-$date1{:}topic1\_date2{:}topic2 \rightarrow cosineSimilarity$, where $date1{:}topic1$ and $date2{:}topic2$ are concatenated as the key, and the value is the cosine similarity. An example of what this mapping looks like can be seen in Table 1. The algorithm is outlined in Algorithm 1.

3.4 Smoothing

The cosine similarity values are then smoothed using Loess Smoothing (Cleveland and Loader, 1996). Figures 1- 4 show the before and after of the cosine similarity graphs smoothed. The bumps that are present in Figure 2(a) and 4(a) do not contain monotonically increasing sections, followed by a plateau, followed by a monotonically decreasing section. Smoothing gives the bumps this property, making it easier to detect.

```
Data: Serialized Daily Topic Models
Result: Loaded topicCosMap
topicCosMap = Map();
foreach Daily Topic Model m do
    foreach Topic t in m do
        foreach Daily Topic Model m' ≠ m do
            topCs = -1;
            topTopic = null;
            foreach Topic t' in m' do
                cs = cossim(t,t');
                if cs > topCs then
                    topCs = cs;
                    topTopic = t';
                end
            end
        end
        topicCosMap.put(String(m,t,m',topTopic),topCs);
    end
end
```

Algorithm 1: Cosine Similarity Pair Mapping

The main parameter, α, in Loess Smoothing determines the percentage of nearest points used in the weighted regressions. Smoothing is done for α= .02, .03, .04, .05, .10 on (x,y) pairs grouped by $date1{:}topic1$ in the mapping table. The $date2$ day index is the x-value, and the cosine similarity is the y-value. The α that we use in Eventy-Topic Detection is significantly lower than the usual .25 to .5 range. This is done to accommodate the sharp, unusual bumps that are found for Eventy-Topics in the cosine similarity pair graphs. The larger the α, the more smooth the graph becomes and the bump becomes less pronounced. These small α values assure a pronounced bump in Eventy-Topics as well as mononically increasing/decreasing sections.

3.5 Bump Detection

We created a detection method to identify Eventy-Topics out of the $D \times K$ collection of topics. We believe that if a topic contains a definite bump in its cosine similarity graph then it is an Eventy-Topic; if not, then it is a Non-Eventy-Topic. After smoothing,

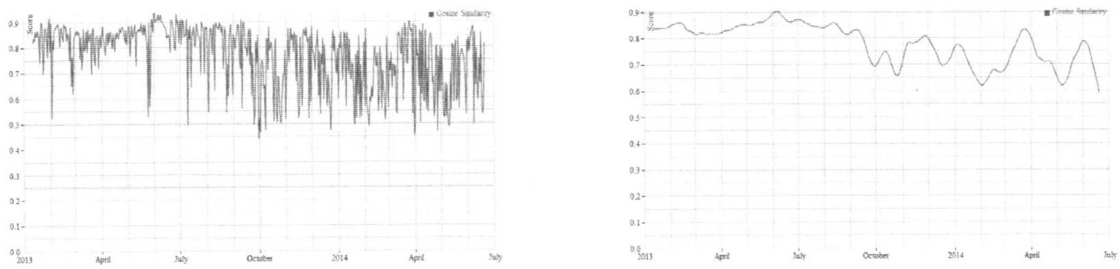

(a) Reuters Non-Event (b) Reuters Non-Event Smoothed α=.05

Figure 1: Cosine similarity graphs for Reuters Topic 20130604:042. "Bonds"- { percent year bond yields yield bonds market debt billion week points basis ... }

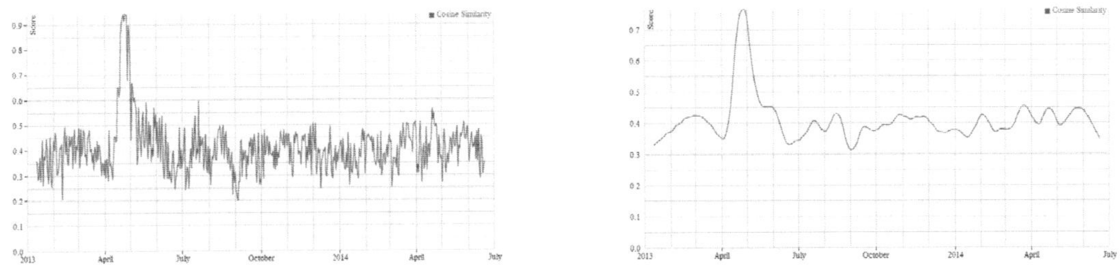

(a) Reuters Event (b) Reuters Event Smoothed α=.05

Figure 2: Cosine similarity graphs for Reuters Topic 20130426:017. "Boston Marathon Bombing"- { boston police marathon people tsarnaev suspect killed monday bombing tamerlan ... }

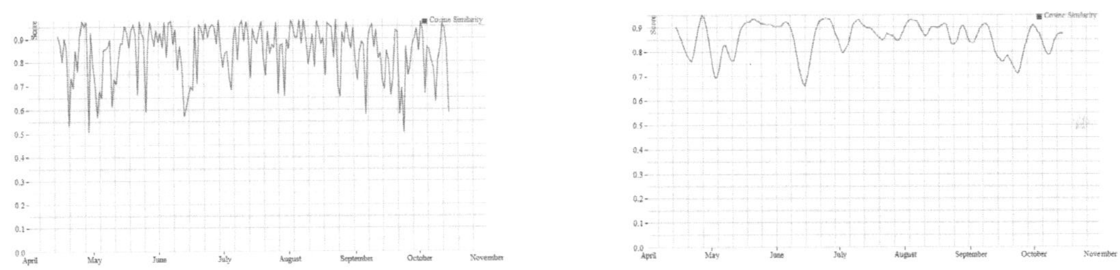

(a) Twitter Non-Event (b) Twitter Non-Event Smoothed α=.05

Figure 3: Cosine similarity graphs for Twitter Topic 20140718:037. "Happy Birthday"- { happy love birthday miss day hope baby beautiful great ya amazing ... }

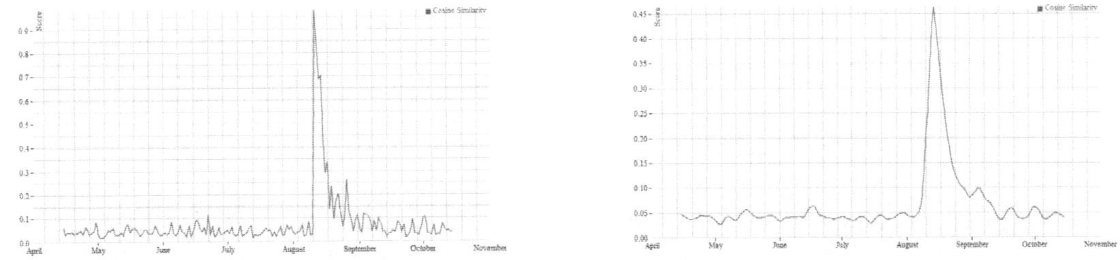

(a) Twitter Event (b) Twitter Event Smoothed α=.04

Figure 4: Cosine similarity graphs for Twitter topic 20140812:003. "Robin Williams' Death"- { robin williams rip dead sad actor mrs doubtfire died #riprobinwilliams news death ... }

the bumps display a monotonically increasing period followed by a monotonically decreasing period. To automatically detect these localized, relatively high cosine similarity bumps we use a novel algorithm called Bump Detection. This algorithm is outlined in Algorithm 2. Bump detection is used on each of the five different smoothed cosine similarity values (α= .02, .03, .04, .05, .10). There are a number of variables and parameters used:

- $coldLevel$ - number where all the non-bump cosine similarity values must be below
- $hotLevel$ - number where all the cosine similarity values in the bump plateau need to be above
- $maxRiseTime$ - max time it takes to get from $coldLevel$ to $hotLevel$
- $maxFallTime$ - max time it takes to get from $hotLevel$ back to $coldLevel$
- $minHot$ - the mininum number of cosine similarity values above the $hotLevel$
- $maxHot$ - the maximum number of cosine similarity values above the $hotLevel$
- $minHotColdDiffThresh$ - parameter where ($hotThresh$-$coldThresh$) must be greater than in order for the topic to be labeled an 'Eventy-Topic'

The hot cosine similarity values must be continuously above the hot threshold. The cold cosine similarity values must be continuous on both the left and right side of the rise and fall values, respectively. The $minHotColdDiffThresh$ is the key parameter that is used to select only graphs that contain large bumps.

Topic 042 from the model with date 2013-06-04 generated from the Reuters corpus represents a "Bond Topic" (Figure 1). Topic 017 from the model with date 2013-04-26 generated from the Twitter corpus represents a "Happy Birthday Topic" (Figure 3). Both of these figures show noisy cosine similarity graphs. This is because these topics are present at all/random times in their respective corpuses and do not correspond to a time specific event. In fact, in almost every serialized topic model in the Twitter corpus, there is a "Happy Birthday" topic with a nearly identical topic-word distribution.

Both the "Boston Marathon Bombing" topic from the Reuters corpus (Figure 2) and the "Robin Williams' Death" topic from the Twitter corpus (Figure 4) have noticable bumps in their cosine similarity graphs around the date of their respective events.

Figure 5 depicts the cosine similarity graph from topic 003 from the model with date 2014-08-12 generated from the Reuters corpus. This topic describes an event where Mt. Gox, a bitcoin exchange, collapsed in minutes. Figure 6 is a closeup on the bump that includes the variables generated from the bump detection algorithm. The difference between the $hotLevel$ and $coldLevel$ for this topics' cosine similarity graph is .536, which is significantly higher than our usual $minHotColdDiffThresh$ of .20.

```
Data: Cosine Similarity Pair Mapping Table
Result: Loaded eventyList
cosMap = loadCosMapTable();
eventyList = List();
foreach date1:topic1 t in cosMap do
    hotColdDiff=0.0;
    dateCosList = getDateCos(cosMap, t);
    reverseSortByCos(dateCosList);
    hotStart = minHot-1;
    coldStart = minHot; hotStop = maxHot;
    coldStop = maxHot+maxRise+maxFall;
    for i <- coldStart to coldStop do
        cold = dateCosList[i].cos;
        for j <- hotStart to min(i,hotStop) do
            hot = dateCosList[j].cos;
            b1 = (hot-cold) > hotColdDiff;
            b2 = consecDates(dateCosList,i);
            b3 = consecDates(dateCosList,j);
            b4 = consecRiseFall(dateCosList,i,j,
            maxRise, maxFall);
            if b1 and b2 and b3 and b4 then
                hotColdDiff = (hot-cold);
            end
        end
    end
    if hotColdDiff>minHotColdDiffThresh
    then
        eventyList.add(t);
    end
end
```

Algorithm 2: Bump Detection

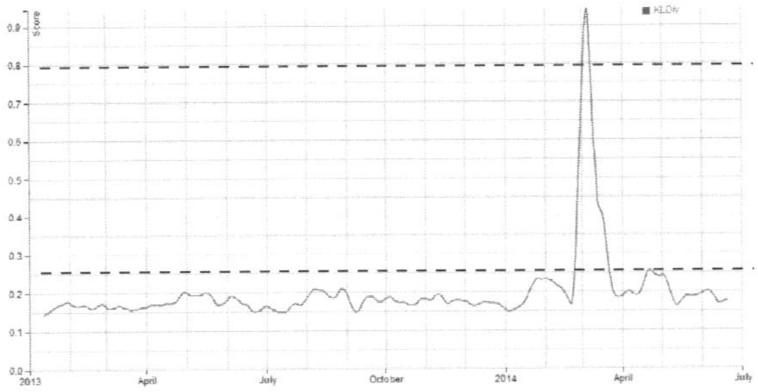

Figure 5: Mt. Gox Bitcoin Collapse Topic Cosine Similarity Pair Graph with Hot/Cold Lines

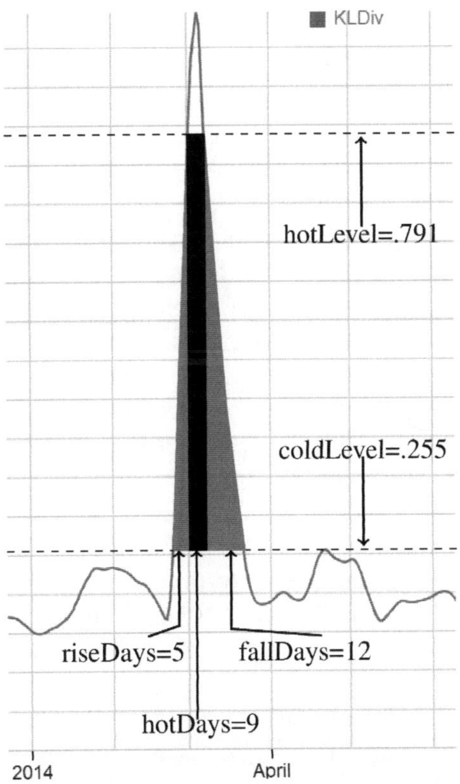

Figure 6: Closeup on the Bump Detection

3.6 Event Grouping

The final step of generating Eventy-Topics is grouping similar Eventy-Topics together. In the Reuters Corpus, for example, topic modeling is run daily over the previous 10 days, and thus each of the documents are input into 10 different, daily topic models. This makes the "Boston Marathon Bombing" Eventy-Topic exist in models run between April 16, 2013 and May 2, 2013. For each Eventy-Topic generated by the Bump Detection algorithm, there is almost surely other near identical Eventy-Topics. Topics with cosine similarity values in the hot zone of one Eventy-Topic are likely labeled Eventy-Topics as well. Thus we want to group these Eventy-Topics into one. We grouped these Eventy-Topics together by creating a graph where the vertices are the Eventy-Topics. If one Eventy-Topic K_1 is in another Eventy-Topic, K_2's, hot zone, then we place an edge between these two vertices in our Eventy-Topic graph. We then run a connected components algorithm over the graph to generate a list of sets of Eventy-Topics. For each set in the list, the vertex with the highest degree is chosen to represent all the Eventy-Topics in that set.

3.7 Multi-Bump Detection

Some events might happen in two or more separate time periods. The topics that describe these events will not be captured by the Bump detection algorithm because the cosine similarity graph will dip into the cold threshold between the two bumps. To modify single Bump Detection algorithm, we added an extra parameter $minTimeBetweenBumps$, which is used to control the minimum time the cosine similarity graph must stay in the cold zone between bumps. This algorithm will then allow multiple bumps as long as they are a certain distance apart from each other.

Figure 7 corresponds to an announcement in January 2013 in which India will raise 57 billion through its first sale of inflation-linked bonds in over a decade . India had periods where it issued these bonds (Mar 2013, Jun 2013, Oct 2013) that correspond to the multiple bumps on the graph. News about this major India debt offering were only present at these particular times and are all tied to that January 2013 announcement.

Event	Date	Topic Words
Mt Gox Bitcoin Collapse	2014-03-22	bitcoin mt gox exchange exchanges currency money
Syrian Chemical Weapon Attack	2013-09-02	syria chemical weapons military russia russian assad
2013 America's Cup	2013-09-24	america cup oracle san francisco ellison zealand bay
The Rim Fire	2013-08-22	fire park national area yosemite blaze san francisco
2013 Korea Crisis	2013-04-13	north korea south korean nuclear missile united states tensions
Israel Election	2013-01-22	israel netanyahu israeli election state west palestinian
Savar Building Colllapse	2013-04-24	building people safety bangladesh stores factory collapse
Thailand Coup	2014-05-22	government army thailand military coup political thai martial
Typhoon Haiyan	2013-11-17	people aid philippines food typhoon water storm hit haiyan
NSA Leak	2013-06-18	government security national information agency snowden nsa
Chinese Bird Flu	2013-04-12	people flu bird health china human cases virus strain

Table 2: Some Reuters' Eventy-Topics Generated

Figure 7: Cosine similarity graphs for Reuters Topic 20130115:052. "Large India Bond Sale" - { percent india gmt eye year inr ns indian oil rupees bond billion ...}

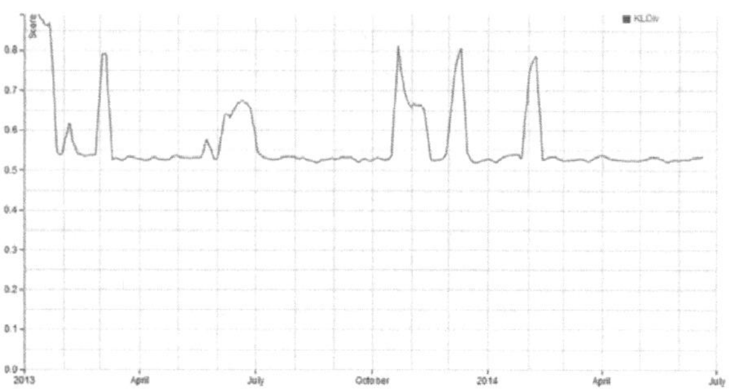

4 Experimental Results

Evaluation of our ETD algorithm was done by annotating a selected set of topics. To expedite and strengthen the annotation process we first ran Bump Detection with a relatively low[1] *minColdHotDiffThresh* and then again with this parameter set to a relatively high[2] value. The sampling for our annotation set was then divided into 3 strata.

- Strata I: topics that were not labeled as Eventy-Topics with a low *minColdHotDiffTresh*.
- Strata II: topics that were labeled as Eventy-Topics with a low, but not a high *minColdHotDiffTresh*.
- Strata III: topics that were labeled as Eventy-Topics with a high *minColdHotDiffTresh*.

The details of our sampling for annotation can be seen in Table 3. Note that the annotation was done on topics and not on the results of the Event Grouping step.

Our annotation set consisted of randomly sampled 84 topics from Strata I, 11 topics from Strata II, and 22 topics from Strata III. The vast majority of topics fell into Strata I (40,270), with the second most in Strata II (1,151), and the rest in Strata III (579).

The reason for dividing the sampled topics into different strata is because the annotation of our Eventy-Topic detection was different in each of these 3 Strata. 80/84 topics in Strata I were labeled as 'Non-Eventy-Topics', while 21/22 topics in Strata III were labeled as 'Eventy-Topics'. 6/11 topics sampled for Strata II were labeled as 'Eventy-Topics'. Strata II topics were the most difficult to annotate.

Now that we had an annotated set of Eventy-Topics, we then tuned the parameters in our Eventy-Topic Detection algorithm to maximize performance over the annotated set. The results of our Reuters News corpus Eventy-Topic Detection with optimal parameters[3] can be seen in Table 4.

[1] low *minColdHotDiffTresh*=[.14, .13, .12, .11, .10} for α = {.02, .03, .04, .05, .10}

[2] high *minColdHotDiffTresh*={.24, .23, .22, .21, .20}, for α = {.02, .03, .04, .05, .10}

[3] optimal *minColdHotDiffTresh*=[.20, .19, .18, .17, .16} for α = {.02, .03, .04, .05, .10}

Strata	Description	# of Topics	# Sampled	# Labeled True	# Labeled False
I	Topics that do not pass low threshold	40270	84	4	80
II	Topics that pass low threshold but not high threshold	1151	11	6	5
III	Topics that pass high threshold	579	22	21	1

Table 3: Sampling of Topics from Reuters Corpus for Annotation

Strata	Correctly Labeled	Incorrectly Labeled	Accuracy
I	80	4	.9545
II	8	3	.7272
III	21	1	.9545

Table 4: Accuracy of Eventy-Topic Detection with Optimized $minColdHotDiffThresh$

5 Discussion

The data sets need to be sufficiently large in size and time horizon in order for our ETD algorithm to be useful. The Reuters News Corpus spanned 525 days, and an even longer spanning corpus could yield better results. The algorithm also requires significant computation. We ran all our computation on Hadoop in the MapReduce framework and wrote all the data to HBase. On our 30-node Hadoop cluster, the daily topic modeling for the Reuters corpus took approximately 1 day, and the cosine similarity calculation took about 2 days. The Bump Detection algorithms for different smoothing parameters and thresholds only took a few minutes.

One limitation of ETD is that it is run on a stale, large corpus of sequential text and not on an online stream of text. Our algorithm can be modified to run the topic modeling, say every 3 hours, on an incoming stream of text, and then cosine similarity pairs and Bump Detection.

Further extensions, such as analyzing the shape of the bump, the rise time, and the fall time to determine if the Eventy-Topic was expected or not expected, could be very useful.

Our Eventy-Topic Detection algorithm was evaluated with a manually annotated corpus. This is similar to the way Retrospective Event Detection is evaluated in previous studies.

References

James Allan, Jamie G. Carbonell, George Doddington, Jonathan Yamron, and Yiming Yang. Topic Detection and Tracking Pilot Study Final Report (1998).

Loulwah AlSumait, Daniel Barbara, and Carlotta Domeniconi. On-Line LDA: Adaptive Topic Models for Mining Text Streams with Applications to Topic Detection and Tracking *Data Mining, 2008. ICDM'08. Eighth IEEE International Conference*. IEEE, 2008.

David M. Blei and John D. Lafferty. Dynamic Topic Models *Proceedings of the 23rd international conference on Machine learning*. ACM, 2006.

David M. Blei, Andrew Y. Ng, and Michael I. Jordan. Latent Dirichlet Allocation *The Journal of Machine Learning Research*, 3 (2003): 993-1022.

Mario Cataldi, Lugi Di Caro, and Claudio Schifanella. Emerging Topic Detection on Twitter based on Temporal and Social Terms Evaluation. *Proceedings of the Tenth International Workshop on Multimedia Data Mining*. ACM, 2010.

William S. Cleveland and Clive Loader. Smoothing by Local Regression: Principles and Methods. *Statistical theory and computational aspects of smoothing*. Physica-Verlag HD, 1996. 10-49.

Wenwen Dou, Xiaoyu Wang, William Ribarsky, and Michelle Zhou. Event Detection in Social Media Data. *IEEE VisWeek Workshop on Interactive Visual Text Analytics-Task Driven Analytics of Social Media Content*. 2012.

Thomas L. Griffiths and Mark Steyvers. Finding Scientific Topics *Proceedings of the National academy of Sciences of the United States of America* , 101.Suppl 1 (2004): 5228-5235.

Jure Leskovec, Lars Backstrom, and Jon Kleinberg. Meme-tracking and the Dynamics of the News Cycle *Proceedings of the 15th ACM SIGKDD international conference on Knowledge discovery and data mining*. ACM, 2009.

Zhiwei Li, Bin Wang, Mingjing Li, and Wei-Ying Ma. A Probabilistic Model for Retrospective News Event Detection. *Proceedings of the 28th annual international ACM SIGIR conference on Research and development in information retrieval*. ACM, 2005.

Andrew K. McCallum. MALLET: A Machine Learning for Language Toolkit *http://mallet.cs.umass.edu*. 2002.

Ramesh Nallapati, William Cohen, Susan Ditmore, John Lafferty, and Kin Ung. Multiscale Topic Tomography *ICWSM*. 2009.

Hassan Sayyadi, Matthew Hurst, and Alexey Maykov. Event Detection and Tracking in Social Streams. *Proceedings of the 13th ACM SIGKDD international conference on Knowledge discovery and data mining*. ACM, 2007.

Russell Swan and David Jensen. TimeMines: Constructing Timelines with Statistical Models of Word Usage *KDD-2000 Workshop on Text Mining*. 2000

Xuerui Wang and Andrew McCallum. Topics over Time: A Non-Markov Continuous-Time Model of Topical Trends *Proceedings of the 12th ACM SIGKDD international conference on Knowledge discovery and data mining*. ACM, 2006.

Xuerui Wang, Natasha Mohanty, and Andrew McCallum Group and Topic Discovery from Relations and Text *Proceedings of the 3rd international workshop on Link discovery*. ACM, 2005.

Limin Yao, David Mimno, and Andrew McCallum. Efficient methods for topic model inference on streaming document collections. *Proceedings of the 15th ACM SIGKDD international conference on Knowledge discovery and data mining*. ACM, 2009.

Detecting Causally Embedded Structures Using an Evolutionary Algorithm

Chen Li
Department of Linguistics
University of Illinois at U-C
707 S Mathews Avenue,
Urbana, IL 61801
chenli@illinois.edu

C. Roxana Girju
Department of Linguistics
University of Illinois at U-C
707 S Mathews Avenue,
Urbana, IL 61801
girju@illinois.edu

Abstract

Causality is an important relation among events and entities. Embedded causal structures represent an important class, expressing complex causal chains; but they are traditionally difficult to uncover automatically. In this paper we propose a method for the efficient identification and extraction of embedded causal relations with minimal supervision, by combining a representation of structured language data with modified *prototype* theory specifically suited to the data type. We then utilize a form of *genetic algorithm* specifically adapted for our purpose to locate the likely candidate linguistic structures that contain causal chains. With this procedure, we were able to identify many embedded structures with complex causal chains in two corpora of different genres, applying this algorithm as a ranking procedure for all structures in the data. We obtained 79.5% percision for top quantiles of both of our datasets (BNC & novels).

1 Embedded Causality

Long chains of causal relations are frequently denoted by a complex embedding of multiple clauses through lexico-syntactic structures, structures which are causally linked. Following previous approaches (Menzies 2009, Beamer & Girju 2009), we define a causal relation as $e_1 \xrightarrow{cause} e_2$, where e_1 precedes e_2 temporally and, had e_1 failed to take place, e_2 would also not have taken place, or more generally, $P(e_2|e_1) > P(e_2|\neg e_1)$. This is a general and agreed upon definition of causality which encompasses various classes of causal types of interest (if one chooses to go deeper into this problem). Our unit of representation (for both the cause and the effect) is a *semantic frame*, given by a predicate and a list of arguments in the form $\phi(ARG_i, ARG_j, ARG_k, ...)$. This corresponds to a clause. Such clauses ocurring in embedded structures can form a causal chain. For example (from *Little Women*):

1. a smart shower at eleven had evidently quenched the enthusiasm of the young ladies who were to arrive at twelve for nobody came and at two the exhausted family sat down in a blaze of sunshine to consume the perishable portions of the feast (prepared in anticipation of the guests) that nothing might be lost (Alcott, 1868)

   (a) a smart shower at eleven had evidently quenched the enthusiasm of the young ladies who were to arrive at twelve

   (b) $\xrightarrow{cause}$ nobody came

   (c) $\xrightarrow{cause}$ the exhausted family sat down in a blaze of sunshire

   (d) $\xrightarrow{cause}$ consume the perishable portions of the feast

   (e) $\xrightarrow{cause}$ nothing might be lost

In this paper we focus on causal relations between clauses (marked or not by discourse markers).

1.1 Distinct characteristics

Each embedded causal structure has a *causer* entity identified by the main clause, and an effect event identified by the embedded (i.e. subordinate) clause. A class of semantically rich verbs is often present, that convey some notion of causation, coloring the causing event with additional *manner* of causation – verbs such as *inspire*, *suggest*, *prompt*, *bribe*, *incite*, *bully*, *force*, *compel*, etc. We call this class $\mathcal{MCC}$-verbs. Other verbs such as *cause*, *bring-about*, however, are just simple causatives (Girju 2003). Depending on its complexity, there may be one or more intermediate clausal structures that represent links in the causal chain, along with intermediate causal agents whose presence could have little specific semantic information, e.g. *"...caused the circumstances to line up in such a way as to..."*, but informs of its properties as a causal chain.

Due to the complexity of these elements and the intervening structures, there are many combinatorial possibilities, and the depths of such structures are potentially unbounded. So rather than finding a comprehensive set of *exemplars* that cover all cases, it is better to assemble patterns that represent a diffuse *prototype*, finding characteristic structures common in embedded causal frames, such as:

Proceedings of the 3rd Workshop on EVENTS at the NAACL-HLT 2015, pages 43–52,
Denver, Colorado, June 4, 2015.

i $ENTITY_{causer}$ ***caused it to come about*** *that* $ENTITY_{causee}$ $[PRED_{emb}$ ....]

ii $ENTITY_{causer}$ ***arranged*** *the events* ***so that it comes about*** *that* $ENTITY_{causee}$ $[PRED_{emb}$ ....]

iii $ENTITY_{causer}$ *had the forsight* ***to prepare the circumstances so that*** *it* ***comes about*** *that* $ENTITY_{causee}$ $[PRED_{emb}$....]

For all examples above, we can see that a subtree producing the terminals would be *"to come about that ....".* A subtree like this can be used to further identify larger embedded structures as causal, and each embedded causative construction thus identified would contain one or more such subtrees.

1.2 Data

We considered two different genres: 1) the British National Corpus (BNC, 2007), and 2) novels from romantic fiction and historical novelas (mostly from Project Gutenberg, 2005), such as *The Great Gatzby*, *Pride and Prejudice*, *Little Women*, *Emma*, and *Lily of the Nile*. The training set consists of 500 positive instances (i.e., manually identified to contain a causal chain of at least one cause - effect relationship) which were selected from the 3rd quarter of BNC. The testing sets consist of the 1st quarter of BNC, and the novels set, respectively.

2 Previous work

There is a variety of approaches to causal relations in the literature, approaches which rely mostly on machine learning methods over high-dimensional semantic-feature spaces (Abe et. al., 2008; Berthard & Martin, 2008; Riaz & Girju; Do et. al., 2011; Radinsky et. al. 2012 / 2013; Oh et. al. 2013; Hashimoto et. al., 2014; etc). Other researchers have focused on pre-identified lexico-syntactic patterns (Khoo et. al. 2001; Girju 2003) which they use to bootstrap an Expectation-Maximization procedure (Chang & Choi 2006; Paul et. al. 2009) for causality and similar semantic relations. Furthermore, these parametric and pattern recognition works are generally fucussed on pair-wise causal relations between event representations. We instead focus on linguistic structures of unbounded complexity that are capable of expressing sequences of events involved in long causal chains. Our work explores novel representations of causality, and procedures rooted in evolutionary computing in order to deal with the structural complexity of these expressions as well as retain the flexibility of parametric approaches.

3 Diffuse prototype

We need to encompass available lexico-semantic (symbolic) and morphosyntactic (structural) information into a single representation that can be compared and transformed. And since our goal is to extract causal chains from complex structures, the representation needs to generalize the information over the member frames/clauses. We mostly focus on the intervening information and structural configuration between clausal subtrees, where the substructures are found based on sub-graph isomorphism between two positive samples treated as trees. The ideal product would be a set of maximally complex sub-structures in the reflection of their causality, which would not compromise their ability to generalize over all embedded causal structures. In this case, a purely parametric approach will not work for any tree structure of sufficient size, given the number of binary parameters that would need to represent the presence or absence of an edge $\langle v_i, v_j \rangle$ is $\mathcal{O}(n(T)^2)$. And thus, the number of possible configurations comes to $\mathcal{O}(2^{n(T)^2})$ without taking into account labels or other sources of complexity. For potential cognitive models of categorization, *prototype* and *exemplars* are the primary theories most frequently considered. A single prototype is ideal for representing a set of similar objects that can be unimodally represented in feature space. A set of *exemplars* has the advantage of allowing distributions in many modes in feature-space, each cluster being represented by a single exemplar.

Thus, we propose and formulate a novel categorial model combining strengths of both prototype and exemplars, with a graph theoretic focus. Like *prototype*, it provides few structures far more concise than sample-set, allowing a high degree of generalization. Like *exemplars*, it is adaptable in a multi-modal distribution over naturally defined feature space, with a wide coverage of subtypes. This we will term a *diffuse prototype* of the class, which are shared graph-theoretic substructures of at least two postitive samples. Given a feature space $X = [x_{[1]}, x_{[2]}, \ .... \ x_{[n]}] \in \{0,1\}^n$, a substructure, as a component within a *diffuse prototype* ($\mathcal{DP}$), is $X_s = \{x_{[\kappa_j]}\} \mid j \in \kappa \sqsubset [1, 2, ..., n]$ such that $\exists Y^p, Y^q \in Y \ \forall j \in \kappa \ [Y^p_{[\kappa_j]} = Y^q_{[\kappa_j]}]$, where Y = set of positive samples for that semantic class. Thus, the samples Y^p, Y^q agree on some substructure within the feature space. When the feature space is structured in some way, an additional constraint of *contiguity* is necessary. X_s above must follow *linear contiguity* for its contiguity definition. This requires that $\forall i, j \in \kappa \wedge X_{[\kappa_i]}, X_{[\kappa_j]} \in X_s$ and where $P_{i \to j} := \lhd i, \ ..., \ j \rhd$ is some consecutive sequence $\sqsubset \mathbb{N}$, we have that $\forall k \in P_{i \to j} \ [\kappa_k \in X_s]$ ($\sqsubset$ here symoblizes sub-sequence relation). So now in this example, any substructure must be restricted by some linearly contiguous region of X. We have a more complex structure of the feature space - the notion of *continguity*, referred to as $N^+_T(v_i)$ and $N^-_T(v_i)$, with which we determine the allowable extensions of any substructure T_s. The allowed substructures are:

$$T_t = G(X_s) \begin{cases} \forall v_p, v_q \in V(T_t) \\ \exists P_{p \to q} := \lhd i, \ ..., k, ... \ j \rhd \ \sqsubset \kappa^P \\ \forall \kappa_k^P, \kappa_{k+1}^P \in \kappa^P \left[v_{[\kappa_{k+1}^P]} \in N_T^+(v_{[\kappa_k^P]}) \right] \end{cases} \quad (1)$$

Where κ^P is a specific ordering of $V(T)$ that conforms to the path P. The only types of X_s sought are those that form a proper subtree T_t of the original T. This is a natural way to allow generalization into members of the $\mathcal{DP}$, and thus some fragmented forest subgraph of T is not desirable. As an illustration, the trees T and T' in Figure 1 contain a pair of substructures T_s and T_t corresponding to red / violet regions. The shared subgraphs are used to find

Figure 1: 2 trees containing common substructures

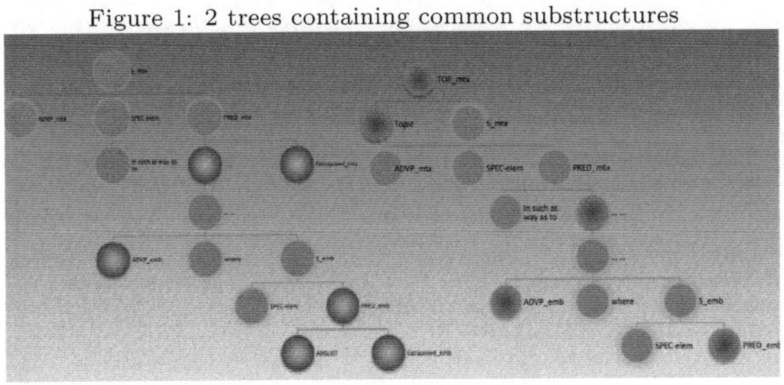

yet some other T'' where variable (blue-grey) regions differ from either T or T'.

4 Extraction procedure

The key difficulty is the *isomorphic* comparison of two trees. For this, we developed a form of graph-theoretic genetic algorithm, simulating the growth of subtrees shared between two reference trees T, T'.

4.1 Baseline genetic algorithm

Inspired by *On the Origin of Species* (Darwin 1859), *genetic algorithms* are a class of adaptive algorithms (Turing 1950; Barricelli 1962; Rechenberg 1973; Holland 1975; de Jong 1975), with wide array of application (Brindle 1981; Baker 1985 / 1989; Goldberg 1989; Goldberg & Deb 1993; Fogel 1998). Our algorithm has similarities to *genetic programming* (Cramer 1985; Schmidhuber 1987), and to aspects of the original biological model, beyond traditional GA, due to greater variability afforded by substructure growth. Two processes are responsible for growth and diversification of chromosomes, *mutation* and *recombination* in GA. An elimination stage culls a part of the population with regard to some notion of *fitness* (*directed selection*), its magnitude determined by *carrying capacity* (Goldberg et. al., 1991).

4.2 Proposed modifications to GA

We adapted the baseline GA, redefining the operators graph-theoretically according to specific structure types in the $\mathcal{DP}$. For our evolutionary algorithm, we have thouroughly reformulated the three primary operators, *non-homogenizing*, *homogenizing*, and *culling*, as well as how gene loci are structured, from the baseline GA. For a minimal ecological niche, we find some lexico-syntactic cues and associated structures discussed in Section 1.1 that is shared by at least a pair of positive samples. To better discriminate between non-causal structures and embedded causal structures, we need to maximize the complexity of the $\mathcal{DP}$ members, in order to minimize the number of possible $T \in \mathbb{T}$ (set of samples) that could contain such, thus maximizing the specificity of $\mathcal{DP}$.

4.2.1 Individual and population

Our genotype is cast as a piece of structural information within some induced subtree T_s of $\langle T, T' \rangle$ that conveys causality, so *'chromosome'* is modeled as the set of parameters necessary to encode T_s denoted as ξ^{T_s}. Thus, the phenotype is simply whether ξ^{T_s}, once decoded into T_s fits inside the ecological niche as induced subgraph. Whether a *"phenotype"* is well adapted for the *"ecological niche"* can simply be a subgraph isomorphism test, which hereon we will denote as $\mathcal{I}^{\mathcal{S}}(T_s, T)$. The baseline GA represents chromosome modeled an ordered set of traits with linear contiguity. Since it is highly inefficient to represent all structural information of a chromosome as individual binary parameters, we redesigned this as a graph-theoretic representation of the linguistic structure. The members of $\mathcal{DP}$ are represented as subgraphs within embedded causal structures, so each GA-operator must be reformulated according to graph-theoretic concepts.

We will use standard graph theoretic notations, where $G = \langle V, E \rangle$ (vertices and edges); and $N_T^{+/-}(v)$ is the operator that locates the neighbors set of $v \in V$ of tree T in the $+/-$ direction. The genetic makeup of an individual is modeled as a single chromosome ξ^{T_s}, so the entire set of such sub-structures of $\langle T, T' \rangle$ becomes our population. Following our definition of *diffuse prototype*, a chromosome is not an ordered set of parameters, but a configuration of subgraph; and location of gene loci is not its linear position, but its relative location WRT to others, in a tree structure.

$$\xi^{T_s} = \begin{cases} \langle v_r, v'_r \rangle \Big| \left[v_r \in V(T) \wedge \nexists v_s \in V(T_s)[v_s \in N_T^-(v_s)] \right] \\ \qquad \bigwedge \left[v'_r \in V(T') \wedge \nexists v'_s \in V(T'_s)[v'_s \in N_{T'}^-(v'_s)] \right] \\ \Big\langle V_l = \left\{ v_l \Big| \exists v_m \in N_T^+(v_l)[v_m \notin N_{T_s}^+(v_l)] \ \vee \ |N_T^+(v_l)| = 0 \right\} \\ V'_l = \left\{ v'_l \Big| \exists v'_m \in N_{T'}^+(v'_l)[v'_m \notin N_{T_s}^+(v'_l)] \ \vee \ |N_{T'}^+(v'_l)| = 0 \right\} \Big\rangle \end{cases} \quad (2)$$

ξ^{T_s} must contain locations of the boundary nodes of substructure within T; such boundaries of both T and T' are contained within ξ^{T_s}, where each point in the boundary is implemented as a pointer to a tree node. So ξ^{T_s} is a collection of pointers WRT $\langle T, T' \rangle$: By moving pointers around $V(T), V(T')$, we can decode T_s. The $\rho-$ and $\lambda-$operators indicate the *'root'* and *'leaves'* of T_s WRT any habitat tree $\check{T}$.

$$\begin{cases} v_r = \rho_{\check{T}}(\xi^{T_s}) \mid v_r \in V(\check{T}) \\ V_l = \lambda_{\check{T}}(\xi^{T_s}) \mid \forall v_l \in V_l[v_l \in V(\check{T})] \end{cases} \tag{3}$$

The initial generation $\mathcal{G}^0$ consists of identical single nodes between T, T', and G is max generation limit, $\{\rho_{\check{T}}(\xi^{T_s})\} = \lambda_{\check{T}(\xi^{T_s})} \wedge \{\rho'_{\check{T}}(\xi^{T_s})\} = \lambda'_{\check{T}}(\xi^{T_s})$.

4.2.2 Non-homogenizing operator

The non-homogenizing operator should be designed to create new gene variations in the population, this is equivalent to *mutation* in baseline GA. Since we cannot efficiently encode all possible subgraphs of T, we use the far more efficient ξ^{T_s}. So we reformulated the non-homogenizing operator as a process that grows a tree sub-structure one edge+node at a time, and thus introduces new degrees of freedom each generation. We define an operation that might add a new vertex $v_i \in V(T) \setminus V(T_s)$ and edge $\langle v_i, v_j \rangle$ or $\langle v_j, v_i \rangle \in E(T), v_j \in V(T_s)$. This is easiest realized in two subtypes, due to the directed nature of T and has no effect on the genetic makeup of the following generation. The previous configuration ξ^{T_s} remains if conditions are not met.

$$\mu_r(\xi^{T_s}, \langle T, T' \rangle) = \begin{cases} \Big\langle \langle v_j, v'_j \rangle, \langle \lambda_T(\xi^{T_s}), \lambda'_{T'}(\xi^{T_s}) \rangle \Big\rangle \\ \quad \Big| \Big(v_j = \rho_T(\xi^{T_s}),\ v_i \in N^-_T(v_j) \Big) \\ \quad \bigwedge \Big(v'_j = \rho'_{T'}(\xi^{T_s}),\ v_i \in N^-_{T'}(v_j) \Big) \\ \quad \bigwedge \Big(\varsigma(v_j) = \varsigma(v'_j) \Big) \end{cases} \tag{4}$$

where l, r are leaf and root directions. When both T, T' agree on a common addition to the current substructure, it returns $\xi^{T'_s}$, grown from the structure of T_s in the r-direction. Here is μ in the l direction (the operator $v_h =_{T_t} v_k$ denotes that they are topologically equivalent with respect to the substructure T_t that is shared within the pair $\langle T, T' \rangle$):

$$\mu_l(\xi^{T_s}, \langle T, T' \rangle) = \begin{cases} \Big\langle \langle \rho_T(\xi^{T_s}),\ \rho'_{T'}(\xi^{T_s}) \rangle, \langle \lambda_T(\xi^{T_s}) \cup \{v_i\}, \\ \quad \lambda'_{T'}(\xi^{T_s}) \cup \{v'_i\} \rangle \Big\rangle \Big| \exists v_i \in V(T), \\ v'_i \in V(T'), v_i =_{T_s} v'_i \Big(v_i \notin V(T_s) \wedge \\ \exists v_j \in \lambda_T(\xi^{T_s}) \,[\, v_i \in N^+_T(v_j) \,] \Big) \bigwedge \\ \Big(v'_i \notin V(T_s) \wedge \exists v_j \in \lambda'_{T'}(\xi^{T_s}) \\ [\, v'_i \in N^+_T(v_j) \,] \Big) \bigwedge \Big(\varsigma(v_i) = \varsigma(v'_i) \Big) \end{cases} \tag{5}$$

During the non-homogenizing stage of a generation, each individual ξ^{T_s} within the population has a chance to undergo either $\mu_r(\xi^{T_s}, \langle T, T' \rangle)$ or $\mu_l(\xi^{T_s}, \langle T, T' \rangle)$. The probabilities are mediated by the random variables $R^{\blacktriangle}$ and $R^{\blacktriangledown}$; the ratio between $R^{\blacktriangle}, R^{\blacktriangledown}$ is governed by the mean branching factor of T, T', so to ensure even growth in all directions.

4.2.3 Homogenizing operator

A homogenizing operator in biological systems or GA randomizes the distribution of alleles and redistribute new allelic types among the population, by exchange of information between distinct units of inheritance between homologous loci; the most prevalent is *recombination*. For our purposes, this is similar to individual haploid organisms exchanging genetic material (e.g. plasmids). So we reformulate the homogenizing operator as process of separating and regrafting tree substructures together to form new tree configurations. These disparate configuration types are analogous to single-point and 2-point cross-overs in linear genomes. The former is a single contiguous region of shared loci between T_s, T_t, $\varkappa_{\Diamond}^{T_s \overset{\mathcal{I}}{\longleftrightarrow} T_t}$. One or more significant regions being shared between to substructures gives us a good anchor for performing cross-over of the remaining, differentiating regions of the substructure, essentially a form of *elitism* (Chakraborty & Chaudhuri, 2003; Mashohor, 2005; Yang, 2007; Chudasama, 2011; Yaman & Yilmaz, 2012; Bora et. al. 2012; etc). We do so by identifying the regions of two substructure with identical graph topology as well as labels of each's vertices. Given some minimum size for the shared region $c_{\Diamond}$:

$$\varkappa_{\Diamond}^{T_s \overset{\mathcal{I}}{\longleftrightarrow} T_t} \begin{cases} V_m(T_s) \ \Big| \ \psi^{T_s, T_t}(V_m), |V_m| \geq c^{\Diamond} \\ \quad \nexists V'_m \subset V(T_s)\, [\psi^{T_s, T_t}(V'_m) \wedge |V'_m| > |V_m|] \,; \\ \quad \psi^{T_s, T_t}(V_p) = \Big(\forall v_i \in V_m[\varsigma(v_i) = \varsigma(v'_i)] \Big) \\ \quad \bigwedge \Big(\langle v_i, v_j \rangle \in V_p(T_s) \leftrightarrow \langle v'_i, v'_j \rangle \in V_p(T_t) \Big) \end{cases} \tag{6}$$

The second type is two discontiguous regions of shared loci between T_s, T_t; denoted as $\varkappa_{\bowtie}^{T_s \overset{\mathcal{I}}{\longleftrightarrow} T_t}$, a pair of disjoint maximum common subgraphs of T_s, T_t. This is analogous to the previous formulation for the shared region of single-point crossover scenario, except that there are two discontiguous regions with a differentiating graph region in between. where we may denote the elements in the pair as $\varkappa_{\bowtie\,[s]}^{T_s \overset{\mathcal{I}}{\longleftrightarrow} T_t}$, & $\varkappa_{\bowtie\,[t]}^{T_s \overset{\mathcal{I}}{\longleftrightarrow} T_t}$. These shared regions of T_s, T_t of $\varkappa^{T_s \overset{\mathcal{I}}{\longleftrightarrow} T_t}$ essentially function as a highly specialized form of *rank elitism* (Chakraborty & Chaudhuri, 2003; Mashohor, 2005; Yang, 2007; Chudasama, 2011; Yaman & Yilmaz, 2012; Bora et. al. 2012; etc), that operates specifically with our sub-structures, where the $\varkappa-$regions function to filter pairs of $\langle T_s, T_t \rangle$ so only the highly compatible pairs would undergo homogenization. We denote subgraph relation as $\trianglelefteq$, a set of all connected componts of G as $\circledast(G)$. We use $\binom{S}{c}$ for denoting the choosing of c elements from the set S, and employ a random variable R^S, so $\binom{S}{c}^{R^S}$ preferentially chooses those of the greatest size. Here, $\varrho_{\Diamond}$, the differentiating regions that may be grafted onto another corresponding substructure, by finding the set of disjoint graph regions ($\circledast$) of a induced subgraph of the substructures T_s, T_t, induced with vertices outside of the shared ($\varkappa_{\Diamond}-$) region.

$$\varrho_{\Diamond}^{T_s \overset{\mathcal{I}}{\longleftrightarrow} T_t} \begin{cases} \left\langle \binom{S}{2}^{R^S}, \binom{S'}{2}^{R^S} \right\rangle \Big| \\ \quad S = \circledast\Big(\phi\Big((V(T_s) \setminus V(\varkappa_{\Diamond}^{T_s \overset{\mathcal{I}}{\longleftrightarrow} T_t}))(T_s) \Big)\Big), \\ \quad S' = \circledast\Big(\phi\Big((V(T_t) \setminus V(\varkappa_{\Diamond}^{T_s \overset{\mathcal{I}}{\longleftrightarrow} T_t}))(T_t) \Big)\Big); \\ \phi(E_p) = G(\{v_q | \langle v_q, v_r\rangle \in E_p \vee \langle v_r, v_q\rangle \in E_p\},\ E_p) \end{cases} \tag{7}$$

We denote the elements within the target loci range: $\varrho_{\Diamond\ [S,0]}^{T_s \overset{\mathcal{I}}{\longleftrightarrow} T_t}$, $\varrho_{\Diamond\ [S,1]}^{T_s \overset{\mathcal{I}}{\longleftrightarrow} T_t}$, $\varrho_{\Diamond\ [T,0]}^{T_s \overset{\mathcal{I}}{\longleftrightarrow} T_t}$, $\varrho_{\Diamond\ [T,1]}^{T_s \overset{\mathcal{I}}{\longleftrightarrow} T_t}$. The corresponding $\bowtie$ type regions is obtained by locating the disjoint regions of the induced subgraph of T_s, T_t, induced by the vertices outside of the shared $\varkappa_{\bowtie}$ region:

$$\varrho_{\bowtie}^{T_s \overset{\mathcal{I}}{\longleftrightarrow} T_t} \begin{cases} \Big\langle T_u,\ T_v \Big\rangle \Big| \psi(T_u, S, T_s) \wedge \psi(T_v, S', T_t) \\ \quad S = \circledast\Big(\phi\Big((V(T_s) \setminus V(\varkappa_{\bowtie\ [s]}^{T_s \overset{\mathcal{I}}{\longleftrightarrow} T_t}))(T_s) \Big)\Big), \\ \quad S' = \circledast\Big(\phi\Big((V(T_t) \setminus V(\varkappa_{\bowtie\ [t]}^{T_s \overset{\mathcal{I}}{\longleftrightarrow} T_t}))(T_t) \Big)\Big); \\ \phi(E_p) = G(\{v_q | \langle v_q, v_r\rangle \in E_p \vee \langle v_r, v_q\rangle \in E_p\},\ E_p); \\ \psi(T_w, S_x, T) = T_w \in S_x \wedge \exists v_i, v_j \in \varkappa_{\bowtie}^{T_s \overset{\mathcal{I}}{\longleftrightarrow} T_t} \Big[\exists P_{i,j} = \\ [v_i, ..., v_j] \trianglelefteq T, [\exists \langle v_h, v_k\rangle \in E(T_w)\ \langle v_h, v_k\rangle \in E(P_{i,j})]\Big] \end{cases} \tag{8}$$

Random variables $R^{\Diamond}$ and $R^{\bowtie}$ give the probabilities of each $\Diamond$ or $\bowtie$ type operator would be applied. $\Diamond$-type operation is shown for the [1]$-$component ([0]$-$component would be analogous), as $\eta_{\Diamond}^{s \rightarrowtail t}(s \rightarrowtail t)$ (t [1]$-$component grafted onto T_s), and $\eta_{\Diamond}^{t \rightarrowtail s}(T_s, T_t)$ (s [1]$-$component grated onto T_t). $\phi_{\Diamond}(\cdot)$ and $\psi_{\Diamond}(\cdot)$ provide configuration of the nodes' relations WRT the ϱ and $\varkappa$ regions, omitted due to space constraints.

$$\eta_{\Diamond}^{s \rightarrowtail t}(T_s, T_t) \begin{cases} V^{s \rightarrowtail t} = (V(T_s) \setminus V(\varrho_{\Diamond\ [S,1]}^{T_s \overset{\mathcal{I}}{\longleftrightarrow} T_t})) \cup V(\varrho_{\Diamond\ [T,1]}^{T_s \overset{\mathcal{I}}{\longleftrightarrow} T_t}) \\ E^{s \rightarrowtail t} = E(\ V^{s \rightarrowtail t}(T_s)\ ) \cup E\Big(\varrho_{\Diamond\ [T,1]}^{T_s \overset{\mathcal{I}}{\longleftrightarrow} T_t}\Big) \cup \{\langle v_i, v'_j\rangle\} \\ \Big| \Big(\phi_{\Diamond}(\langle v_i, v_j\rangle) \vee \phi_{\Diamond}(\langle v_j, v_i\rangle)\ \Big) \\ \bigwedge \Big(\psi_{\Diamond}(\langle v'_i, v'_j\rangle) \vee \psi_{\Diamond}(\langle v'_j, v'_i\rangle)\Big); \end{cases} \tag{9}$$

It takes the necessary vertices from the graft [1]$-$component of T_t, and the remainder of T_s, and add a new edge so that they are still attached in the same configuration as they were in T_s and T_t. The $t \rightarrowtail s$ process is the mirror image of $s \rightarrowtail t$ when the same $\varrho_{\Diamond}^{T_s \overset{\mathcal{I}}{\longleftrightarrow} T_t} \Leftrightarrow \varkappa_{\Diamond}^{T_s \overset{\mathcal{I}}{\longleftrightarrow} T_t}$, omitted due to space. Correspondingly, the $\bowtie$ $-$type operation is similar to a two-point cross-over, with two new edges $\langle v_i, v'_j\rangle$, $\langle v_p, v'_q\rangle$ necessary for the new composite form. We define $\bowtie$ type operation, with the two recombinations as $\eta_{\bowtie}(T_s, T_t)$, and demonstrate one direction of grafting of component onto the remainder of T_s, the opposite direction is analogous.

$$\eta_{\bowtie}(T_s, T_t) \begin{cases} V^{\bowtie} = (V(T_s)\ \setminus V(\varrho_{\bowtie\ [S]}^{T_s \overset{\mathcal{I}}{\longleftrightarrow} T_t})) \cup V(\varrho_{\bowtie\ [T]}^{T_s \overset{\mathcal{I}}{\longleftrightarrow} T_t}) \\ E^{\bowtie} = E(V^{\bowtie}(T_s)) \cup E(\varrho_{\bowtie[T]}^{T_s \overset{\mathcal{I}}{\longleftrightarrow} T_t}) \cup \{\langle v_i, v'_j\rangle, \langle v'_p, v_q\rangle\} \\ \Big| v_i \neq v_q \bigwedge \Big(\Big(\phi_{\bowtie}(\langle v_i, v_j\rangle) \vee \phi_{\bowtie}(\langle v_j, v_i\rangle)\Big) \bigwedge \\ \Big(\phi_{\bowtie}(\langle v_p, v_q\rangle) \vee \phi_{\bowtie}(\langle v_q, v_p\rangle)\Big)\Big) \bigwedge \Big(\Big(\psi_{\bowtie}(\langle v'_i, v'_j\rangle) \vee \\ \psi_{\bowtie}(\langle v'_j, v'_i\rangle)\Big) \bigwedge \Big(\psi_{\bowtie}(\langle v'_p, v'_q\rangle) \vee \psi_{\bowtie}(\langle v'_q, v'_p\rangle)\Big)\Big) \end{cases} \tag{10}$$

Similar to $\Diamond$, the $\bowtie$ $-$type operator takes the necessary nodes from the two shared regions between T_s, T_t and any non-shared regions not between shared regions. It then locates the nodes in the graft component and edges between them. Finally, it includes two new edges, making the connection between graft and host, while preserving the local configurations at the attachment points. It is easier illustrated pic-

Figure 2: before single-point crossover

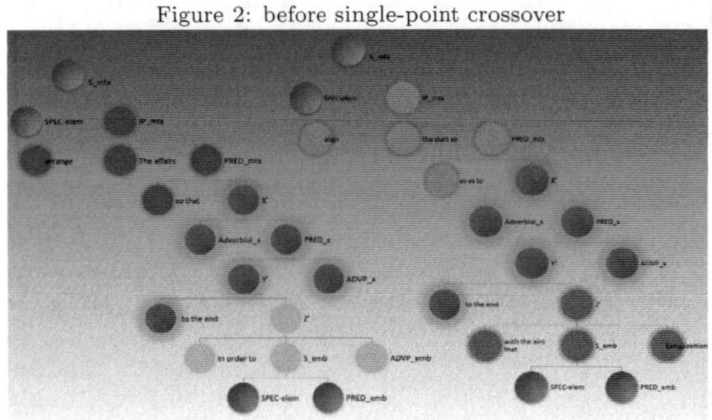

Figure 3: after single-point crossover

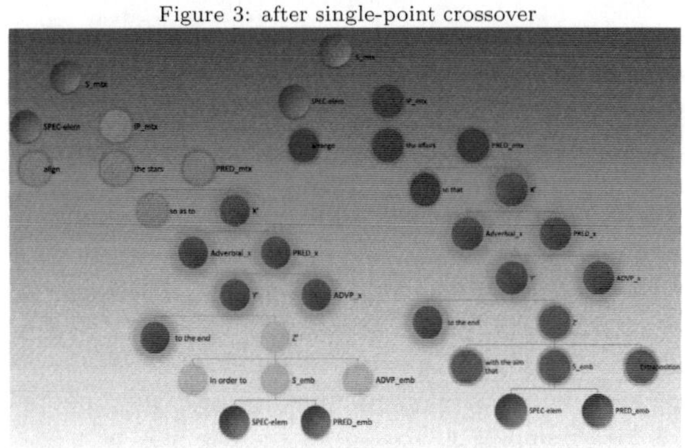

torially, such as $\Diamond-$type operation in Figures 2 - 3; the single red region are shared between the substrutures, while the orange, green regions within T_s, and yellow, purple regions in T_t, undergo re-grafting into new host structures from one figure to the next.

4.2.4 Culling operator & genetic drift

Death is an essential component of evolution in nature; with significant death rate, natural selection has an opportunity to apply its pressure. In a biological system, this process is a mixture of *directed selection*, (depends on the fitness of an organism in an ecological niche), or migration patterns among niches; and some *randomization* in selection, which in nature include *genetic drift* and *immigration/emmigration*. Directed selection is the primary driver for adaptation, when the environment remains static over several generations. The primary metric of usefulness of any T_s is its complexity measured as $n(T_s)$, which entails the maximization of the number of potential non-homogenizing operations on T_s^l. So the base formulation of *fitness* is based the total capacity to reproduce (potential rate * reproductive span), termed *fecundity*, and the actual rate given population and environmental factors, termed *fertility*. This important ratio is $f(T_s) = \frac{fertility}{fecundity} = \frac{\mathfrak{f}^{T_s}}{\mathfrak{e}^{T_s}}$. Also a factor in the usefulness of sub-structure T_s is the distribution of terminal symbols of T_s within the corpus. We incorporated *lift* of tokens of tree terminals within positive sample, against all tokens in the training data. Let $\tau(T_s)$ be a function linearizes the terminals of the tree T_s, and where X_E is the set of terminal sequences from the positive samples, and $X_{E\&i}$ are samples showing both traits; the fitness F is:

$$F(T_s) = \begin{cases} f(T_s) \propto \frac{\mathfrak{f}^{T_s}}{\mathfrak{e}^{T_s}} \cdot \frac{\sum\limits_{x_j \in \tau(T_s)} \mathcal{L}(X_E \Longrightarrow x_j)}{|\tau(T_s)|} \\ \mathcal{L}(X_E \Longrightarrow x_j) = \frac{\mathcal{S}(X_{E\&i})}{\mathcal{S}(X_E) \times \mathcal{S}(X_i)} \mid x_j \in X_i \\ \mathcal{S}(X_i) = \frac{\sum\limits_{x_j \in X_i} \mathcal{N}_j}{\sum\limits_{x_k \in X} \mathcal{N}_k} \,\Big|\, \mathcal{N}_j \propto n(X_j) \end{cases} \tag{11}$$

Since degrees of freedom increase over generations, Boltsmann selection is unnecessary and may even delay arrival at global maximum. The procedure used is a *roulette selection*, since variability of fitness within a single generation is small. *Genetic drift* is not an issue here, since the degree of freedom available increases with each generation's non-homogenizing operation. Each testing sample is tested against the extracted substructures. This process still has high time complexity, potentially $\mathcal{O}(n^{k+4.5})$ (k is the degree limit) (Bodlaender, 1988). Additional pre-filters (i.e., number of vertices, degree-list, label-histogram of V) are applied to further reduce complexity.

5 Test results

5.1 Dataset and model parameters

The BNC is a mixed corpus with complex genres such as parliamentary proceedings and news articles. The training set needs to have sufficiently complex frames to have a significant probability of being embedded causals. Other non-training parts of BNC, as well as the novels corpus, were used for testing. The labelled data is lexed and parsed, and some tree transformations are detected and reconstructed, and separated into semantic frames. The BNC-testing data contained 196314 lines, and novels set 129695 lines. For the **novels** testing set, 26356 instances of semantic frames were detected, and for the **BNC** testing set, 31807 instances of frames were detected. This procedure provides no specific threshold, since it is not binary, but produces a score for likelihood of complex causality. For evaluation, due to output frame count, and the fact that embedded causal structures are a small fraction of all possible clauses, standard precision + recall over the corpus is not feasible. The most sensible method is a sparse *quantile*-based annotation. We annotated three sets of $k = 100+$ (actually 115 each, to ensure at least 100 determinable). The annotation of this initial testing phase was performed by one of the authors. The labels for sample are Y (causal), N (non-causal), and U (undeterminable)

5.2 Ranking evaluation

The results are ranked sets of samples. A positive causal chain sample will contain at least some clearly identifiable $e_i \xrightarrow{cause} e_j$, where e_i, e_j are events expressed by clauses in the surface sequence. It is not required that each pair of adjacent pair of events e_i, e_{i+1} would be causal; and some causal relation $\langle e_i \xrightarrow{caus} e_j \rangle$ may not be immediately adjacent pairs (may skip some event in sequence). We explored how quickly the result by annotating the next several quantiles, each with the aforementioned approximately 115 samples to guarantee each quantile having at least 100 determinable ones. Since it is very labor intensive, we annotated each until a trend in quantile precision emerges, which was 7 for BNC-testing, and 10 for novels, when we observe a large difference from the highest quantile and a trend tending to a distribution tail. There are now 805 annotated samples from top 7 quantiles (Y:225, N:457, U:93) from the BNC-testing, where the top quantile had precision of 0.795, next highest quantile 0.677, and 7th quantile 0.133 (quantile precision is shown in Figure 4). There is a total of 1150 from top 10 quantiles (Y:401, N:672, U:77) from novels; the top quantile had a precision of 0.800, next highest 0.574, 7th quantile 0.206 (shown in Figure 5). The top 2 quantiles for each set is significantly above %50, thus a relatively high-confidence threshold can be set at top 200 for a binary classification task. The samples mostly contain 2-5 events in a causal chain, with the longest of 7.

Figure 4: BNC precision in its top 7 absolute quantiles

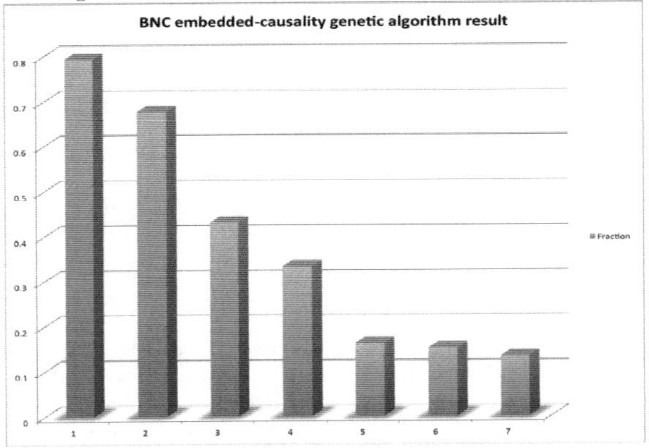

Figure 5: Novels precision in their top 10 absolute quantiles

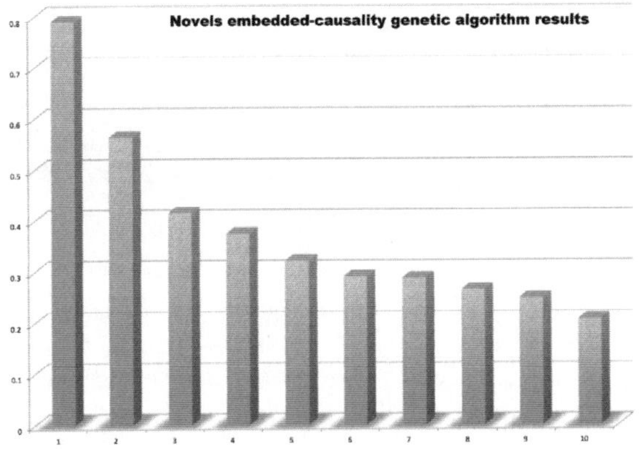

5.3 Comparison with baselines

We compared the results of our system to baselines, a textual entailment system as well as an n-gram model; since annotation is highly labor intensive, the annotated data are from the top 10 quantiles of our ranking. Thus these samples are already pre-selected by our system to be relatively likely to be causal; so we mainly test to see if a correlation with our system exists, and whether they produce the same gradient of precisions that rank from highest quantile to the lowest among these 1150 samples. For each, we expect some positive correlation with ours; but our system, being more specifically designed for complex causality, should outperform each.

We are unaware of any comparable system for complex causality, so textual-entailment (TE) is the most similar to our task. Thus, we used the TE system VENSES (Delmonte et. al. 2007/2009). This test is not approrpiate for the original purpose of VENSES, but is done with our data and annotation to see any correlation to our results, a comparison of the closest system. For any given sample of testing set, we determine whether any pair of the multiple clauses, is identified as entailed by VENSES. We compared the results against our gold standard (for embedded causality). The samples are the top 10 quantiles of the novels data-set (set with the most annotated samples), ranked according to our algorithm. Figure 6 contain the TE fraction of each quantile according to VENSES (red), whether VENSES judgement on TE is consistent with our human annotation on causality (green), and our system's output (blue). TE results

Figure 6: fractions of TEs according to VENSES, fraction of VENSES Y/N output same as human judgement on causality, and our system; for each of the top 10 quntiles for *novels*. The black lines with shading are the corresponding trend lines

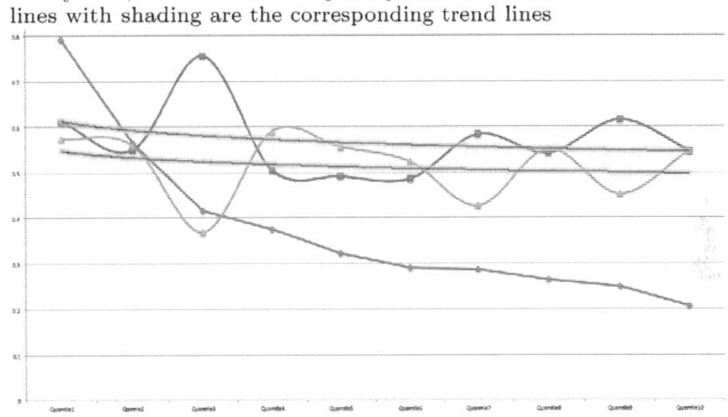

labels contained many false negatives, since it is not designed for causality. This also serves as a baseline for our system, given TE is the closest system available for testing, where our system overperformed significantly given the task of complex causality.

Causal chains are highly sequential structures, so an n-gram model is a reasonable method for comparison. We also produced a standard n-gram model with smoothing and back-off, trained on the same training data as our system. Each sample of multiple clauses/frames is presented a a single sequence of terminal tokens. We determined that a trigram model is the optimum to obtain good specificity and avoid over-training. Thus, we tested it against each of the annotated testing samples, and produced a ranked score using the harmonic mean of probability of each token in the sequence according to the trigram model. Given that the testing samples are preselected by our system to be top-10 quantile, the n-gram model provides a re-ranking of these. We examined this re-ranking to see whether we get the same differentiation in precision in the new 10-quantiles of the same size after re-ranking (Figure 7). Thus the results of our system are also weakly correlated with n-gram re-ranking; but our system provides much better Y/N separation of the gold-standard in the trajectory over the top quantiles, and provides a more consistent and monotonic trend.

Figure 7: precision in re-ranked quantiles according to n-gram, with trendline, and original ranked quantiles from our system

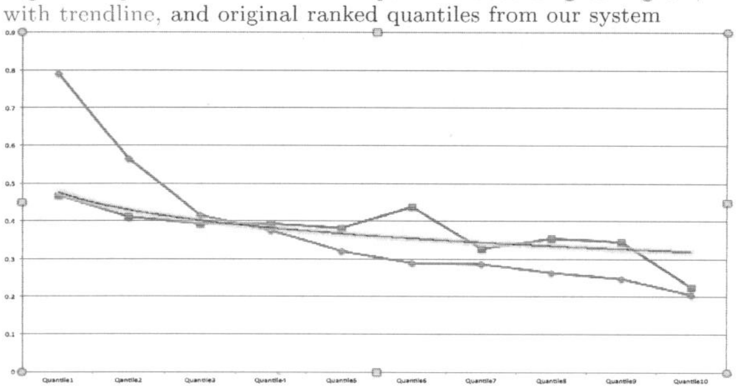

5.4 Further Analysis

Given *causality* has many divergent definitions, we used a detailed characterization scheme allowing each annotator to select from "categories" of causations. Each of these characterizes one frequently accepted aspect of causation, including the four classical *'material' (constitution of component sub-events)*, *'formal'*, *'efficent'*, and *'final' (purpose)* causes (Aristotle 350 B.C. / 322 B.C.), which are often regarded in cognative studies as relevant aspects of causation that humans use in recognition of causality (Rachlin 1992, Hogan 1994, Killeen 2001, Killeen & Nash 2003, Alvarez 2009); as well as other common aspects of causality, *'cause of necessity (enablement)'*, *'cause with intermidate volition' (inducement)'*, and *'latent causal chain (outcome)'*. We also labelled the top 150 samples of the novels set, for the presence/absence of each of these 7 classes. Since long causal chains may contain multiple relations of different semantic types in one sequence, a sample may have multiple labels. The number and percent of the top 150 ranked samples are ❶ *efficient:* 17, 11.3%; ❷ *necessity:* 36, 24.0%; ❸ *formal:* 42, 28.0%; ❹ *final:* 40, 26.7%; ❺ *inducement:* 44, 29.3%; ❻ *material:* 17, 11.3%; ❼ *latent:* 10, 6.7%; which has a wide distribution among the 7, and has no particular dominant class. It is unsurprising that *latent causal chain* is contained in the least number of samples, since it is also the most difficult for people to detect. We here provide some top-quantile samples with the said annotation with a variety of classification scheme labels:

- eurotunnel is already in default of its credit agreement with the bank synidcate, [that it] is seeking an extra xx billions on top of the xx billions raise so far .
  eurotunnel is already in default of its credit agreement with the bank syndicate $\xrightarrow{efficient}$ *it is seeking an extra xx billions on top of the xx billions raised so far*

- before the housewives could rest several people called and there was a scramble to get ready to see them (receive them with hospitality)
  several people called [the housewives to visit] $\xrightarrow{efficient}$ *there was a scramble to get ready* $\xrightarrow{purpose}$ *to see them* (here meaning receiving the guests)

- she tries to find highborn women to bear him a son that she can take in as her own
  she tries to find highborn women $\xrightarrow{enables}$ *to bear him a son* $\xrightarrow{enables}$ *she can take in as her own*

- by late afternoon, I (Cleopatra Selene II) joined the rest of the women of the household Lady Octavia took it upon herself to [Lady Octavia] teach me (Cleopatra Selene II) to spin whorl *I joined the rest of the women of the household* $\xrightarrow{constitute}$ *Lady Octavia took it upon herself* $\xrightarrow{purpose}$ *teach me* $\xrightarrow{purpose}$ *spin wool*

- I (Cleopatra Selene II) was a Ptolemy princess (meaning descended from Hellenic-pharonic bloodline), a queen in exile who must bide her time until she could think of some plot, some plan to [some plot/plan] return her to her throne
  I was a Ptolemy princess $\xrightarrow{constitute}$ *[I was] a queen in exile* $\xrightarrow{implication}$ *who must bide her time* $\xrightarrow{enables}$ *she could think of some plot, some plan* $\xrightarrow{purpose}$ *return her to her throne*

- one of the guards searched Euphronius he actually put his unclean hands on our wizard's hold person I (Cleopatra Selene II) watched, aghast, trying to ignore the curious motion within the basket an echo of fear that snaked around my heart then the ill-mannered Roman guard approached me and I held my basket out to him hoping he'd reach inside (Counterfactual) hoping that whatever evil spirit lurked there would fly out strike him dead
  one of the guards searched Euphronius $\xrightarrow{efficient}$ *I watched aghast trying to ignore the curious motion within the basket* $\xrightarrow{outcome}$ *the ill-mannered Roman guard approached me* $\xrightarrow{induces}$ *I held my basket out to him* $\xrightarrow{purpose}$ *he'd reach inside* $\xrightarrow{efficient}$ *whatever evil spirit lurked there would fly out* $\xrightarrow{efficient}$ *strike him dead*

6 Conclusion & future direction

For this study, we designed and demonstrated a procedure to rank the likelihood of causality from complex linguistic structures. The process takes lexico-semantic as well as morpho-syntactic information in the expressions into a single form of representation; a collection of which then is extended into a *diffuse prototype*, a composite cognitive categorization model, for a complex multi-modal description of causality. An evolutionary algorithm, with a graph theoretic focus, is developed specifically to obtain the *diffuse prototype* from a limited number of training samples. The output model then can be used to score unseen samples according to a variegated notion of causality. Due to the nature of the model representation and the GA-like procedure, it is adaptable for a wide variety of human definitions of causality. This system in the future needs to be further developed from a ranking procedure to a discrete classification task. It will also be worth to look at further sub-classifications of causality, to see whether a similar procedure can provide a yet more fine-grained recognition of different deep semantic types of this relation.

References

S. Abe, K. Inui and Y. Matsumoto 2008. *Two-phrased event relation acquisition: Couplingthe relation-oriented and argument-oriented approaches. Proceedings of the 22nd International Conference on Computational Linguistics (COLING2008)*, 1–8

L. M. Alcott 1997. *Little women.* Roberts Brothers Publishing, Boston.

M. P. Alvarez 2009. *The four causes of behavior: Aristotle and Skinner. International Journal of Psychology and Psychological Therapy*, 9(1):45–57

Aristotle 300 B.C. φυσικὴ ἀκρόασις (Physics). Translated by R. P. Hardie and R. K. Gaye, MIT Press 1994.

Aristotle before 322 B.C. τὰ μετὰ τὰ φυσικά (Metaphysics), ed. J. Verner. Oxford Classical Texts: Oxford University Press, 1957.

J. E. Baker 1985. *An Analysis of the Effects of Selection in Genetic Algorithms. International Conference on Genetic Algorithms and Their Applications*, 101–111

J. E. Baker 1989. *An Analysis of the Effects of Selection in Genetic Algorithms. Ph.D. Thesis, Vanderbilt University*, Nashville, 1989

N. A. Barricelli 1989. *Numerical testing of evolution theories : Part I Theoretical introduction and basic tests. Acta Biotheoretica*, Issue 16 (1-2):69–98

R. Girju and B. Beamer 2009. *Using a bigram event model to predict causal potential. In Proceedings of Conference on intelligent text processing and computational linguistics 2009*, Mexico City, Feb 26–28

S. Berthard & J. H. Martin 2008. *Learning semantic links from a corpus of parallel temporal and causal relations. Proceedings of ACL-08: HLT, Short Papers (Companion Volume)*, 177–180, Association for Computational Linguistics

H. Bodlaender 1988. *Dynamic programming on graphs with bounded treewidth. Proceedings of 15th International Colloquium on Automata, Languages, and Programming*, volume 317 of Lecture Notes in Computer Science, 105118. Springer-Verlag, Berlin Heidelberg

T.C. Bora, L. Lebensztajn, L.D.S. Coelho 2012. *Non-Dominated Sorting Genetic Algorithm Based on Reinforcement Learning to Optimization of Broad-Band Reflector Antennas Satellite. IEEE Transactions in Magnetics*, 48(Number 2 Supplement 4 Part 1):767–770, Piscataway, NY

A. Brindle 1981. *Genetic algorithms for function optimization, Technical Report*, 81–82, University of Alberta, Canada

British National Corpus 2007. *University of Oxford Press, Longman Publishing, W & R Chambers Publishing, in conjunction with British Library, University of Oxford, and Lancaster University* url:http://www.natcorp.ox.ac.uk/

B. Chakraborty and P. Chaudhuri 2003. *On The Use of Genetic Algorithm with Elitism in Robust and Non-parametric Multivariate Analysis.* Austrian Journal of Statistics, Volume 32

D.S. Chang, K.S. Choi 2006. *Incremental cue phrase learning and bootstrapping method for causality extraction using cue phrase and word pair probabilities Information Processing and Management*, 42(3):662678

C. Chudasama, S. M. Shah, M. Panchal 2011. *Comparison of parents selection methods of genetic algorithm for TSP. International Conference on Computer Communication and Networks*, published by International Journal of Computer Applications (IJCA)

N. L. Cramer 1985. *A Representation for the adaptive generation of simple sequential programs. Proceedings of International Conference on Genetic Algorithms ans their Applications*, Carnegie-Mellon University

C. Darwin 1859. *on the Origin of species: (by Means of Natural Selection, The Preservation of Favoured Races in the Struggle for Life)* John Murray Publishing

R. Delmonte, A. Bristot, M.A. Piccolino Boniforti, S.Tonelli 2007. *Entailment and anaphora resolution in RTE3. Proceedings of ACL Workshop on Text Entailment and Paraphrasing*, 48–53, Association of Computational Linguistics, Prague

D. B. Fogel 1998. *Evolutionary computation: the Fossil record*, IEEE Press, Piscataway, NJ

R. Girju 2003 *Automatic detection of causal relations for question answering, The 41st Annual Meeting of the Association for Computational Linguistics (ACL 2003)*, Workshop on Multilingual Summarization and Question Answering : Machine Learning and Beyond

D. Goldberg 1989. *Genetic Algorithms in Search, Optimization and Machine Learning*, Addison-Wesley Publishing, Reading MA

D. Goldberg and K. Deb 1993. *A comparative analysis of selection schemes used in genetic algorithms. Foundations of Genetic Algorithms*, 69–93

D. Goldberg, K. Deb, J. Clark 1991. *Genetic algorithms, noise, and sizing of population. Complex System*, 6:333-362

Project Gutenberg, M. Hart 2005. *Gutenberg corpus*, http://www.gutenberg.org/

C. Hashimoto, K. Torisawa, J. Kloetzer, M. SanosIstvan, V. J.H. Oh, Y. Kidawara 2014. *Toward future scenario generation: extracting event causality exploiting semantic relation, context, and association features. Proceedings of the 52nd Annual Meeting of the Association for Computational Linguistics (ACL)*

J. D. Holland 1975. *Adaptation in Natural and Artificial Systems.* University of Michigan Press, Ann Arbor, Michigan

K. A. de Jong 1975. *an Analysis of the behavior of a class of genetic adaptive systems*, Ph. D. Dissertation, University of Michigan Press, Ann Arbor, Michigan

C. Khoo, S. Myaeng, R. Oddy 2001. *Using cause-effect relations in text to improve information retrieval precision, Information Processing and Management*, 37:119145

P.R. Killeen 2001. *The four causes of behavior, Current Directions in Psychological Science*, 10:136–140

P.R. Killeen and M.R. Nash 2003. *The four causes of hypnosis. The International Journal of Clinicaland Experimental Hypnosis*, 51:195–231

S. Kirkpatrick, J. C.D. Gelatt, M. P. Vecchi 1983. *Optimization by simulated annealing. Science*, 220:671–680

S. Mashohor 2005. *Elitist selection schemes for genetic algorithm based printed circuit board inspection system. Evolutionary Computation, The 2005 IEEE Congress*, 2:974–978

P. Menzies 2009. *Counterfactual theories of causation. Stanford Encyclopedia of Philosophy, Fall 2009*, ed: E. N. Zalta, web published: plato.stanford.edu/entries/causation-counterfactual Stanford University Department of Philosophy

J.H. Oh, K. Torisawa, C. Hashimoto, M. Sano, S. de Saeger, K. Ohtake 2013. *Why-question answering using intra- andinter-sentential causal relations Proceedings of the 51st Annual Meeting of the Association for Com-putational Linguistics (ACL 2013)*, 51:17331743

M. Paul, C. Girju, C. Li 2009. *Mining the web for reciprocal relationships, Proceedings of the Thirteenth Conference on Computational Natural Language Learning (CoNLL)*, Boulder, Colorado

H. Rachlin 1992. *Teleological behaviorism. American Psychologist*, 47:1371-1382, American Psychological Association

K. Radinsky, S. Davidovich, S. Markovitch 2012. *Learning causality for newsevents prediction. Proceedings of International World Wide Web Conference 2012 (WWW 2012)*, 909–918

I. Rechenberg 1973. *Evolutionsstrategic: Optimierung technicher System nach Principen der Biologischen Evolution*, Frommmann-Holzboog Verlag, Stuttgart

M. Riaz and C. R. Girju 2010. *Another look at causality: Discovering scenario-specific contingency relationships with no supervision, Proceedings of ICSC*, CERN School of Computing

J. Schmidhuber 1987. *Evolutionary principles in self-referential learning: On Learning now to learn: the meta-meta-meta...*, Doctoral Thesis, Technische Universität Munchen, Germany

A. Turing 1950. *Computing machinery and intelligence Mind: a Quarterly Review of Psychology and Philosophy*, LIX(236):433–460, The Mind Association

F. Yaman, A. E. Yilmaz 2012. *Elitist genetic algorithm performance on the uniform circular antenna array pattern synthesis problem, PRZEGLD ELEKTROTECHNICZNY (Electrical Review)*

S. Yang 2007. *Genetic algorithms with elitism-based immigrants for changing optimization problems, EvoWorkshops 2007*, LNCS 4448:627–636, Springer Verlag, Berlin.

Evaluation Algorithms for Event Nugget Detection : A Pilot Study

Zhengzhong Liu, Teruko Mitamura, Eduard Hovy
Carnegie Mellon University
5000 Forbes Avenue
Pittsburgh, PA 15213, USA
liu@cs.cmu.edu, teruko@cs.cmu.edu, hovy@cmu.edu

Abstract

Event Mention detection is the first step in textual event understanding. Proper evaluation is important for modern natural language processing tasks. In this paper, we present our evaluation algorithm and results during the Event Mention Evaluation pilot study. We analyze the problems of evaluating multiple event mention attributes and discontinuous event mention spans. In addition, we identify a few limitations in the evaluation algorithm used for the pilot task and propose some potential improvements.

1 Introduction

Textual event understanding has attracted a lot of attention in the community. Recent work has covered several areas about events, such as event mention detection(Li et al., 2013; Li et al., 2014) , event coreference (Bejan et al., 2005; Chen and Ji, 2009; Lee et al., 2012; Chen and Ng, 2013; Liu et al., 2013), and script understanding (Chambers and Jurafsky, 2008; Chambers and Jurafsky, 2009). Event Mention detection is the fundamental preprocessing step for these tasks. However, downstream event researches often make minimal effort for event mention detection. For example, in event coreference work, Lee et al. (2012) do not make clear distinction between event and entity mentions. Bejan et al. (2005) and Liu et al. (2013) use oracle event mentions from human annotations. Building robust event mention detection system can help promote research in these areas and enable researchers to produce end-to-end systems. In this paper, we discuss our recent effort in providing a proper evaluation metric for event mention detection.

1.1 The Event Nugget Detection Task

As defined in Mitamura (2014), event nugget detection involves identifying semantic meaningful units (**mention span detection**) that refer to an event[1]. The task also requires a system to identify other attributes (**attribute detection**). In this pilot study, the attributes are *event type* and *realis status*.

(1) President Obama will `nominate` [realis: Other type: Personnel.Nominate] John Kerry for Secretary of State.

(2) He `carried out` the `assassination` [realis: Actual type: Life.Die] .

Example 1 shows one annotated event nugget `nominate`, which has the realis type "other" and event type "Personnel.Nominate". Example 2 annotates one event nugget with discontinuous event span `carried out assassination`. The evaluation corpus is annotated with event nuggets that fall into 8 types of event[2]. Please refer to Mitamura (2014) for detailed definitions of the attributes.

1.2 Past Evaluation Methods

The Automatic Content Extraction 2005 evaluation task involves event extraction. The Event Detection and Recognition (VDR) task in the Automatic Content Extraction 2005 evaluation (NIST, 2005) evaluate the accuracy of event arguments and multiple other event attributes. However, event mention recognition is not directly evaluated (§3.2).

[1]This is similar to Event Trigger in ACE 2005, which is adopted in other work (Li et al., 2013; Li et al., 2014)

[2]These are *Life, Movement, Business, Conflict, Contact, Personnel, Transaction, Justice*

Proceedings of the 3rd Workshop on EVENTS at the NAACL-HLT 2015, pages 53–57,
Denver, Colorado, June 4, 2015.

Li et al. (2013; 2014) evaluate event trigger detection using a mention-wise F-1 score. An event trigger is considered correct only when the span and event type are matched exactly. Errors from different sources are not separately presented.

In addition, most previous evaluations on event mention evaluation do not give partial credits to partial matches. Partial scoring is more important in the current setting because of the mention span detection task is difficult with discontinuous event nuggets.

2 The Evaluation Algorithm in Pilot Study

In this section, we describe our mention detection algorithms[3]. We will use the terms Event Nugget and Event Mention interchangeably.

2.1 Prerequisites

The main prerequisite for the evaluation is tokenization. In our pilot study, we provide a standard tokenization for all participants. System responses represent each event mention in terms of predefined token ids[4]. Discontinuous mentions can be easily represented using tokens.

2.2 Partial Span Scoring

The proposed evaluation produces a span similarity score for a pair of mentions (system and gold standard) between 0 and 1. Given a pair of mentions (G, S), we represent the span of each mention by a set of token ids (T_G , T_S). The span similarity score is defined as the Dice coefficient between the two sets (which is the same as the F-1 score).

$$\begin{aligned} Dice(T_G, T_S) &= \frac{2|T_G T_S|}{|T_G| + |T_S|} \\ &= \frac{2}{|T_G|/|T_G T_S| + |T_S|/|T_G T_S|} \\ = F1(T_G, T_S) &= \frac{2}{1/P + 1/R} \end{aligned}$$

2.3 Mention Mapping

To evaluate mention attributes, the evaluation algorithm needs to decide which system mention corresponds to a gold standard mention. We refer to this step as mention mapping. The input of our mention-mapping algorithm is the pairwise scores between all gold standard vs. system mention pair. We use the token-based Dice score (§2.2). Algorithm 1 shows our mapping algorithm to compute the mapping in one document.

Algorithm 1 Compute a mapping between system and gold standard mentions

Input: A list L of scores $Dice(T_G, T_S)$ for all pair of G, S in the document

1: $M \leftarrow \varnothing; U \leftarrow \varnothing$
2: **while** $L \neq \varnothing$ **do**
3: $\quad G_m, S_n \leftarrow \arg\max_{(G,S)\in L} Dice(T_G, T_S)$
4: $\quad$ **if** $S_n \notin U$ **and** $Dice(T_{G_m}, T_{S_n}) > 0$ **then**
5: $\quad\quad M_{G_m} \leftarrow M_{G_m} \cup (S_n, Dice(T_{G_m}, T_{S_n}))$
6: $\quad\quad U \leftarrow U \cup \{S_n\}$

Output: The mapping M

Algorithm 1 iteratively searches for the highest Dice score in all remaining mention pairs. Line 4 ensures that each system mention can only be mapped to one gold standard mention to avoid multiple counting. One gold standard mention is allowed to be mapped to multiple system mentions, which will be used in calculating attribute accuracy scores.

2.4 Overall Span Scoring

In the pilot study, we first evaluate the system's performance on span detection[5]. We use F-1 score (referred as mention level F-1 score to distinguish with the token level F-1 score in §2.2) for this task.

The definition of True Positive (TP) and False Positive (FP) for mention-level F-1 are slightly adjusted to reflect partial matching. TP values are accumulated according to Algorithm 2.

Precision, Recall, F-1 are calculated as followed:

$$P = \frac{TP}{TP + FP}; R = \frac{TP}{N_G}; F1 = \frac{2PR}{P + R}$$

N_G is the number of gold standard mentions.

In the study, we use $TP + FP$ as the denominator for Precision. We later identify a problem of this formulat. When FP is 0, even if the span range is

[3]Code base: github.com/hunterhector/EvmEval

[4]Some other KBP evaluations use character span evaluation, which will favor long words than short words. We argue that the difficulties in tokenizing a long word and a short word in English should be virtually the same; hence scoring these two cases differently is not fair.

[5]For simplicity, we describe our algorithm on a single document, the scorer will produce aggregate results for each metric with standard Micro and Macro average methods.

Algorithm 2 Compute TP and FP

Input: The set of gold standard $\mathcal{G}$; The mapping M indexed by G; Number of system mentions N_S

$TP \leftarrow 0; FP \leftarrow 0$
for $\forall G \in \mathcal{G}$ **do**
  if $|M_G| = 0$ **then**
    $FP \leftarrow FP + 1$
  else
    $S_T \leftarrow \arg\max_{Dice}(S, Dice) \in M_G$
    $TP \leftarrow TP + Dice(G, S_T)$

Output: TP

not exactly correct, the system can still get perfect precision (though imperfect recall), which is counter-intuitive. If we calculate FP with $N_S - TP$, the precision, recall calculation will naturally resolve to:

$$P = \frac{TP}{N_S}; R = \frac{TP}{N_G}$$

The new formula is also aesthetically symmetric on precision and recall. We present the influence of this fix in §4.1.

2.5 Attribute Scoring

For each attribute and gold standard mention, we calculate the accuracy according to algorithm 3. This algorithm will give a system full credit even when the span matching is not perfect. In addition, when one system incorrectly splits one gold standard mention into two, we still give it credit as long as attributes are all predicted correctly.

Algorithm 3 Compute Attribute Accuracy for one Gold Standard Mention

Input: The gold standard mention G; The mapping M indexed by G; The set A indexing target attributes for all mentions;

$Accuracy \leftarrow 0$
for $S, Dice(T_S, T_G) \in M_G$ **do**
  if $A_S = A_G$ **then**
    $Accuracy \leftarrow Accuracy + 1/|M_G|$

Output: $Accuracy$

Gold He `carried out` the `assassination` [type: Life.Die] .

System 1 He `carried`[type: Life.Die] out the `assassination` [type: Life.Die] .

System 2 He `carried`[type: Business.MERGE] out the `assassination` [type: Life.Die].

In the above examples, there is one gold standard mention while both systems report two event mentions, and they both omit the word "out". According algorithm 3, **System 1** gets full credit while **System 2** gets 0.5. The algorithm is designed this way to prevent a system being penalized again for its span error. However, this make it difficult to find a natural way to combine span scores with attribute scores.

2.6 Combining multiple scores

Algorithm 2 and 3 are limited in that there is no one simple score for final system ranking. Furthermore, the span score only reflects the system's ability to distinguish the 8 types of event mentions from everything else, which is not a useful metric by its own.

A naive way to combine the scores is to multiply these individual scores. However, theoretically, the errors in attribute scoring and the span scoring are not independent, thus it is inappropriate to perform a simple multiplication. We propose a natural adjustment by directly augmenting attribute evaluation into F1 score calculation (Algorithm 4). Line 3 in the algorithm finds a system mention with the highest mapping score that also fits all the attributes of interest as true positive. We can choose the set $\mathcal{A}$ to contain the desired attributes we would like to evaluate on. In our implementation, we iterate all possible attribute combinations and produce all the scores (§4.2).

Algorithm 4 Compute True Postive with Attributes

Input: The set of gold standard mentions $\mathcal{G}$; The mapping M indexed by gold standard mentions; Number of system mentions N_S; The set $\mathcal{A}$ indexing the attributes that will be evaluated for all mentions

1: $TP \leftarrow 0$
2: **for** $G \in \mathcal{G}$ **do**
3:   $S_{max} \leftarrow \arg\max_{Dice}(S, Dice) \in M_G$ Subject to $\mathcal{A}_{S_{max}} = \mathcal{A}_G$
4:   $TP \leftarrow TP + Dice(S_{max}, G)$

Output: TP

3 Comparison with Previous Methods

3.1 Comparison with MUC

The Message Understanding Conference provides a scoring algorithm for the information extraction task (Chinchor, 1992). Though there is no event mention evaluation, some algorithm design can still be compared with our methods.

The MUC scorer first calculates an alignment between gold standard mention and system, and then counts the number of exact matches COR, the number of partial matches PAR, the number of gold standard keys POS, the number of system responses ACT. The precision and recall are calculated as[6] :

$$P = \frac{COR + 0.5PAR}{POS}; R = \frac{COR + 0.5PAR}{ACT}$$

The MUC scorer then takes the highest F-Score from all possible alignments.

Our method makes several different decisions. First, we use a simple greedy method for choosing an alignment based on span matching instead of trying to find the best alignment.

Second, we give a partial score between 0 to 1 using the Dice Coefficient, while MUC uses a universal partial credit of 0.5. A variable partial score can reflect more subtle differences between systems.

3.2 Comparison with ACE

The Automatic Content Extraction 2005 task included an event related evaluation (NIST, 2005). The Event Mention Detection (VMD) task described in the evaluation guideline defines the event mention as a sentence or phrase. The ACE event task evaluates the systems on the attributes and arguments of a whole event (which may contains multiple event mentions). Such evaluation also requires a system to resolve event coreference. Thus, there is no direct evaluation for event nuggets in ACE 2005.

4 Experiments

We conduct evaluation on the 15 pilot study submissions using the LDC2015E3 dataset, which contains 200 documents with 6921 annotated event mentions. The results we show in this section are all micro average across these mentions.

[6]We simplified the discussion by assuming there is no optional gold standard key, which will be removed by the MUC scorer if exists but not aligned

4.1 Fixing the Precision Formula

The simple fix on precision calculation (§2.4) does not affect the overall trend of the evaluation. The scores of the participant systems only change by a very small value, and the span-based ordering remains the same. We argue that this fix is both more theoretically sound and mathematically pleasing.

4.2 Combining Multiple Scores

As discussed in §2.6, scoring each metric individually will make it difficult to provide one unified score to rank all systems. This can be seen from Figure 1, which plot the evaluation results using the original scoring (sorted on Span F1). In addition, because attribute scores are only calculated on the gold standard mentions, the false alarms on the rest of the predicted mentions are not penalized.

Figure 2 shows the results using multiplicity combination. We observe that the resulting scores will soon become too small after multiplication, which are less interpretable.

Figure 3 presents the results after applying Algorithm 4. The combined score of all attributes now falls into a more reasonable range (bounded by the performance of the hardest attribute, namely realis status). We also observe that all performances decrease monotonically.

We can also use the results from Figure 3 to understand the performance bottleneck of the systems. For example, in system 7, there is a big gap between the mention type F1 score and the span F1. This indicates that the type detection accuracy is low and should be improved. In system 5, the mention span F1 and mention type F1 are very close. Therefore the bottleneck might be in event span identification. This information is not immediately clear from the other figures.

5 Conclusions

In this paper we describe our proposed evaluation metric for event nugget task and identify two problems in evaluation design. We propose solutions to these problems and find out that the new methods produce more interpretable results.

Acknowledgments

This research was supported in part by DARPA grant FA8750-12-2-0342 funded under the DEFT program.

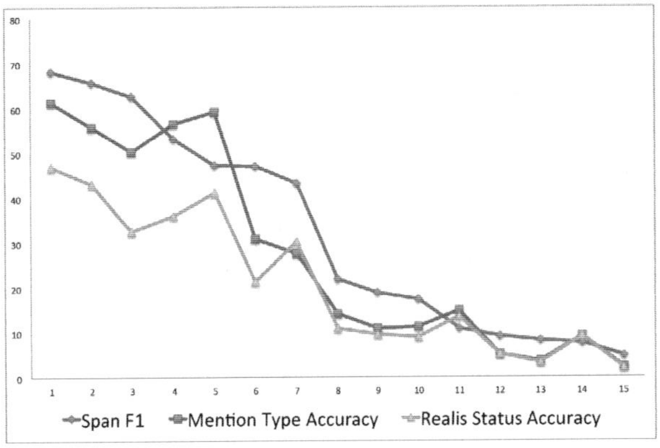

Figure 1: System results sorted by Span F1 score

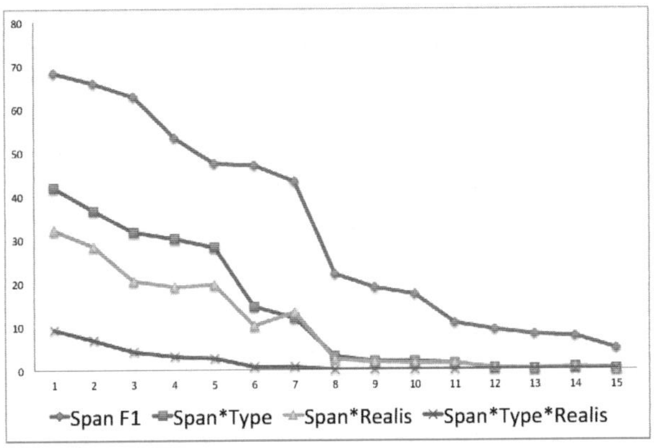

Figure 2: Combining scores with multiplicity (sorted on combined score)

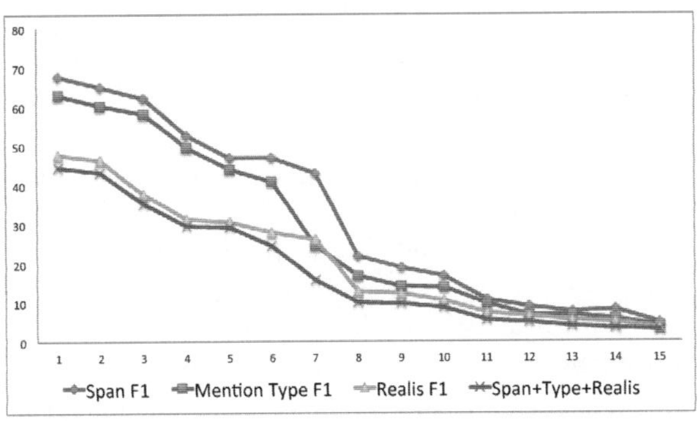

Figure 3: Attribute augmented scoring (sorted on combined score)

References

Cosmin Adrian Bejan, Matthew Titsworth, Andrew Hickl, and Sanda Harabagiu. 2005. Nonparametric Bayesian Models for Unsupervised Event Coreference Resolution. In Y Bengio, D Schuurmans, J Lafferty, C K I Williams, and A Culotta, editors, *Advances in Neural Information Processing Systems 22 (NIPS)*, pages 1–9.

Nathanael Chambers and Dan Jurafsky. 2008. Unsupervised Learning of Narrative Event Chains. In *ACL '08 Meeting of the Association for Computational Linguistics*, pages 789–797.

Nathanael Chambers and Dan Jurafsky. 2009. Unsupervised learning of narrative schemas and their participants. In *ACL '09 Proceedings of the Joint Conference of the 47th Annual Meeting of the ACL and the 4th International Joint Conference on Natural Language Processing of the AFNLP*, pages 602–610. Association for Computational Linguistics.

Zheng Chen and H Ji. 2009. Graph-based event coreference resolution. *Proceedings of the 2009 Workshop on Graph-based Methods for Natural Language Processing*, pages 54–57.

Chen Chen and Vincent Ng. 2013. Chinese Event Coreference Resolution: Understanding the State of the Art. In *Proceedings of the 6th International Joint Conference on Natural Language Processing*, pages 822–828.

Nancy Chinchor. 1992. Muc-5 evaluation metric. In *Proceedings of the 5th Conference on Message Understanding*, pages 69–78.

Heeyoung Lee, Marta Recasens, Angel Chang, Mihai Surdeanu, and Dan Jurafsky. 2012. Joint Entity and Event Coreference Resolution across Documents. In *Proceedings of the 2012 Conference on Empirical Methods in Natural Language Processing and Natural Language Learning*.

Qi Li, Heng Ji, and Liang Huang. 2013. Joint Event Extraction via Structured Prediction with Global Features. In *Proceedings of the 51st Annual Meeting of the Association for Computational Linguistics (ACL2013)*.

Qi Li, Heng Ji, Yu Hong, and Sujian Li. 2014. Constructing Information Networks Using One Single Model. In *Proceedings the 2014 Conference on Empirical Methods on Natural Language Processing (EMNLP2014)*.

Zhengzhong Liu, Jun Araki, Eduard Hovy, and Teruko Mitamura. 2013. Supervised Within-Document Event Coreference using Information Propagation. In *Proceedings of the Ninth International Conference on Language Resources and Evaluation (LREC'14)*, pages 4539–4544, Reykjavik, Iceland. European Language Resources Association (ELRA).

Teruko Mitamura. 2014. TAC KBP event detection annotation guidelines, v1.7. Technical report, Carnegie Mellon University, September.

NIST. 2005. The ACE 2005 (ACE05) Evaluation Plan: Evaluation of the Detection and Recognition of ACE. Technical report, National Institute of Standards and Technology.

Event characterization for information extraction from business-based technical documents

Bell Manrique Losada
Universidad de Medellín
Cra. 87 30-65 Belén
Medellín, AQ, Colombia
bmanrique@udem.edu.co

Carlos M. Zapata Jaramillo
Universidad Nacional de Colombia
Cra. 80 65-223 Robledo
Medellín, AQ, Colombia
cmzapata@unal.edu.co

Abstract

Event identification plays a crucial role in several natural language processing applications such as information extraction, question answering, and text analysis. In this paper, we describe a novel approach for analyzing events, their distribution, and the event mentions from a corpus of unlabeled business-based technical documents—a specific genre. In order to infer such mentions, we analyze the subject-verb-object structure for semi-automatically extracting several lexical, syntactic, and semantic features for each event mention from the corpus. Extracting event mentions allows us to cast grouping together the mentions with same features and propose properties leading to the differences of the specific genre. The obtained results are used for supporting an event-centered processing level, from an automated machine for processing texts.

1 Introduction

Information extraction (IE) is a process for extracting structured information from unstructured texts (Sangeetha *et al.*, 2010). Event identification plays a crucial role in IE and other natural language processing applications (*e.g.,* question answering, text analysis, etc.). Identification of event structures can exploit cross-document techniques. A special attention is given to the recognition of events from heterogeneous document sources, stemming from several genres and domains (Petrenz and Webber, 2011).

According to Pivovarova *et al.* (2013), in the context of IE, events represent real-world facts and they should be extracted from plain text. By the unique nature of events, they receive in-depth attention in current research, by trying to identify what events are mentioned within texts and how they are related semantically (Do *et al.*, 2011).

In this paper we propose an unsupervised approach for identifying events, from unannotated sentences of business-based technical documents contained in a training corpus. We base our approach on text expressions referring to real-world events—also called event mentions— for identifying events (Bejan & Harabagiu. 2013) from a set of clusters.

We define training documents based on lexical chains by holding the set of semantically related words of given sentences. WordNet lexicon was used for constructing lexical chains with the event mentions. A set of features and properties for each event has been identified in order to obtain a characterization of the specific genre concerned to the technical document.

The preliminary results, in terms of events features and properties, are the based on a processing level in an automated system for processing texts. Then, such event-centered processing level is the basis for identifying the organizational domain knowledge and some business information as the first instances of the requirement elicitation process.

The remainder sections of this paper are organized as follows: in Section 2 we describe the related work in the field of information extraction and event extraction. In Section 3 we present our approach to event identification for extracting information from the genre *business-based technical documents*. Finally, in Section 4 we draw conclusions and we outline future work.

Proceedings of the 3rd Workshop on EVENTS at the NAACL-HLT 2015, pages 58–65,
Denver, Colorado, June 4, 2015.

2 Overview and related work

This Section provides a short overview and related work of the most relevant research in terms of event analysis, information extraction, and event extraction.

2.1 Events

Events represent real-world facts. Also, they may have several relationships to such facts, and different sources may have contradictory views on the facts (Saurí & Pustejovsky, 2012). Thus, the structure and content of an event is influenced by both the structure of the specific real-world fact and the properties of the surrounding text. The role of the events in a text depends directly on the context, real-world domain, or scenario in which the text is used. In this sense, events are representations of facts and also linguistic units. Whereby, and according to Pivovarova *et al.* (2013), in the analysis and research of events should be considered the particular language, genre, scenario and medium of the text—*i.e.,* events should be analyzed in the context of particular corpora.

Our motivation yields on the event study in practice, looking for identifying domain-specific characteristics of events in a business-based corpus. We hope this preliminary study of the corpus can be used in the same or greater depth of linguistic analysis by a language processing system or an IE system.

2.2 Basics of lexical-semantic analysis

WordNet is a lexical semantic resource which defines word senses by using methods for grouping senses of the same word and thus producing coarser word sense groupings (Fellbaum, 1998). For the aim of this work and looking for analyzing events, we consider the syntactic categories of verbs. Verbs form language-specific structures in the WordNet ontology and they are included in the category of 2nd Order Entity. According to Vossen (2002), such a category comprises entities referring to any situation—being static or dynamic—which cannot be grasped, heard, seen, or felt as an independent physical thing. These situations can occur or take place in a time or place/space, rather than exist (*e.g.* happen, cause, occur, apply, etc.). Also, they are related to: i) verbs or events denoting nouns, and ii) events, processes, states-of-affairs, or situations located in time. Verbs in this category can be further subrogated according to the physical entities involved in the following subcategories:

Process. This category implies all physical entities, *i.e.*, those located in space-time. Entities related to objects and processes are involved in it. Verbs in this category are mostly related to processes since they are things that 'happen' and have 'temporal parts/stages'. A process can be considered as a set of denotations related to dual object process, intentional process, motion, internal change, shape, or change.

Situation Type. Refers to a situation—event or set of events, featured as a conceptual unit—happening over time. This kind of verbs is represented in terms of the event-structure or the predicate properties.

Conceptual Domain. EuroWordNet is a multilingual database for multiple languages containing 200 domain labels organized in a hierarchical structure for grouping the words in categories based on a domain hierarchy. Semantic domains are knowledge areas—*e.g.* economy or politics—used to describe texts according to general subjects characterized by domain specific lexica. The domain hierarchy is represented as an ontology which comprises conceptual levels for each language. The levels of the domain hierarchy are called basic domains.

2.3 Language processing techniques

Several language processing techniques centered in events have been used in areas such as text-mining and information extraction. They have been applied by considering many kinds of documents, *e.g.*, technical documents, patents, and software requirement documents, as follows.

Cascini *et al.* (2004) present a functional analysis of patents and their implementation in the PAT-Analyzer tool. They use techniques based on the extraction of the interactions from the entities described in the document and expressed as subject-action-object triples, by using a suitable syntactic parser. Rösner *et al.* (1997) generate multilingual documents from knowledge bases by using automated techniques. The resulting documents can be represented in an interchangeable way centered in events.

2.4 Information Extraction and Text Analytics

Information Extraction includes techniques for extracting any kind of information from texts. Relation extraction techniques require the identification of significant entities and relationships between entities and significant properties of entities (Grimes, 2008). The goal of IE is storing the extracted entities and relationships in a database—structured information. The *prototypical document extraction* relies on the identification of frequent sequences of terms in the documents, and uses language processing techniques, such as POS tagging and term extraction, for pre-processing the textual data (Rajman & Besancon, 1997). Such a technique can be considered as an automated, generalized indexing procedure for extracting linguistically significant structures from documents.

According to Wilcock (2009), *Text Analytics* (TA) refers to a subfield of information technology dealing with applications, systems, and services for doing some kind of text analytics as a way to extract information from them. Several techniques for TA have been developed, among them: named entity recognition, co-reference resolution, information extraction, chunking, semantic role labeling, text mining, and semantic search.

The state-of-the-art review present several approaches in the previous areas for studying events, as follows.

Meth *et al.* (2012) propose an automated and knowledge-based support system for eliciting activities and process, in the context of knowledge engineering. RARE project (Cybulski & Reed, 1998) is focused on parsing texts based on a semantic network assisted by a thesaurus; they combine NLP with faceted classification for identifying and analyzing needs and expectations of stakeholders. Hahn *et al.* (1996) develop a methodology for knowledge acquisition and concept learning from texts written in German. The method relies on a quality-based model for reasoning on terminology, by using concepts from NLP.

Focused on goal identification we found several approaches (Dardenne *et al.*, 1993; Darimont *et al.*, 2005; Giorgini *et al.*, 2005). Such goals describe desired states or actions performed by actors regardless of specific consideration for normative positions (*e.g.*, permissions, recommendations, and obligations). Young and Antón (2010) propose the analysis of the commitments, privileges, and rights conveyed within online policy documents.

2.5 Event extraction

The event extraction has been approached by several authors as we present in the following paragraphs.

Huttunen *et al.* (2002a) propose linguistic cues for identifying the overlapping or partial events including specific lexical items, locative and temporal expressions, and usage of ellipsis and anaphora. Grishman (2012) emphasizes in unsupervised event extraction by using extensive linguistic analysis. Do *et al.* (2011) develop a minimally supervised approach, based on focused distributional similarity methods and discourse connectives, for identifying causality relations between events in context. Sun *et al.* (2007) are focused on detecting causality between search query pairs in temporal query logs.

Riaz and Girju (2010) propose cluster sentences into topic-specific scenarios, and then focus on identifying causal relations between events and building a dataset of causal text spans headed by a verb. Etzion and Niblett (2010) work with event processing and present a software system including specific logic to filter, transform, or detect patterns in events as they occur. The event analysis in specific genres has been approached as follows:

- Beamer and Girju (2009) work on detecting causal relations among verbs in a corpus of screen plays, limited to consecutive or adjacent verb pairs.
- Szarvas *et al.* (2012) study the linguistic cues of events in three genres: news, scientific papers, and Wikipedia articles. They demonstrate significant differences in lexical usage across the genres by using syntactic cues.
- Pivovarova *et al.* (2013) propose the event analysis for generating particular statistics and capturing the scenario-specific characteristics of event representation in a particular corpus.
- The PULS[1] system is based on the event structure for discovering, aggregating, verifying, and visualizing events in various scenarios.

Finally, relevant proposals for event extraction have been developed: Chambers and Jurafsky (2011) propose a template-based IE algorithm for

[1] http://puls.cs.helsinki.fi

learning sets of related events and semantic roles from an unlabeled corpus; Kasch and Oates (2010) define script learning and narrative schemas to capture knowledge from unlabeled text. Scripts are sets of related event words and semantic roles learned by linking syntactic functions with coreferring arguments; Benson *et al.* (2011) propose a method for discovering event records from social media feeds. Such a method operates on a noisy feed of data and extracts canonical records of events by aggregating information across multiple messages.

3 Approach for event analysis

3.1 Corpus and Analysis Tools

The corpus definition starts by collecting possible technical documents circulating on the web related to the genre *business domain*. We have not so many restrictions by selecting the texts for building the corpus, because the focus is getting as many samples as possible, but not the entire track rolling stock. We collect and analyze a set of documents from such a domain in different subject fields (*e.g.* medicine, forestry, and laboratory). The corpus used as the basis for this preliminary study comprises 50 English-written documents with independence of its variety. Assuming the population is evenly distributed, we selected a sample of 32 documents, corresponding to 64% of the total corpus population—the minimum percentage statistically random, calculated with proportions Z test. The variety of subject fields is important to the analysis of the events identified in the corpus.

The training documents belong to the 'Standard Operating Procedure (SOP) category. All the documents sum 167,905 tokens and 9,252 word types. The initial exploration of this experimental corpus was supported by AntConc 3.3.5w® (Anthony, 2009) and TermoStatWeb™ (Drouin, 2003). AntConc was used to manually and systematically find frequent expressions and select their contexts, and TermoStatWeb™ was used to list most frequent verbs, for analyzing its organization in the texts.

3.2 Analysis approach

This analysis is based on the semantic behavior of the events, under the premise the analysis of meanings or senses of the verbs should be closely linked to the analysis of events and terms used in a context. This event-centered analysis is approached from the point of view of the possible meanings suggested by the Multilingual Central Repository (MCR)[2].

Based on the training corpus (SOP), we identify the set of most frequent verbs. Prioritized verbs are classified by categories, according to Vossen (2002). Then, we use the types of verb in order to identify patterns. Such patterns will be the basis of rules for inferring and extracting organizational relationships from business-based information. In this way, we guide the analysis to all situations concerning the verb regarding its usage in the SOPs. Based on an incremental method, we performed this step-by-step analysis as follows:

Review. In this phase we look for identifying the verbs in the relevant sections of the documents, according to the rhetorical organization units defined by Manrique (2015). For the sake of identifying verbs, we first prioritize the most used verbs in the SOPs according to the occurrence frequency. Analysis of the occurrence frequency of verbs in the corpus was supported by corpus analysis tools. We selected the first 58 verbs corresponding to the interval of hits [501–72], with 501 the highest frequency and 72 the lower occurrence. In Table 1 we present the 10 most used verbs in the corpus.

Term	Frequency
use	501
include	458
provide	355
follow	314
require	314
ensure	226
submit	175
approve	166
prepare	156
identify	143
involve	143
perform	136
describe	133

Table 1. Sample of prioritized verbs

[2] http://adimen.si.ehu.es/web/MCR

Verb feature identification. The semantic features of each prioritized verb are addressed, and the discriminant features for relevant and irrelevant verbs, according to some categories—conceptual, functional, process-based, and situational—are identified. The classification of verbs is based on the meanings reported by WordNet 3.0 by using the Interlingual Index (ILI 3.0) included into the EuroWordNet Interface (WEI consult mode)[3]. For each prioritized verb, we define the categories of classification according to the classes defined in section 2.2, by following an iterative and sequential process:

i) For each verb, checking the meanings reported in WEI. For the first four meanings reported:

- Assign an occurrence indicator (value) for each associated conceptual category.
- Assign a value for each functional category the verb has.
- Assign values to situational category (unique value for situation type) and multiple value for the situation component.

ii) Generating the sum of all values for each category

iii) Identifying which categories correspond to the highest sum of the corresponding analysis. The complete verb classification was presented by Manrique (2015), as a result of the previous analysis. In Table 2 a sample of such results is presented, where: column 1 is de list of prioritized verbs; columns 2 to 6 correspond to the conceptual classification category of verb (based on WordNet 3.0 and ILI). The number appearing in each cell verb/category corresponds to the frequency of verb is taking such a category. We generate the sum of all values by category and identify the categories corresponding with the highest sum.

iv) Analyzing and presenting results. Based on the defined classification and categorization of verbs, we make an analysis and identify findings in terms of features and properties capturing the particularities of the specific genre.

[3] http://adimen.si.ehu.es/cgi-bin/wei/public/wei.consult.perl

3.3 Characterization of events from business-based technical documents

As a result of the previous process and according to the each analyzed and prioritized category, we identify the following findings, characterizing the genre:

Conceptual Category. The conceptual domains are based on a relation of specificity. We identified the events are not assigned to a particular conceptual category, due to their nature. Unlike nouns which somehow can be grouped by domains, the events/verbs can be used in similar senses by several different domains. For instance we can find that '*apply*' is used in a specific domain like '*Medicine*' for saying '*a nurse is applying medication to a patient*,' or in a general domain involving an intentional process for saying '*The operator works applying rules.*'

	Conceptual classification of verb (Category)												
Verb	facto tum	social	free-time	applied science	humanities	pure-sciences	social	Possession	change	cognition	stative	communication	creation
assign							1						
use	3	1					1						
include	3						1			1			
provide	2	1	1					1				1	
follow	4								2				
require	4											2	
review	2	1			1					3		1	
process	1	1		2		1	2		1	1			
ensure	2									1		1	
request	3											3	
submit	4							1				2	
work	3	1					3						
approve	2									1		1	
prepare	3		1						1				3

Table 2. Sample of prioritized verbs

As we show in the results of classification, the prioritized verbs are mostly used in any domain, for example the one appearing under the label *Factotum*, which is assigned when none of the labels were assigned. When verb is not labeled as factotum, the second mostly used conceptual category is *social label.*

Functional category. According to the tracks of the analysis, most of verbs are marked as an *intentional process* (general), whose intention is no longer identified (*e.g.* attaching, comparing, substituting, and separating). Generally speaking, an *intentional process* is deliberately set in motion by a Cognitive Agent, *i.e.* it is a human action, act, or activity of a thing for accomplishing or achieving a work.

The second most frequent functional category is *social interaction* as a kind of intentional process involving interactions between Cognitive-Agents. This category relates a social relation, an interaction, or a socially accepted situation.

Situation Category. The *situation type* for most of the verbs is *dynamic*. Such verbs are related to the situations implying either a transition from one state to another or a continuous transition perceived as an unbounded process (*e.g.* event, act, action, become, happen, take place, process, habit, change, and activity). No change in their properties or relation is involved by the verb.

Dynamic situations. More than half of verbs occur with *bounded event*, when they are implied with a specific transition from one situation to another, which is bounded in time and directed to a result (*e.g., to implement, to remove, to develop, etc.*). Regarding to the *situation component*, the results show the main semantic components characterizing the situation are the following:

- *Cause*. Component of situations involving causation. This component is coherent with the *situation type* since the *causation* is always combined with *dynamic* and it can take several forms. Such forms depend on the grade of intervention of an agent. The form with the higher frequency is *agentive* which can be related to a controlling agent who intentionally tries to achieve some change. The agentive situations imply a controlling agent causing a dynamic change (*e.g.* to implement, to write, to record, etc.).
- *Purpose*. Abstract components reflecting the intentionality of acts and activities. Situations intended to have some effect are implied. As the previous situation component, this one reflects consistency with the context as applied to *dynamic situations*. Also, this component strongly correlates to *agentive* and *cause*, clustering mainly human acts and activities. *Situation Components* such as *usage*, *social,* and *communication* often combine with *purpose*.
- *Communication*. Component of situations involving communication (*e.g.* designate, request, describe, issue, etc.). Communication verbs are often speech-acts (*bounded events*) or denote more global communicative activities (*unbounded events*). Also, they include different phases of the communication referring to causation of communication effects (*e.g.,* to explain or to show) or creation of a meaningful representation (*e.g.,* to write or to draw).
- *Physical*. Component of situations involving perceptual and measurable properties of objects (*e.g.,* to shape, to prepare, to describe, etc.); or dynamic changes and perceptions of its physical properties (*e.g.,* to monitor, to collect, to copy, to notice, etc.).

Based on the previous characterization (features and properties) and the prioritized verbs, we finally develop a dependency parsing. For the parsing process we use the Freeling dependency parser[4]. The goals of such parsing are:

- Defining patterns of occurrence of the identified verbs and defining a set of semantic/dependency rules for transforming each pattern to a controlled language structure.
- Defining a script for preprocessing the SOPs, trying to extract simple sentences for the parser to maximize its performance.
- Processing the evaluation corpus with a dependency parser.
- Evaluating the extracted relations and the findings.

According to the event characterization and feature identification resulted from the dependency parsing, we propose a set of semantic rules for transforming each feature into a controlled language. We used the UN-Lencep (named by its Spanish acronym for 'Universidad Nacional de Colombia—Lenguaje Controlado para la Especificación de Esquemas Preconceptuales'), as an intermediate representation between natural language and conceptual schemas for software engineering.

[4] http://nlp.lsi.upc.edu/freeling/

We present the rules defined for such mapping in Manrique & Zapata (2013). Each mapping rule is assigned to one category expressed in terms of the pattern in the SOP and the expression in UNLencep generated. The pattern composing each defined rule considers attributes relating the tags (*e.g.*, syntactic or semantic tag—synt—, function tag—func—, etc.) assigned by the dependency parser.

By means of the basic interface of the parser library, we analyzed the text files of the corpus from the command line. We extract the relations matching the semantic rules from the parser. Based on them, we performed a preliminary evaluation in terms of the useful relations being extracted, the number of relevant extracted relations with the necessary components for measuring precision and recall. According to the results, we could identify the potential of the parsing, the quality of the defined rules, and the aspects improved by the text preprocessing.

4 Conclusions

This study aims at characterizing SOPs by revealing key features and properties of events used in an English corpus belonging to the business genre. We proposed an approach for analyzing events from a training corpus, which can be processed as input for further knowledge engineering processes. The appropriateness of JSDs in requirements elicitation was verified with this study.

We analyze the structure of training text for semi-automatically extracting several features for each event mention from the corpus. Extracting a rich set of features allows us propose properties capturing the differences of this specific genre. We contribute to the research about the identification of events from heterogeneous document sources stemming from different genres and domains

Our proposal is focused on the events study in the practice, for identifying domain-specific characteristics of them in a business-based corpus. This is a preliminary study which we expect can be used in the same or greater depth of linguistic analysis by language processing systems or IE systems.

We are testing the performance of the rules derived from this event analysis approach in NAHUAL, our functional prototype of a software system for processing texts.

As future work, we expect to increase the number of documents in the corpus and refine the study of event features. Statistical measures can be also considered as a way to support the presented event analysis and the event representation in this particular corpus, as suggest Pivovarova *et al.* (2013). The automated event extraction in the frame of knowledge acquisition from business-based documents is also our interest.

Likewise, given the importance of the event structure, the supervised event causality identification and the causal relations analysis seems to be a promising approach in the current research.

Acknowledgments

This work has been partly founded by the Vicerrectoría de Investigación from both the Universidad de Medellín and the Universidad Nacional de Colombia, under the following projects: "Método de transformación de lenguaje natural a lenguaje controlado para la obtención de requisitos, a partir de documentación técnica"; "Especificación de un lenguaje controlado de Dominio Específico: Fundamentos Lingüísticos y bases de Transformación desde Documentos Técnicos Corporativos en Lenguaje Natural". Also, it was supported in part by the COLCIENCIAS, under the doctoral program "Generación del Bicentenario, Colombia 2010."

References

Anthony, L. 2009. *Issues in the design and development of software tools for corpus studies: The case for collaboration.* Contemporary corpus linguistics, London: P. Baker Ed.: 87-104.

Bejan, C.A. and Harabagiu, S. 2013. Unsupervised Event Coreference Resolution. *Computational Linguistics*, 40: 2.

Benson, E., Haghighi, A. and Barzilay, R. 2011. Event discovery in social media feeds. In Proceedings of the 49th Annual Meeting of the Association for Computational Linguistics, ACL, Stroudsburg, PA, USA, 1: 389-398.

Cascini, G. Fantechi, A. and Spinicci E. 2004. Natural Language Processing of Patents and Technical Documentation. *Lecture Notes in Computer Science*, 3163:508-520.

Chambers, N. and Jurafsky, D. 2011. Template-Based Information Extraction without the Templates, ACL-2011, Portland, OR.

Cybulski, J. and Reed, K. 1998. Requirements Classification and Reuse: Crossing domains boundaries. *6th Intl. Conf. on Software Reuse (ICSR'2000)*. Vienna, Austria. Springer.

Dardenne, A., van Lamsweerde, A. and Fickas, S. 1993. Goal-directed Requirements Acquisition. *Science of Comp*. Prog., 20:3-50.

Darimont, R., Delor, E., Massonet, P., van Lamsweerde, A. 2005. GRAIL/KAOS: An Environment for Goal-driven Requirements Engineering. *IEEE 19th International Conference on Software Engineering*, pp. 612-613.

Do, Q.X., Chan, Y.S., and Roth, D. 2011. Minimally Supervised Event Causality Identification. *EMNLP'2011*.

Drouin, P. 2003. *TermoStat Web 3.0*. Désormais utilisable qu'après enregistremen. Available in: http://olst.ling.umontreal.ca/~drouinp/termostat_web/

Etzion O., Niblett P. 2010. *Event Processing in Action*. Manning Publications, Co. NY, USA.

Fellbaum, C. 1998. *WordNet*. An Electronic Lexical Database. The MIT Press. NY, USA.

Giorgini, P., Massacci, F., Mylopoulos, J., Zannone, N. 2005. Modeling Security Requirements through Ownership, Permission and Delegation. *13th IEEE International Requirements. Engineering Conference*, pp. 167-176.

Grimes, S. 2008. Text technologies in the mainstream: Text analytics solutions, applications and trends. Available in: http://altaplana.com

Grishman, R. 2012. Structural linguistics and unsupervised information extraction. *Automatic Knowledge Base Construction and Web-scale Knowledge Extraction* (AKBC-WEKEX 2012), pp. 57–61.

Hahn, U. Klenner, M. and Schnattinger, K. 1996. A Quality-Based Terminological Reasoning Model for Text Knowledge Acquisition. *Advances in Knowledge Acquisition*. Shadbolt, O'Hara & Schreiber (Eds.). Springer-Verlag, Berlin.

Huttunen, S., Yangarber, R. and Grishman, R. 2002. Diversity of scenarios in information extraction. *Proceedings of the Third International Conference on Language Resources and Evaluation* (LREC 2002), Las Palmas de Gran Canaria, Spain.

Manrique, B. 2015. A formalization for mapping discourses from business-based technical documents into controlled language texts for requirement elicitation. Ph.D. Thesis. Universidad Nacional de Colombia, Medellín.

Meth, H., Li, Y., Maedche, A. Mueller, B. 2012. Advancing task elicitation systems–An experimental evaluation of design Principles. *Proceeding of 33 International Conference on Information Systems*, pp. 54-68.

Petrenz, P. and Webber, B. 2011. Stable classification of text genres. *Computational Linguistics*, 37(2):385–393.

Pivovarova, L., Huttunen, S. and Yangarber, R. 2013. Event representation across genre. *Proceedings of the 1st Workshop on EVENTS: Definition, Detection, Coreference, and Representation*, pp. 29–37.

Rajman, M. and Besancon, B. 1997. *Text Mining: Natural Language techniques and Text Mining applications*. IFIP 1997. Chapman & Hall. NY, USA.

Riaz, M. and Girju, R. 2010. Another look at causality: Discovering scenario-specific contingency relationships with no supervision. *Proceedings of the 2010 IEEE Fourth International Conference on Semantic Computing*, pp. 361-368.

Rösner, D., Grote, B., Hartmann, K. and Höfling, B. 1997. From Natural Language Documents to Sharable Product Knowledge: A Knowledge Engineering Approach. *Journal of Universal Computer Science*. 3(8): 955-987.

Sangeetha S, R.S. Thakur, and Arock, M. 2010. *Event detection using lexical chain*. Hrafn Loftsson, Eirikur Rögnvaldson, Sigrun Helgadottir (eds.). In: IceTAL 2010, LNAI 6233: 314-319.

Saurí, R. and Pustejovsky, J. 2012. Are you sure that this happened? Assessing the factuality degree of events in text. *Computational Linguistics*, 38(2):261–299.

Sun, Y., Liu, N., Xie, K., Yan, S., Zhang, B. and Chen, Z. 2007. Causal relation of queries from temporal logs. *Proceedings of the 16th international conference on World Wide Web*, NY, USA.

Szarvas, G. Vincze, V., Farkas, R., Mófra, G. and Gurevych, I. 2012. Cross-genre and cross-domain detection of semantic uncertainty. *Computational Linguistics*, 38(2):335–367.

Vossen, P. 2002. *EuroWordNet General Document*. Version 3. Piek Vossen (ed.). University of Amsterdam. Amsterdam, Holanda.

Wilcock, G. 2009. *Introduction of linguistics annotation and texts analytics*. Synthesis Lectures on Human Language Technologies. Morgan & Claypool (eds). Toronto, CA.

Young, J. D. and Antón, A. I. 2010. A Method for Identifying Software Requirements Based on Policy Commitments. *18th IEEE International Requirements Engineering Conference*. Available in: http://ieeexplore.ieee.org.ezproxy.unal.edu.co/stamp/stamp.jsp?tp=&arnumber=5636634

Event Nugget Annotation: Processes and Issues

Teruko Mitamura, Yukari Yamakawa, Susan Holm
Language Technologies Institute, Carnegie Mellon University, Pittsburgh PA
teruko@cs.cmu.edu, {yukariy, sh4s}@andrew.cmu.edu

Zhiyi Song, Ann Bies, Seth Kulick, Stephanie Strassel
Linguistic Data Consortium, University of Pennsylvania, Philadelphia PA
{zhiyi, bies, skulick, strassel}@ldc.upenn.edu

Abstract

This paper describes the processes and issues of annotating event nuggets based on *DEFT ERE Annotation Guidelines v1.3* and *TAC KBP Event Detection Annotation Guidelines 1.7.* Using Brat Rapid Annotation Tool (brat), newswire and discussion forum documents were annotated. One of the challenges arising from human annotation of documents is annotators' disagreement about the way of tagging events. We propose using Event Nuggets to help meet the definitions of the specific type/subtypes which are part of this project. We present case studies of several examples of event annotation issues, including discontinuous multi-word events representing single events. Annotation statistics and consistency analysis is provided to characterize the inter-annotator agreement, considering single term events and multi-word events which are both continuous and discontinuous. Consistency analysis is conducted using a scorer to compare first pass annotated files against adjudicated files.

1 Introduction

Annotating event mentions is useful for event detection tasks. It also is useful for detecting event coreference, subevent relations, event arguments, and realis values in corpora. This paper describes the processes and issues of annotating event nuggets based on the *DEFT ERE Annotation Guidelines v1.3* (LDC, 2014) (henceforth referred to as *Light ERE Guidelines*) and the *TAC KBP Event Detection Annotation Guidelines v1.7* (LTI, 2014) (henceforth referred to as *TAC KBP Event Guidelines*). Using the Brat Rapid Annotation Tool (brat)[1], we annotated files in newswire and discussion forums genres to create the corpus that supports the TAC KBP pilot evaluation for Event Nugget Detection as part of the DEFT program.

In this paper, we introduce the notion of event nugget and how event nuggets are annotated in the corpus. We discuss the issues that arose in the process of developing *TAC KBP Event Guidelines*, because they are important challenges for manual annotation and impact the quality of annotation for gold standard creation. Two major issues are (1) determining if an event meets the event type/subtype definitions and (2) deciding which words should be tagged within the span of a multi-word event nugget that represents a single event. We provide screen images of our annotation tool in order to give a complete picture of the annotation process. Finally, we present statistics to explain the characteristics of the corpus, such as the size of the corpus and the distribution of event type/subtypes. We discuss consistency analysis of inter-annotator agreement in terms of single word, multi-word continuous, and multi-word discontinuous event nuggets.

2 What is an Event Nugget?

It is challenging to provide clear-cut definitions of events, because many researchers define events differently. For example, in the Light ERE annotations, as well as in ACE, *Automatic Content Extraction) English Annotation Guidelines for Events* (LDC, 2005), an event is defined as an explicit occurrence involving participants. An event is something that happens at a particular place and time, and it can frequently be described as a change of state. The *Light ERE Guidelines* expect annotators to tag an event trigger, which is the smallest extent of text that expresses the occurrence of an event. Both ACE and Light ERE, only examples of a particular set of types/subtypes are tagged. An event trigger is usually a word or phrase. In many cases, event triggers are main verbs in sentences that in-

[1] Brat Rapid Annotation Tool (brat) was developed by Pontus Stenetorp et al. (2014). It is a web-based annotation tool.

Proceedings of the 3rd Workshop on EVENTS at the NAACL-HLT 2015, pages 66–76,
Denver, Colorado, June 4, 2015.

dicate the occurrence of the events. Annotating a main verb is relatively easy and is likely to produce a higher rate of inter-annotator agreement, because it allows annotators to pay more attention to a syntactic attribute of an event as well as its semantic feature. However, event triggers are not just verbs. Some nouns and adjectives can also express events (See examples in Section 3.1.).

In this study, we took a different approach to event annotations so that we would be able to annotate more complex events, which consist of multiple words taggable as events. For this reason, we decided to take a semantically oriented approach for annotation. New annotation guidelines were produced (*TAC KBP Event Guidelines*), based on the *Light ERE Guidelines* and *ACE*. To clarify the tagging of multiword events, we propose the idea of "event nugget," which is comprised of a semantically meaningful unit that expresses the event in a sentence. An event nugget can be either a single word (main verb, noun, adjective, adverb) or a continuous or discontinuous multi-word phrase.

The main reason why we propose event nugget annotation is to identify events accurately enough to meet the definitions of event types/subtypes in the *Light ERE Guidelines*. The type/subtype definitions restrict annotation to very specific types of events. Figuring out which events fall within the type/subtype definitions is a key issue to annotation. In the process of annotation, we have encountered cases in which multiple words could equally be considered as an event trigger. In many cases the multiple words are hard to separate from one another in terms of meaning (e.g., "hold a meeting", "serve a sentence", "send email"). Thus, we decided to annotate the maximum extent of text which meets the definition of the event types/subtypes provided by the *Light ERE Guidelines*. This approach allows annotators to tag all possible words that meet the definition of the event types/subtypes.

In addition to the annotation of the maximum extent of events, discontinuous tagging is another characteristic of event nugget annotation. (In order to clarify which words are in the same event nugget in this paper, we underline from the first word in a discontinuous multiword event nugget to the last word in the nugget. A dotted underline appears under words that are not part of the event nugget.) Discontinuous tagging allows annotators to tag words that do not lie next to each other but still belong to a multiword event nugget because they are all required to meet the definition, such as "The company **laid** 10 workers **off**," and "His **death sentence** was **carried out**."

Discontinuous tagging is very effective because it can be used to prevent violations of rules for annotation. For example, *TAC KBP Event Guidelines* as well as *Light ERE Guidelines* mention that non-main verbs should not be tagged. In sentences such as "His death sentence was carried out," annotators may want to tag "death sentence was carried out" to meet the definition of Justice_Execute events, since carrying out a death sentence means executing someone. However, tagging "was" violates the rule that non-main verbs are not taggable. In this case, tagging "death sentence" and "carried out" together as a discontinuous multiword event nugget not only meets the definition of Justice_Execute events but also does not violate the rule that "be" verbs should not be tagged.

The merits of event nugget annotation are summarized as follows: identification of events in a more semantically meaningful way and flexible annotation without violating annotation rules. In the next section, we present examples of event nuggets, using the following format to indicate the annotation: [Event Type_Subtype, REALIS]. Realis will be discussed in Section 3.3.

3 Types of Event Nuggets and REALIS

3.1 Single-Word Event Nuggets

As in ACE and Light ERE annotation, single-word event nuggets meet the definitions of event triggers for particular types/subtypes. Slightly modified in *TAC KBP Event Guidelines*, single-word event nuggets refer to words that meet the definitions of event types/subtypes by themselves. They are verbs (usually main verbs), nouns, adjectives, or adverbs. Below are some examples of single-word event nuggets. The words in **bold face** are event nuggets.

- The **attack** by insurgents occurred on Saturday. [Conflict_Attack, ACTUAL]
- Hillary Clinton was not **elected** president in 2008. [Personnel_Elect, OTHER]

There are some cases where multiple single-word event nuggets appear in the same sentence.

- Kennedy was **shot dead** by Oswald. [Conflict_Attack, ACTUAL], [Life_Die, ACTUAL]
- Three years ago, investors **bought** two stagnant web-hosting companies and **merged** them into what is now known as The Planet. [Transaction_Transfer-Ownership, ACTUAL], [Business_Merge-Org, ACTUAL]

Pronouns and other anaphors are also considered as single-word event nuggets if they refer to previous event mentions that meet the definitions of event types/subtypes.

- The **talks** between the Koreas were largely unsuccessful. **They** ended without agreement on Monday. [Contact_Communicate, ACTUAL], [Contact_Communicate, ACTUAL]

3.2 Complex (Multi-Word) Event Nuggets

Complex event nuggets are multi-word phrases (or compounds) that construct semantic units that meet the definitions of event types/subtypes. Those units can be continuous or discontinuous. Multi-word event nuggets take various forms such as verb+noun, verb+particle/adverb, noun+noun, and so on. The words underlined and in **bold face** are multi-word event nuggets that represent a single event.

- Foo Company had **filed Chapter 11** in 2000. [Business_Declare-Bankruptcy, ACTUAL]
- The police investigated the **murder incident**. [Conflict_Attack, ACTUAL]

Discontinuous tagging is one of the characteristics of annotation of multi-word event nuggets. This type of tagging is useful because it captures event nuggets accurately without missing important components of meaning. Below are the examples of discontinuous tagging of multi-word event nuggets.

- The court **found** him **guilty**. [Justice_Convict, ACTUAL]
- His **death sentence** was **carried out**. [Justice_Execute, ACTUAL]
- All **charges** were **dropped** against him last year. [Justice_Acquit, ACTUAL]

Multi-word event nuggets that represent single events are tagged either continuously or discontinuously depending on the particular construction of the semantic units that meet the definitions of the event types/subtypes in each sentence.

For example, consider the definition of Justice_Sue: "A SUE event occurs whenever a court proceeding has been initiated for the purposes of determining the liability of a PERSON, ORGANIZATION or GPE accused of committing a crime or neglecting a commitment." The three examples below illustrate event nuggets for Justice_Sue events. (For clarification, strikethrough denotes an event that is not part of the event nugget being illustrated.)

- His lawyer should **file** a **lawsuit**. [Justice_Sue, OTHER]
- His lawyer should **sue**. [Justice_Sue, OTHER]
- His lawyer should ~~contest~~ the **lawsuit**. [Justice_Sue, OTHER]

The noun+verb combination of "file" and "lawsuit" meet the definition of Justice_Sue as a court proceeding having been initiated. A lawsuit is a court proceeding, and filing refers to its initiation, which is a part of the court proceeding. The two words in combination express the "doing" of the SUE event and meet the definition of Justice_Sue. The single verb "sue" can also be used to meet this definition, as can the single noun "lawsuit". However in the third sentence, "contest" is separate from the lawsuit event and does not belong to the event nugget. To contest a lawsuit is an action of the defense team in response to an existing lawsuit. There is currently no Justice Subtype defined in the *Light ERE Guidelines* to fit this contest event.

3.3 REALIS

In our annotation, event nuggets are annotated with three types of REALIS: ACTUAL, GENERIC, and OTHER. REALIS relates to whether or not an event occurred (LTI, 2014).

The REALIS of ACTUAL is used when the event actually happened at a particular place and time, involving specific entities. Both ongoing events and events that have ended are tagged ACTUAL. For example, "He **emailed** her about their plans [Contact_Communicate, ACTUAL]."

The REALIS of GENERIC is used for events that refer to general events involving types or categories of entities. GENERIC is also used for taggable event nuggets which appear in statistics or demographic information. For example, "People **die** [Life_Die, GENERIC]."

The REALIS of OTHER will be used for events that are neither ACTUAL nor GENERIC. If it is determined that an event meets the definition of a type/subtype and it is not an ACTUAL or GENERIC event, it can simply be tagged OTHER. For example, "He plans to **meet** with both political parties [Contact_Meet, OTHER]."

In the case of GENERIC events which also qualify as OTHER (e.g., negated generic) or ACTUAL (e.g., past generic, habitual generic), GENERIC is used, not OTHER or ACTUAL.

4 Event Types/Subtypes

The *TAC KBP Event Guidelines* and the *Light ERE Guidelines* share the same 33 event types/subtypes in particular areas, such as Life, Movement, Business, Conflict, Personnel, Transaction, and Justice, which were originated in the *ACE Guidelines* (LDC, 2005).

The complete set of event types/subtypes is: Life (Be-Born, Marry, Divorce, Injure, Die), Movement (Transport-Person), Business (Start-Org, End-Org, Declare-Bankruptcy, Merge-Org), Conflict (Demonstrate, Attack), Contact (Meet, Communicate), Personnel (Start-Position, End-Position, Nominate, Elect), Transaction (Transfer-Ownership, Transfer-Money), Justice (Arrest-Jail, Release-Parole, Trial-Hearing, Charge-Indict, Sue, Convict, Sentence, Fine, Execute, Extradite, Acquit, Appeal, Pardon).

- John Doe was **born** in Casper, WY. [Life_Be-Born, ACTUAL]
- Roosevelt and his family immediately **departed** for Buffalo. [Movement_Transport-Person, ACTUAL]
- A car bomb **exploded** in central Baghdad. [Conflict_Attack, ACTUAL]

5 Annotation Challenges

One of the main challenges in the development of annotation guidelines is that there is always some disagreement about what should (not) be taggable. In this section, we present some examples of disagreements, which we experienced in the process of developing annotation guidelines, as case studies.

The first case is related to annotating implied events which are contained within nouns referring to persons (e.g., "protestor", "assailant", "killer"). The second case concerns prepositional phrases (e.g., "in prison", "behind bars"), which seem to meet the definitions of event types/subtypes. The third case involves annotating nouns that refer to the consequences or results of events (e.g., "injury", "body", "funeral"), which could be considered as either an entity or an event by individual annotators. The fourth case occurs when only a portion of a word indicates an event (e.g., "antiwar", "postwar", "ex-husband", "ex-wife"). The last case is discontinuous tagging of event nuggets. Although discontinuous tagging is effective for capturing the semantically meaningful unit of event nuggets, the consistency (See Table 5) of discontinues event nuggets is not as good as singe token event nugget.

In the case studies below, the words in ***italic bold*** are controversial or in issue.

Case Study 1: Is a person an event?

- Two other ***assailants*** have committed suicide.
- Here is the KICKER: As reported by local news stations DOZENs of ***protestors*** showed up to protest.
- On the grounds of legality, according to the Geneva Convention, members of regular armed forces – involved in conflicts – are the only persons who may be considered lawful ***combatants*** and authorized to use lethal force.

The words such as "assailants", "protesters", and "combatants" imply the occurrence of events, as we can see by paraphrasing them as "a person who assailed (assaulted) someone," "people who are protesting," and "people who combat." If annotators take the implied occurrences into consideration, those words will be tagged as event nuggets. However, those words actually refer to the "people" themselves. People are not events. Tagging them as events means that we tag implied events. In a similar fashion, some annotators may be tempted to tag "the **dead**" as an event nugget, but others do not because they think that "the dead" refers to dead people. It is critical for annotators to consider the implications of implied events when they tag. If implied events are to be tagged, rules should be explicitly stated to guide annotators as to which implied events should be tagged, and which implied events should not be tagged.

Case Study 2: Is a prepositional phrase taggable?

- A former militant of the French far-left group Action Directe, Georges Cipriani, left prison on parole on Wednesday after 23 years ***behind bars*** for two high-profile murders.

- Prosecutors have said Chen could face life ***in prison*** if convicted on all counts, including embezzlement and bribe-taking."

The phrases "behind bars" and "in prison" indicate that the agent was (or would be) imprisoned and could be tagged as Justice_Arrest-Jail events. They are, however, prepositional phrases that describe a certain state (i.e. the state of physically residing in a particular place). There is some debate whether or not states are taggable as events. Especially in the case of prepositional phrases, it is difficult for annotators to decide whether those phrases should be tagged, since they could be considered to refer to states and sound less eventive.

Case Study 3: Is it an event or the result of an event?

- Why was Trayvon's ***body*** laying 12 hours in the Morgue?
- A cry for the men to be hanged went up almost immediately after the woman died of her ***injuries***, …
- And those already existing time place and manner restrictions were utilized at Matthew Snyder's ***funeral***, with the result that the family never even knew WBC was there.

The words in ***italic bold*** indicate the consequence or result of certain events. For example, the type of "body" referred to in the first example only exists after a Life_Die event has occurred. "Injuries" exist on or in a person's body after (s)he has experienced a Life_Injure or Conflict_Attack event. A "funeral" is a ceremony that occurs after a Life_Die event has happened. Since "body", "injuries" and "funeral" are words that are closely related to taggable event types/subtypes, annotators may be tempted to tag those words as event nuggets. However, it is necessary to differentiate the consequence/result of an event from an event itself.

Case Study 4: Is a portion of a word taggable?

- U.N. Secretary General Kofi Annan said this week that the body has no interest in policing a ***postwar*** Iraq, …
- We were so proud of forming an ***antiwar*** bloc with France and Germany …
- Jurassic Park creator Crichton agrees to pay ***ex-wife*** 31 million dollars

The decision on whether a portion of a word should be tagged also causes disagreement among annotators. Some annotators may think it not appropriate to break a word into chunks, or others may tag a part of a word only if it is hyphenated. This case study raises the issue on how events are defined in relation to word level structure. Semantically, both "war" and "ex" meet the definitions of event types/subtypes. However, it is unclear whether the entire word ("postwar", "antiwar", "ex-wife") should be tagged. Is "antiwar" a Conflict_Attack event, for instance? It is necessary to have a clear rule for this type of tagging.

Case Study 5: Tagging Discontinuous Multiword Event Nuggets

In our corpus with 3,798 event nuggets, there were 209 discontinuous nuggets, a ratio of 5.5%. The discontinuous event nuggets appear in various forms such as verb+noun, verb+particle/adverb, verb+adjective, and verb+prepositional phrase. Among those patterns, the most frequent one is a verb+noun compound (83%), where a noun is the direct object of the verb. This pattern appears in a passive form as well.

- today I **got** a **letter** from the hospital [Contact_Communicate, ACTUAL]
- where was the father when the **shot** was **fired** not more than a 1000 feet away? [Conflict_Attack, ACTUAL]

These discontinuous events are tagged because multiple words in the sentence are important semantic components of their event type/subtype definitions. For example, the word, "get" is used to create various event types such as "get money" (Transaction_Transfer-Money) and "get a job" (Personnel_Start-Position). Thus, tagging a verb and a noun together as one event seems important to differentiate a particular event type from the others. In the second example, both "shot" and "fired" are taggable as events and it is hard to ignore either of them as not taggable due to the close relationship between the "doing" of an event and event itself. A verb+noun compound appears very often in the following event types/subtypes: Transaction_Transfer-Money (23%), Contact_Communicate (18%), and Conflict_Attack (10%).

Part of speech patterns for discontinuous tagging include verb+particle/adverb, which is 14% of the entire discontinuous tagging. This form appears most often in Movement_Transport-Person (68%).

- ...**took** us **in** for a interview...[Movement_Transport-Person, ACTUAL]
- ... i **put** the thread **up** because i really did want some opinions...[Contact_Communicate, ACTUAL]

Some annotators may only tag main verbs because they think adverbs and particles are modifying the verbs, but others may tag verb+adverb/particles together because they feel that the adverb/particles signify a different meaning from just the verbs alone. As shown Table 5, it is not as easy to consistently annotate multi-word event nuggets as it is to consistently annotate single-word event nuggets. However, the percentage of multi-word event nuggets is so low that it may not significantly affect overall event nugget detection performance.

We continue to work on reaching agreement on the optimal method of handling of these four types of controversial event nuggets in order to better represent the deeper semantics of texts. The very low frequency of discontinuous event nuggets does not mean that they should be ignored to achieve higher inter-annotator agreement. Clear rules for these cases should be laid out for future tasks on event nugget detection.

6 Brat Rapid Annotation Tool (brat)

Our annotation was conducted using Brat Rapid Annotation Tool (brat). This tool allows for customization of tags, such as event types/subtypes, realis types, types of entities/arguments, types of event links, and provides a means to add notes for questionable mentions. In addition, brat supports discontinuous tagging and side-by-side comparison of two files.

The actual procedure of annotation and the review of applied tags are relatively simple with this user-friendly application. Clicking on a word to be tagged opens a window where annotators can select tags, such as event types/subtypes and realis. After a word has been tagged, when the cursor is moved over the tag, a small box appears, displaying the assigned event type and realis for review. Screenshots of brat are shown in the Appendix.

7 Data Selection and Preparation

We produced training and evaluation (eval) data to support the Event Nugget evaluation as a pilot TAC KBP evaluation. The data includes both formal newswire text (NW) and informal discussion forums (DF), drawn from a pool of data also labeled for the DARPA DEFT Program's Light Entities, Relations and Events (Light ERE) task (Song et al., 2015), and/or the NIST TAC KBP Evaluation Event Argument Task (Ellis et al., 2014), with the goal of ultimately being able to take advantage of multiple styles of event annotation on the same data. Documents for the current task were carefully selected from this pool to optimize coverage of as many of the event types and subtypes as possible, with a goal of at least five instances of each type-subtype combination. The training data consists of 151 documents, while the eval data contains 200 documents. Table 1 shows the genre distribution as well as token counts for each partition.

Partition	Training		Eval	
Genre	NW	DF	NW	DF
Documents	77	74	101	99
Tokens	44,962	70,427	50,997	169,740

Table 1. Event Nugget Data Profile

While the Light ERE and KBP Event Argument tasks rely on character offsets for annotation and scoring, the Event Nugget Tuple Scorer[2] (Liu, Mitamura & Hovy, 2015) requires tokenized data. Therefore, prior to annotation, all selected documents were automatically tokenized in the Penn English Treebank style. No manual correction was performed on the tokenization due to time constraints.

8 Corpus and Consistency Analysis

8.1 Corpus

Experience with event annotation for Light ERE and ACE (Doddington et al., 2004) and related tasks suggests that a major challenge for annotation consistency is poor recall – human annotators are not highly consistent in recognizing that a mention has occurred. To reduce the impact of this known issue for the Event Nugget task, two anno-

[2] Event Nugget Tuple refers to the tuple made up of the nugget, event type/subtype, and realis.

tators independently labeled each document (two first pass annotation passes, referred to as FP1 and FP2 below); a senior annotator then adjudicated discrepancies to create a gold standard. The team consisted of four first pass annotators, two of whom were also adjudicators. The effort was made to ensure that annotators did not adjudicate their own first pass files, but due to time constraints and the pilot nature of the task, in some cases there was overlap.

The gold standard training data has 3,798 event nuggets annotated in total, while the eval data has 6,921 event nuggets. Table 2 shows the distribution of event nuggets by genre and realis type for each partition.

Realis Attribute	Training		Eval	
	NW	DF	NW	DF
Generic	202	383	245	981
Other	346	406	448	1271
Actual	1313	1132	1752	2224
Total	3798[3]		6921	

Table 2. Realis Annotation of Event Nuggets

Figure 1 (in Appendix) shows the distribution of each type-subtype combination in the training and eval data. Conflict_Attack has the highest representation in both training (579) and eval (791). Justice_Extradite has the lowest count in training data (3), while Life_Be-Born is least frequent in the eval data (19). Despite our efforts to manually select documents to maximize coverage for all type-subtype combinations, the corpus does not include any occurrences of Business_End-Org or Personnel_End-Position.

8.2 Consistency Analysis

We examined annotation consistency and quality by comparing different passes of the eval set annotation using the Event Nugget Tuple Scorer (Liu, Mitamura, & Hovy, 2015) developed for the event nugget evaluation task. This scorer treats one file as "gold" and the other as "system", and matches each nugget in the gold file to one or more nuggets in the system file. This mapping is based on the overlap of the nugget spans. By nugget span, we mean the exact list of tokens, continuous or discontinuous, that make up an event nugget. However, each system nugget can only be mapped to one gold nugget. For each gold nugget, the scorer computes type and realis accuracy scores based on the values for the gold nugget and all the system nuggets that are mapped to it.

The scorer produces three scores for each file. The first is an F-measure for the nugget spans, based on the mapping from gold to system nuggets, as well as ''false alarms" in the system file that are not mapped to any nuggets in the gold file. The type and realis scores for each gold mention are also cumulatively summed up, producing a type and realis score for the file. The type and realis scores are therefore tied to the F-measure score of the nugget spans. We used this scorer rather than the ACE (NIST, 2005) scorer since this scorer was designed for the event nugget evaluation task, and so seemed the most appropriate to use for evaluation of annotation consistency and quality of this corpus.

We examined annotation consistency by comparing the two independent first passes of annotation (FP1 and FP2), with the results shown in the column FP1 vs. FP2 in Table 3. We also evaluated improvement in annotation quality in the workflow by comparing the adjudicated (ADJ) and first (FP1 and FP2) passes, shown in the columns ADJ vs. FP1 and FP2 in Table 3. The noticeable improvement in score shows the advantage of including adjudication as part of the annotation process. (For IAA purposes, there is obviously no gold or system, but in order to use the scorer we arbitrarily treated one file as the "gold".)

	FP1 vs. FP2	ADJ vs. FP1	ADJ vs. FP2
Span	69.0	78.2	89.3
Type	68.2	71.7	84.3
Realis	60.0	63.2	85.7

Table 3. Scores for Event Nugget Eval Set Annotation

To gain some further insight into these numbers we expanded the analysis in two directions. First, we compared the FP1 vs. FP2 event nugget consistency with the FP1 vs. FP2 annotation consistency on the ACE 2005 training data (Walker et al., 2006). There is also a scorer that was developed for ACE (NIST, 2005), but we used the Event Nugget Tuple evaluation scorer so that we could score both sets of data for this comparison as in the

[3] 16 event nuggets in the training set did not receive a realis attribute, due to annotation error.

event nugget evaluation. This necessitated converting the ACE files into the format for event nuggets used for the current scorer. We used the ''anchor'' string of the ACE event mention as the nugget span, the ''type'' and ''subtype'' of the ACE event mention as the nugget type, and the ''modality'' of the ACE event mention as the nugget realis value. The results are shown in Table 4. The ACE FP1 vs. FP2 scores in Table 4 are somewhat lower than the FP1 vs. FP2 scores for the event nugget annotated data. However, while we have converted the format and used the same scorer, the annotation task is not identical, so this can only be taken as a rough comparison. There is greater difference between the ADJ vs. FP1, FP2 scores for the event nugget data than the ACE data. The event nugget task had a smaller annotation team than for ACE, and it is likely that more of the adjudication annotators for event nugget annotation also did the FP2 pass than was the case for ACE.

	FP1 v. FP2	ADJ v.FP1	ADJ v. FP2
Span	64.8	79.3	81.8
Type	62.2	70.4	75.6
Realis	56.1	68.0	73.0

Table 4. Scores for ACE 2005 Training Annotation

Second, we wished to determine also if there was a difference in the annotation consistency and quality of event nugget spans depending on whether the span consists of only one token as compared to those that are multiple tokens, either continuous or discontinuous. We decomposed the span F-measure in Tables 3 and 4 based on these criteria. We did this by modifying the event nugget scoring program to optionally ignore nuggets depending on their span. For example, when we wished to compare annotations for which the span is a single token, we simply ignored all nuggets with spans of more than one token. Likewise, when comparing nuggets for which the span consists of discontinuous multiple tokens, all nuggets for which the span was either a single token or multiple continuous tokens were ignored.

We ran this modified scorer in different modes to use (1) all nuggets (as before), (2) only nuggets that consist of a single token, ignoring all others, (3) only nuggets that consist of multiple continuous tokens, (4) only nuggets that consist of multiple discontinuous tokens, and (5) only nuggets that consist of multiple tokens, whether continuous or not. Mode (1) is the same as the score reported for the spans in Tables 3 and 4, and modes (2)-(5) in effect break this down into subcomponents. The results are shown in Table 5. ACE annotation did not allow discontinuous multiple token mentions, and so there are no results listed for ACE for (4) and (5).

The results for the consistency agreement between FP1 and FP2 show a similar fall in score for both the event nugget data and the ACE 2005 training data, when considering only multiple continuous tokens. The score climbs back up a little for the event nugget FP1 vs. FP2 score when considering (5) either continuous or discontinuous multiple tokens, as compared with either (3) only multiple continuous or (4) only multiple discontinuous. The reason for this is that there are cases where one file has an event nugget with a continuous multiple token span such as "got jail time" while the other has the corresponding event nugget with a multiple discontinuous span such as ''got time''. In (3) or (4), only one or the other would be included in the comparison, whereas in (5) and (1) both would be included, allowing for partial match instead of a miss. Similarly, there are cases where one file has a single token span for a nugget while the other file has a multiple token span for the corresponding nugget, and so it is only in (1) that both would be included, allowing for a partial match instead of a miss.

These more fine-grained nugget span scores for FP1 vs. FP2 show that single-token nuggets are annotated more consistently than multi-token nuggets. Considering just the multi-token nuggets, there is little difference in consistency of annotation between continuous and discontinuous spans. The ADJ vs. FP1 / ADJ vs. FP2 results show that including adjudication annotation lessens any difference in annotation quality for nuggets depending on whether the span is single or multi-token.

In future work on this consistency analysis, we will also go in the other direction, and convert the event nugget data into the ACE format so that it can be evaluated using the ACE scorer (NIST, 2005), ensuring that the comparison of inter-annotator consistency is not overly affected by details of particular scoring algorithms.

	Event Nugget				ACE 2005 Training			
	FP1 vs. FP2		ADJ vs. FP1 / ADJ vs FP2*		FP1 vs. FP2		ADJ vs. FP1 / ADJ vs. FP2	
	Span F-meas	Ratio**	Span F-meas	Ratio	Span F-meas	Ratio	Span F-meas	Ratio
(1) All mentions	69.0	100%	78.2/89.3	100%	64.9	100%	79.3/81.8	100%
(2) Single-token	67.7	90.0%	77.0/88.9	87.7%	65.0	94.6%	79.2/81.6	95.2%
(3) Multiple cont.	45.3	6.1%	57.7/84.4	6.8%	44.2	5.4%	70.8/70.6	4.8%
(4) Multiple discont.	43.0	4.0%	57.5/84.1	5.5%	NA	NA	NA	NA
(5) Multiple all	46.0	10.1%	59.0/85.4	12.3%	NA	NA	NA	NA

Table 5: Decomposing the Span Scores for Nugget and Trigger Span

* The two figures represent ADJ compared to FP1 (before the slash) and ADJ compared to FP2 (after the slash).

** Event nugget type per all event nuggets.

9 Conclusion

This paper first describes the processes of event nugget annotation using a brat tool and issues which arose in the process of developing *TAC KBP Event Guidelines*. We present complex cases that cause annotators' disagreement on tagging. Questions are raised about implied events, states vs. events, results of events, tagging portions of words, and discontinuous tagging. Second, the paper explains the creation of a tagged event nugget corpus and provides annotation statistics and consistency analysis comparing the first pass annotations, and also a comparison of adjudicated files with first pass files using the Event Nugget Tuple Scorer. The analysis shows that single-word nuggets are tagged more consistently than multi-word nuggets and that adjudication is very important for improving the quality of annotation.

Reconciliation of annotation disagreement is crucial in terms of not only the development of annotation guidelines but also the quality of annotation. This is closely associated with how an event nugget is defined and clarification of tagging rules. Resolving the issues surrounding event type/subtype definitions will be very helpful not only for future studies on event nugget detection but also studies on event coreference, subevent relations, and event arguments.

Acknowledgments

This material is based on research sponsored by Air Force Research Laboratory and Defense Advanced Research Projects Agency under agreement numbers FA8750-13-2-0045 and FA8750-12-2-0342. The U.S. Government is authorized to reproduce and distribute reprints for Governmental purposes notwithstanding any copyright notation thereon. The views and conclusions contained herein are those of the authors and should not be interpreted as necessarily representing the official policies or endorsements, either expressed or implied, of Air Force Research Laboratory and Defense Advanced Research Projects Agency or the U.S. Government.

We are thankful to Jun Araki, Zhengzhong "Hector" Liu, and Volkan Cirik for their assistance in the annotation tool and data calculation.

References

George Doddington, Alexis Mitchell, Mark Przbocki, Lance Ramshaw, Stephanie Strassel, and Ralph Weischedel. 2004. The Automatic Content Extraction (ACE) program – tasks, data, and evaluation. In *Proceedings of the Fourth International Conference on Language Resources and Evaluation (LREC 2004)*, Lisbon, May 24-30.

Joe Ellis, Jeremy Getman, and Stephanie M. Strassel. 2014. Overview of Linguistic Resources for the TAC KBP 2014 Evaluations: Planning, Execution, and Results. In *Proceedings of TAC KBP 2014 Workshop*, National Institute of Standards and Technology, Gaithersburg, Maryland, USA, November 17-18, 2014.

Language Technologies Institute. 2014. *TAC KBP Event Detection Annotation Guidelines, Version 1.7*, Language Technologies Institute, CMU, September 12, 2014.

Linguistic Data Consortium. 2014. *DEFT ERE Annotation Guidelines: Events Version 1.3*, March 13, 2014.

Zhengzhong Liu, Teruko Mitamura, Eduard Hovy. 2015. "Evaluation Algorithms for Event Nugget Detection: A Pilot Study". To appear in the Proceedings of the 3rd Workshop on EVENTS: Definition, Detection, Coreference, and Representation. NAACL-HLT 2015.Linguistic Data Consortium. 2005. *ACE (Automatic Content Extraction) English Annotation Guidelines for Events, Version 5.4.1 2005.05.09.*

National Institute of Standards and Technology. 2005. *The ACE 2005 Evaluation Plan.* http://www.itl.nist.gov/iad/mig/tests/ace/2005/doc/ace05-evalplan.v3.pdf

Zhiyi Song, Ann Bies, Tom Riese, Justin Mott, Jonathan Wright, Seth Kulick, Neville Ryant, Stephanie Strassel, Xiaoyi Ma. Submitted. From Light to Rich ERE: Annotation of Entities, Relations, and Events.

Pontus Stenetorp, Sampo Pyysalo, Goran Topić, Tomoko Ohta, Sophia Ananiadou and Jun'ichi Tsujii (2012). brat: a Web-based Tool for NLP-Assisted Text Annotation. In *Proceedings of the Demonstrations Session at EACL 2012.*

Christopher Walker, Stephanie Strassel, Julie Medero, Kazuaki Maeda. 2006. *ACE 2005 Multilingual Training Corpus*. Linguistic Data Consortium Catalog No.: LDC2006T06.

Appendix

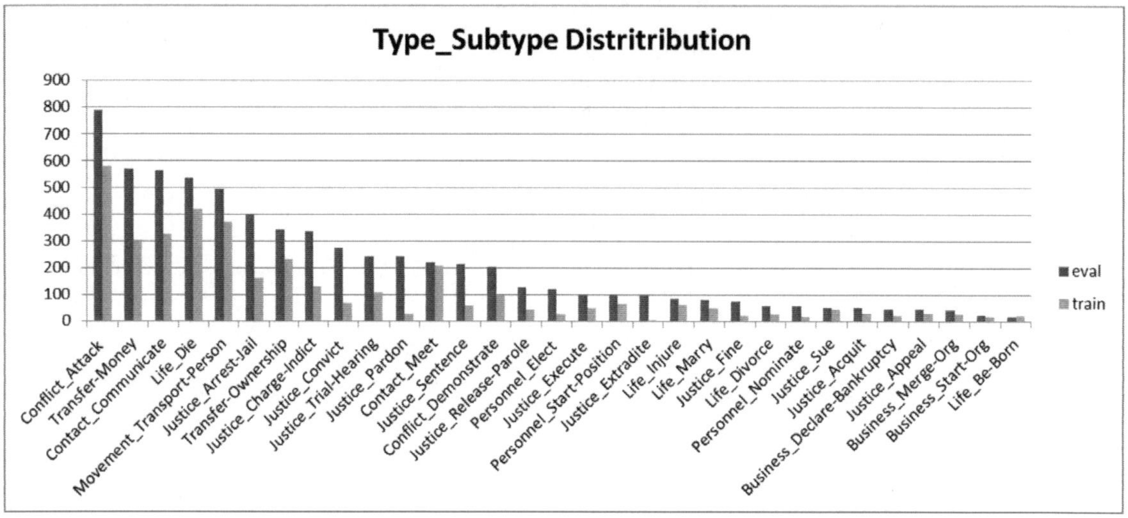

Figure 1. Type and Subtype Distribution in Event Nugget Annotation

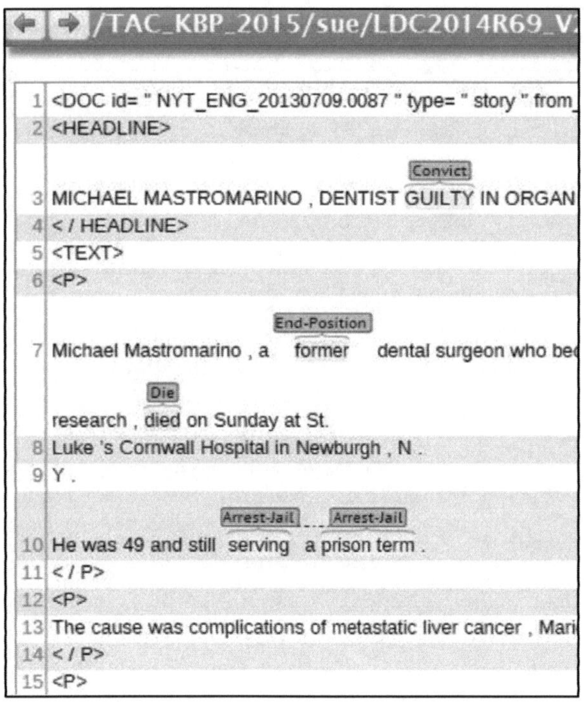

Screenshot 1. Brat tool main annotation screen

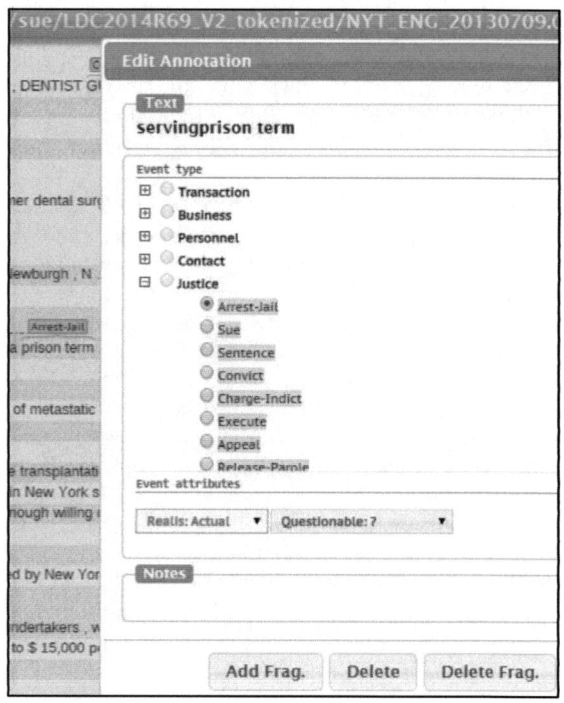

Screenshot 2. Brat tool pop-up window

Game-Changing Event Definition and Detection in an eSports Corpus

Emily Grace Olshefski
Montclair State University
1 Normal Avenue
Montclair, NJ 07043, USA
olshefskie1@montclair.edu

Abstract

Despite the growing cultural presence of eSports, no corpus contains this genre of entertainment. This paper presents how a preliminary corpus was created from broadcast speech from a professional game of the eSport *Counter-Strike: Global Offensive* (*CS:GO*). The corpus was initially annotated following the Automatic Contact Extraction (ACE) event subtype definitions for game-changing events: deaths, injuries, and attacks. Event subtype definitions were modified for further annotation to detect a wider range of game-changing events otherwise not defined by ACE. A high degree of inter-annotator agreement for most event subtypes suggests that modifying event subtype definitions for an eSports corpus is necessary to detect the breadth of game-changing events.

1 Introduction

The phenomenon of eSports (electronic sports, or competitive video gaming) is relatively new but has quickly become a global sensation. The advent of local area networks (LAN) has made eSports as competitive, if not more, than traditional sports, especially in countries like South Korea and China and, "this emerging market segment produces billions of dollars and contributes economically to the growth of the sport industry as a whole" (Lee and Schoenstedt, 2011).

Despite the popularity, growth, and cultural impact of eSports, few studies examine the nature of eSports. Furthermore, no linguistic studies of eSports exist due to the lack of eSports as a genre in corpora. For example, the Manually Annotated Sub-Corpus (American National Corpus Project) contains multiple genres of entertainment, like fiction, essays, and movie scripts. eSports, like film, is a multi-billion dollar industry that is growing rapidly, and by collecting data for eSports other corpora can become representative of emerging language use. While projects such as FrameNet (International Computer Science Institute) and other genre specific corpora like GENIA (Kim et al., 2005), a bio-textmining corpus, have undergone extensive event annotation, eSports has not been included in prior event annotation work, and doing so may provide insight into event detection and definition.

This paper aims to explain how a preliminary eSports corpus was created from the speech of eSports broadcasters who provide play-by-play and color commentary of one of the most popular eSports, *Counter-Strike: Global Offensive*, or *CS:GO*. The corpus was annotated by two annotators with extensive knowledge of not only *CS:GO* but also language the community and broadcasters use to describe the events of *CS:GO* games. Creating and annotating a corpus of *CS:GO* speech also provides a controlled model for the annotation of real-life attack, injury, and death events in, for example, a military based corpus.

The corpus was annotated twice to explore the nature of game-changing events (events that significantly impact the outcome or course of gameplay) in *CS:GO*. The corpus was first annotated following definitions designated by the Automatic Content Extraction (ACE) Program. Annotations were then made after event subtype modification. A new event

Proceedings of the 3rd Workshop on EVENTS at the NAACL-HLT 2015, pages 77–81,
Denver, Colorado, June 4, 2015.

subtype was created to more accurately detect game-changing events. This paper is the first step in detecting game-changing events in a corpus comprised entirely of language from eSports.

2 Approach

The first step in the approach to detecting game-changing events in an eSports corpus began with choosing an eSport (*CS:GO*) and creating a corpus from the speech of professional *CS:GO* broadcasters. Annotators were chosen based on knowledge of the eSport, and event definitions and modifications were made to better detect game-changing events.

2.1 *CS:GO* Classic Competitive - Bomb Scenario

Although there are five different game modes in the first-person shooter *CS:GO*, the only one played professionally is Classic Competitive - Bomb Scenario. This game mode is played between a team of five terrorists and five counter-terrorists, loosely modeling a terrorist bomb plant scenario.

The goal of the terrorist team is to plant the bomb and have it explode, and/or to kill all of the counter-terrorists. The goal of the counter-terrorist team is to defuse a planted bomb, kill all of the terrorists, or have a minimum of one player alive in the absence of a bomb plant. The teams switch sides (from counter-terrorist to terrorist, and vice versa) at the halfway mark of 15 rounds, and the first team to win 16 rounds wins the game. In the event of a tie (30 rounds, each team with 15 round wins) the game extends into overtime to determine a winner.

Each player starts each round with 100 health and zero armor points unless they purchase armor in the form of a Kevlar vest and/or helmet. Players lose health and armor points by taking damage from guns, knives, tasers, bomb and grenade explosions, and grenade contact, and damage can be dealt from the opposing team, one's own teammates, or oneself. When a player loses all of their health and armor points they die and are unable to participate in the game until the next round. Professional players often plan their strategies around planting bombs, killing and/or injuring opposing players, and creating space with smoke and flash grenades (referred to as flashbangs in *CS:GO*).

2.2 The *CS:GO* Corpus

The corpus consists of 47 minutes of speech comprised of 10,000 words from an August 2014 video broadcast of a professional *CS:GO* game posted on YouTube between a French team, Titan, and a North American team, Cloud9. The speech was manually transcribed by the author due to a lack of transcripts or closed captioning. This broadcast took place during the Electronic Sports League One Cologne 2014 tournament, and since the broadcasters were not in soundproof booths background noise rendered speech-to-text programs useless in obtaining data.

This video was chosen primarily on the basis of the broadcasters, Auguste "Semmler" Massonant and Anders "Anders" Blume. Semmler and Anders, as they are known in the *CS:GO* community, were chosen due to their expert knowledge of *CS:GO*, their extensive experience broadcasting, and the clarity of their speech. Written permission to use their speech as the basis of this corpus was obtained from both broadcasters. An example of the speech in the corpus is as follows: "Hiko tries to put shots through with the Five Seven, and Seangares looking to do some damage but the bomb will get planted and Cloud9, they just don't have the firepower or the nades to really get in here and have an impact."

2.3 Annotators

The annotation task was completed by two annotators, referred to as Annotator A (the author) and Annotator B. Both annotators have spent over 1000 hours playing *CS:GO*, watch broadcast games weekly, and have not completed any prior annotation tasks.

2.4 Original Event Definitions

Originally the annotators agreed that the ACE English Annotation Guidelines for Events Version 5.4.3 2005.07.01 definitions for LIFE.DIE, LIFE.INJURE, and CONFLICT.ATTACK event subtypes represent the majority of game-changing events in a *CS:GO* game. Player kills (LIFE.DIE events) can significantly alter the outcome of rounds, and even lowering a player's health (LIFE.INJURE events) affects strategy and gameplay. When players are not killing or injuring each other different types of attack events (CONFLICT.ATTACK) occur that change the course of the game. The ACE (Linguistic Data Consortium, 2005) definitions for these aforementioned event subtypes are as follows:

"An INJURE Event occurs whenever a PERSON Entity experiences physical harm. INJURE Events can be accidental, intentional or self-inflicted.

A DIE Event occurs whenever the life of a PERSON Entity ends. DIE Events can be accidental, intentional or self-inflicted.

An ATTACK Event is defined as a violent physical act causing harm or damage. ATTACK Events include any such Event not covered by the INJURE or DIE subtypes, including Events where there is no stated agent. The ATTACK Event type includes less specific violence-related nouns such as 'conflict', 'clashes', and 'fighting'. 'Gunfire', which has the qualities of both an Event and a weapon, should always be tagged as an ATTACK Event, if only for the sake of consistency. A 'coup' is a kind of ATTACK (and so is a 'war')."

2.5 Modified Event Definitions

After the first round of annotation where the annotators followed the ACE definitions, a new event subtype was created in order to better detect more game-changing events and eliminate definition ambiguity. Both annotators agreed that the LIFE.DIE and LIFE.INJURE definitions were unambiguous enough to complete the task.

There was a strong consensus between the annotators, however, that the CONFLICT.ATTACK event subtype did not accurately specify the idea of what an attack always is in *CS:GO*. The annotators took issue with phrasing a CONFLICT.ATTACK event as, "a violent physical act causing harm or damage" when there exist attacks in *CS:GO* that do not cause quantifiable damage or harm but are still violent and physical.

For example, *CS:GO* players have the option of buying grenades, like the HE (high explosive) grenade that explodes on contact, and the Molotov cocktail/incendiary grenade that ignites players and the ground, that are primarily used to injure or kill other players. While these grenades can be used strategically to create space or block access to areas of contention, the general aim of throwing these two types of grenades is to inflict damage. Thus, events depicting these types of attack events fit into the ACE definition for CONFLICT.ATTACK.

Event Subtype	A	B	Agreement
DIE	140	140	0.976
INJURE	1	1	1.00
ATTACK-D	70	63	0.653
ATTACK-ND	22	19	0.952

Table 1: Number of Annotated Events and Degree of Inter-Annotator Agreement

Smoke grenades, on the other hand, which create a smoke cloud and block vision, and flashbangs, which create a blinding light on the player's screen if they look in the direction of the grenade as it is thrown, are solely used for a strategic purpose. These attacks do not cause any quantifiable damage but are violent and physical in nature, and despite the ACE definition, would be considered an attack by the *CS:GO* community. The creation of a new event subtype makes a necessary distinction of events that are both game-changing but vary regarding damage and harm. Attacks fitting the old definition were simply relabeled as CONFLICT.ATTACK-D, specifying that the event causes damage. The definition for non-damaging attack events, labeled CONFLICT.ATTACK-ND, is identical to that of CONFLICT.ATTACK-D except the phrase "causing harm or damage" is changed to "cannot or would not cause harm or damage."

3 Results and Discussion

Table 1 details the total number of game-changing events depicted in the corpus as well as inter-annotator agreement calculated by Cohen's kappa coefficient. LIFE.DIE events were depicted most in this corpus. Killing opposing players provides a strategic advantage in *CS:GO*, and the majority of games are won by the team with the most kills. The high degree of inter-annotator agreement is due to the familiarity with how the broadcasters generally describe LIFE.DIE events during *CS:GO* games.

Both annotators detected the same LIFE.INJURE event and agreed that although the data for LIFE.INJURE events in this corpus is sparse, the likelihood of encountering more LIFE.INJURE events in a larger corpus is high. Play style varies greatly in *CS:GO* amongst teams and regions, and including speech from matches between different teams could produce more LIFE.INJURE events.

The lowest degree of agreement between the annotators was for CONFLICT.ATTACK-D events, despite a similar number of events of this subtype detected by both annotators. This lower degree of agreement should be attributed to the fact that certain language was perceived differently, causing one annotator to detect an event where the other did not. For example, in the sentence, "He's gonna find one headshot, tries to control the spray..." one annotator labeled the act of trying to control gun spray as a CONFLICT.ATTACK-D event and the other annotator did not. However, in other instances where the word 'spray' is used as a verb the annotators detected it as a CONFLICT.ATTACK-D event. The annotators agreed that the definition for CONFLICT.ATTACK-D events should be revised to eliminate existing ambiguity, and possibly include a list of words or phrases in *CS:GO* that could signal a CONFLICT.ATTACK-D event.

CONFLICT.ATTACK-ND agreement was also high between annotators despite the relatively small set of event depictions. This high degree of agreement can be attributed to the fact that this event subtype was created specifically to fulfill the need to detect game-changing non-damaging attacks. Regardless, the high degree of inter-annotator agreement indicates that this event subtype definition was generated in such a way that game-changing non-damaging attack events could be consistently and accurately detected. Like LIFE.INJURE both annotators agree that a larger corpus would lead to more CONFLICT.ATTACK-ND events, especially if either team's strategy relied heavily on the use of non-damaging grenades (flashbangs and smoke grenades).

4 Conclusion and Future Work

The high degree of inter-annotator agreement for the majority of event subtypes demonstrates that modifying event subtype definitions is necessary to more widely detect game-changing events in an eSports corpus. Lower inter-annotator agreement for the minority of event subtypes, however, suggests that further modifications should be made to event subtype definitions.

There are multiple ways to continue improvement in event detection in eSports corpora. First, the *CS:GO* corpus could be lengthened to achieve a larger set of annotated events. This task could be accomplished efficiently with the addition of multiple transcribers of *CS:GO* broadcasts.

Second, event subtype definitions could be modified further. While the majority of game-changing events was detected in this corpus, others could be detected as well in a larger and more varied corpus. For example, bomb defusals are a round win condition for the counter-terrorist team in *CS:GO* and can have a major impact on gameplay. Creating an event subtype to detect less common but equally as important event types like bomb defusals can contribute to the detection of more game-changing events.

One advantage of conducting an artificial task such as this on an eSports corpus is that more clear-cut relations between events can be detected. While this paper specifically focused on event detection in the context of a *CS:GO* game, there is the possibility of using these event subtype definitions for annotation tasks of real-life events. This could prove especially successful in any corpora comprised of military texts where, what are considered game-changing events in a *CS:GO* game actually occur in real-life scenarios.

Ultimately, with extensive further development this corpus could be used as training data for an automated event detection system. A gold standard corpus could be produced not only for automation but also as the standard for the creation of further eSports corpora.

5 Acknowledgments

The author would like to thank Matthew Shanks for completing the annotation task, Auguste Massonant and Anders Blume for permission to use their speech as the basis of the *CS:GO* corpus, and Eileen Fitzpatrick for advice and guidance.

References

American National Corpus Project. MASC - The Corpus Web. 9 March 2015.

Donghun Lee and Linda J. Schoenstedt. 2011. Comparison of eSports and Traditional Sports Consumption

Motives. *ICHPER-SD Journal of Research.* 6(2), 39-44.

International Computer Science Institute. FrameNet Data Web. 17 April 2015.

Jin-Dong Kim, Tomoko Ohta, Yuka Tateisi, and Jun'ichi Tsujii. 2003. GENIA corpus - a semantically annotated corpus for bio-textmining *Bioinformatics.* 19(1), 180-182.

Linguistic Data Consortium. 2005. ACE (Automatic Content Extraction) English Annotation Guidelines for Events Version 5.4.3 2005.07.01. Web. 9 March 2015.

Identifying Various Kinds of Event Mentions in K-Parser Output

Arpit Sharma, Nguyen H. Vo, Somak Aditya & Chitta Baral
School of Computing, Informatics & Decision Systems Engineering
Arizona State University
Tempe, AZ 85281, USA
{asharm73, nhvo1, saditya1, chitta}@asu.edu

Abstract

In this paper we show how our semantic parser (Knowledge Parser or K-Parser) identifies various kinds of event mentions in the input text. The types include recursive (complex) and non recursive event mentions. K-Parser outputs each event mention in form of an acyclic graph with root nodes as the verbs that drive those events. The children nodes of the verbs represent the entities participating in the events, and their conceptual classes. The on-line demo of the system is available at http://kparser.org

1 Introduction

Identifying the events mentioned in a text is an essential task for any semantic parsing system. Many Natural Language Understanding applications such as Question Answering (Berant et al., 2013; Kwiatkowski et al., 2013) and semantics-based machine translation (Bazrafshan and Gildea, 2013; Jones et al., 2012) use semantic parsers to translate both questions and answer sources into a desired representation. Several semantic parsers, both application-independent (Bos, 2008b; Allen et al., 2007; Dzikovska et al., 2003) and the ones for specific application (Berant and Liang, 2014; Fader et al., 2014; Kwiatkowski et al., 2013; Yao and Van Durme, 2014) have been developed for the assistance. However, most of them do not very effectively represent the different kinds of event mentions.

In this paper we demonstrate, with the help of examples, how our semantic parser (Knowledge Parser or K-Parser) is able to identify the semantics of various event types and output them in form of an acyclic graph.

The sections below explain, in order, the basic overview of K-Parser (along with its output), a brief explanation of various kinds of event mentions and examples demonstrating how K-Parser output is able to identify event mentions in those examples.

2 The Knowledge Parser (K-Parser)

K-Parser[1] is a semantic parser which produces a graphical semantic representation of the input text. The output of the parser is a mapping between the dependency parse of input text and the ontological relations from KM component library (Clark et al., 2004). The mapping process uses Word Sense Disambiguation and a set of rules to map syntactic dependencies to appropriate semantic relations. Furthermore, the output of the parser contains commonsense information about the words in the text i.e. the conceptual classes. For example in Fig. 1 *Barack-Obama_1* has superclass *person*. To sum up, the output of the parser has following properties:

1. An acyclic graphical representation in the form of interconnected event mentions.

2. A rich ontology (KM) to represent semantic relations (Event-Event relations such as *causes, caused_by*, Event-Entity relations such as *agent*, and Entity-Entity relations such as *related_to*).

[1]The system is available online at http://kparser.org

Proceedings of the 3rd Workshop on EVENTS at the NAACL-HLT 2015, pages 82–88,
Denver, Colorado, June 4, 2015.

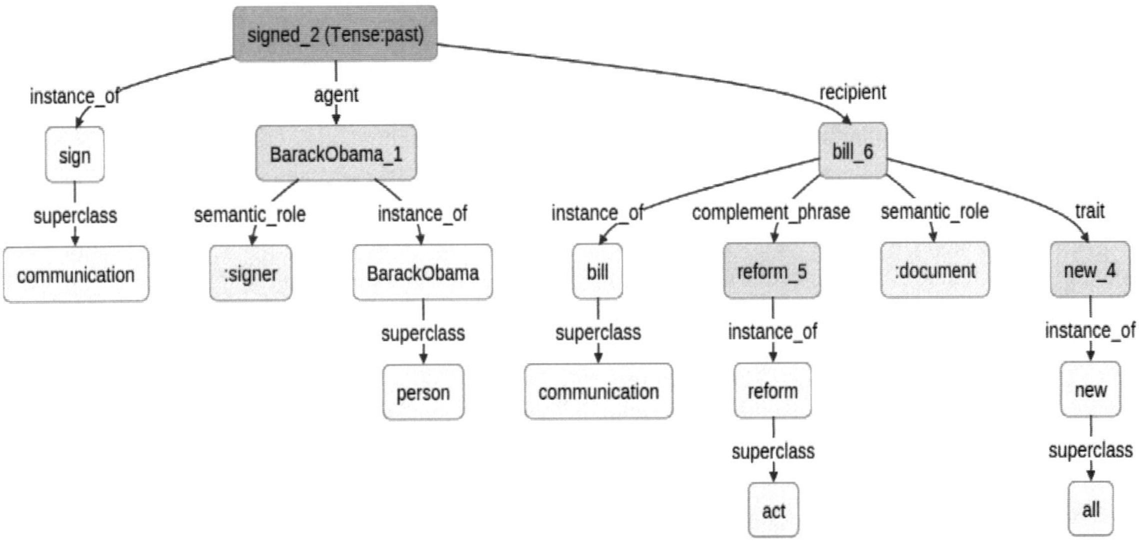

Figure 1: K-Parser output for *"Barack Obama signed the new reform bill."*

3. Special relations (*instance_of* and *prototype_of*) to represent the existential and universal quantification of entities. (For example, sentences *Every boxer walks.* and *Some boxer walks.*)

4. Conceptual class information about words in the text.

5. Semantic roles of entities (For example in sentence *John loves Mia.*).

6. Tenses of the events in the input text.

7. Other features such as an optional Co-reference resolution.

The basic algorithm of K-Parser contains five modules. The first module is used to extract the syntactic dependency graph from the input text. We used Stanford Dependency Parser (De Marneffe et al., 2006) for the purpose. The second module is used to map the syntactic dependency relations to KM relations (Barker et al., 2001; Clark et al., 2004) and a few newly created relations (such as *related_to*). There are three techniques used for semantic mapping. First, we used the rules to map syntactic dependencies into semantic relations. For example the *nominal subject* dependency is mapped to *agent* relation. Second, we developed a multi-class multilayer perceptron classifier to disambiguate different senses of prepositions and assign the semantic relations appropriately. The training data for classification is taken from "The Preposition Project" (Litkowski, 2013) and the sense ids for prepositions are manually mapped to the KM relations. The third method uses the discourse connectives in the text to label the event-event relations. Different connectives correspond to different labels. For example, the coordinate connectives such as *but*, *and*, *comma (,)* and *stop(.)* are labeled as *next_event*. Other connectives are also labeled based on their effect, such as *because* and *so* are labeled *caused_by* and *causes* respectively. The third module in K-Parser algorithm adds two level of classes for each node in the output of Semantic Mapping module. Word Sense Disambiguation (Basile et al., 2007) along with the lexical senses from WordNet (Miller, 1995) are used for this task. The fourth module corrects the mappings done by the mapping function by using class information extracted by the third module. For example, if there is a relation *is_possessed_by* between two nodes with their superclass as *person*, then the relation is corrected to *related_to* (because a person can not possess another person). Lastly, the fifth module implements other features such as semantic roles of the entities by using Propbank Framesets (Bonial et al., 2012; Palmer et al., 2005). An option for coreference resolution is also provided in the system which uses state of the art, Stanford Co-reference resolver (Raghunathan et al., 2010). Furthermore, many other tools are also used at various steps in the above mentioned modules, such as Named Entity Tagging, WordNet database and Weka statistical classifier library (Witten et al., 1999).

We used KM library for labeling the relationship edges between nodes in the output graph. There are 118 total relations available in KM. Out of 118, there are 24 (12 bi-directional[2]) relations that define the relationship between events. These relations are used in K-Parser to capture event-event relations. We also defined four new relations to represent some of the edge labels that were not captured in KM. These relations are *instance_of*, *superclass*, *participant* and *related_to*. The first two are used to represent two levels of conceptual class information associated with nodes in the graph. The other two relations represent special relations between an event node and an entity node.

As mentioned before, apart from recognizing event mentions, K-Parser also have other features such as conceptual classes, semantic roles and an optional co-reference resolution.

3 Event Mentions

We believe that the event mentions in the text are driven by the verbs in it. For example in Fig. 2 the left side shows the output for the phrase *Jerry and Tom*. There are no verbs in this phrase, hence no events. The right side of the figure shows the output for *Jerry and Tom were lying in the bed*. There is a verb (*lying_5*) in this sentence, hence the output shows an event graph with root as *lying_5*. In our system, we identify event mentions based on the actions or verbs found in the text. The environment of the events i.e. the subgraph with its root as a verb, is defined using the entities and attributes found in the input text. For example, the graph in Fig. 1 represents an event mention driven by the action *signed_2*.

3.1 Types of Event Mentions

There are four aspectual types of events (namely achievements, accomplishments, process or activity and states). Pustejovsky (1991) demonstrates how same verbs can be used in different types of events (see example sentences 1(a) and 2(a) in Table 1). The difference between these types is determined by the arguments of the verb. For example in 1(a), the event is an unbounded *process* whereas in 2(a) it is an *accomplishment* because of the bounding (by the phrase *to the store*). Our parser captures these arguments and hence is useful in differentiating between the types of events. Table 1 shows example sentences for these types.

Another criteria for categorizing events is based on the complexity. An event is defined recursive or complex if there exist events with other events as their arguments. For example, the sentence *The knife was used for killing the dog* has a complex event consisting of two events *used* and *killing*. The *killing* event is an argument to the *used* event. The K-Parser output for the sentence is shown in Fig. 3. The relationship between the two events is shown with an argumentative Event-Event relation i.e *objective* (see Fig. 3).

On the other hand, there is no argumentative relationship between events in the non-recursive or simple event mentions. Example sentence 6(b) in Table 1 contains two events *killed* and *ran*. These events are not arguments of each other but they are related via an ordering edge that specifies that *ran* is the event happened after *killed* event. Temporal ordering is another criteria for categorization of events. This is used to specify the order of occurrence of atomic events in a chain of events. K-Parser parser such events by using special event-event relations such as *next_event* and *previous_event*.

Example sentences of all the types are provided in Table 1. K-Parser outputs for only a few are demonstrated in this paper because of space constraints. We encourage the reader to try out all other examples in the table in the on-line demo of K-Parser, which is available at *www.kparser.org*

4 Evaluations

K-Parser is developed based on the training sentences collected from many sources such as the example sentences from stanford dependency manual (De Marneffe and Manning, 2008) and dictionary examples for sentences with conjunctions. We eval-

[2] *causes, defeats, enables, inhibits, by-means-of, first-subevent, objective, next-event, prevents, resulting-state, subevent, supports*

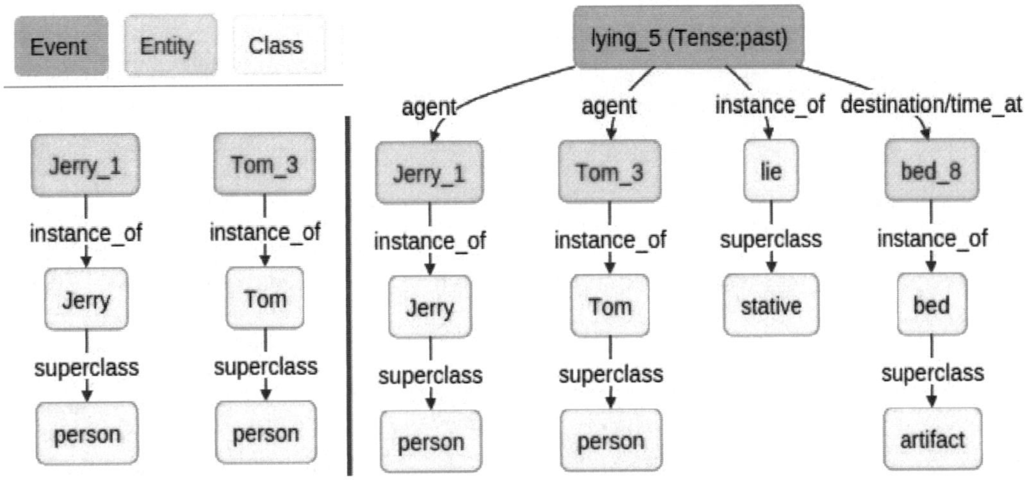

Figure 2: K-Parser output for *"Jerry and Tom"*(left) and *"Jerry and Tom were lying in the bed"*(right)

Table 1: Event Types and Example Sentences

Event type	Example Sentences
Process or Activity	*1(a) Mary walked.* *1(b) John ran.*
Accomplishment	*2(a) Mary walked to the store.*
Achievement	*3(a) Tim ran two miles.* *3(b) John arrived at his destination.*
State	*4(a) John loves Mia.* *4(b) I knew about the incident.* *4(c) He fell asleep during the meeting.*
Complex Events	*5(a) The knife was used to kill the dog.* *5(b) George was bullying Tim so we rescued him.*
Simple Events	*6(a) John loves Mia, and Mia hates John.* *6(b) Tom killed John before Tom and Jane ran away.*
Temporal Events	*7(a) Tom killed John before Tom and Jane ran away.* *7(b) She sat opposite him and looked into his eyes.*

uated the K-Parser output based on the types of events identified. This is done by manually defining gold standard representation for a corpus of 282 Winograd Schema Challenge (WSC) (Levesque et al., 2011) sentences (there is no overlap between test and training corpus). WSC is a well accepted corpus known to demonstrate complex semantics. We identified some important categories to assess the accuracy of event mentions and relations between events in the output of K-Parser. The categories are *number of Events, number of Entities, number of Classes, number of Event-Event relations* and *number of Event-Entity relations*. Each of the categories are compared with the gold standard based on measures mentioned below.

t_1 = identified and relevant and the label is correct.
t_2 = identified and relevant and the label is wrong.
t_3 = identified, but not relevant.
t_4 = not identified, but relevant.

Table 2: Evaluation Results

	Precision	Recall
Events	0.94	0.92
Entities	0.97	0.96
Classes	0.86	0.79
Event-Event Relations	0.91	0.79
Event-Entity Relations	0.94	0.89

We defined Precision and Recall of our system based on the above terms
Precision = $t_1/(t_1 + t_2 + t_3)$
Recall = $t_1/(t_1 + t_2 + t_4)$

Table 2 shows the evaluation results. We have also used the output of our system in solving a subsection of the Winograd Schema Challenge (Sharma et al., 2015).

5 Related Works

There are many semantic parsers available, such as the SEMAFOR parser (Das et al., 2010). While it assigns semantic roles to entities and verbs in the text, they lack in defining event mentions and relations between them. Furthermore, these systems do not correctly process the implications, quantifications and conceptual class information about the text (eg. *John* is an instance of *person* class). Among the others, there is Boxer system (Bos, 2008b) that translates English sentences into first order logic. Despite its many advantages, this parser fails to represent the event-event and event-entity re-

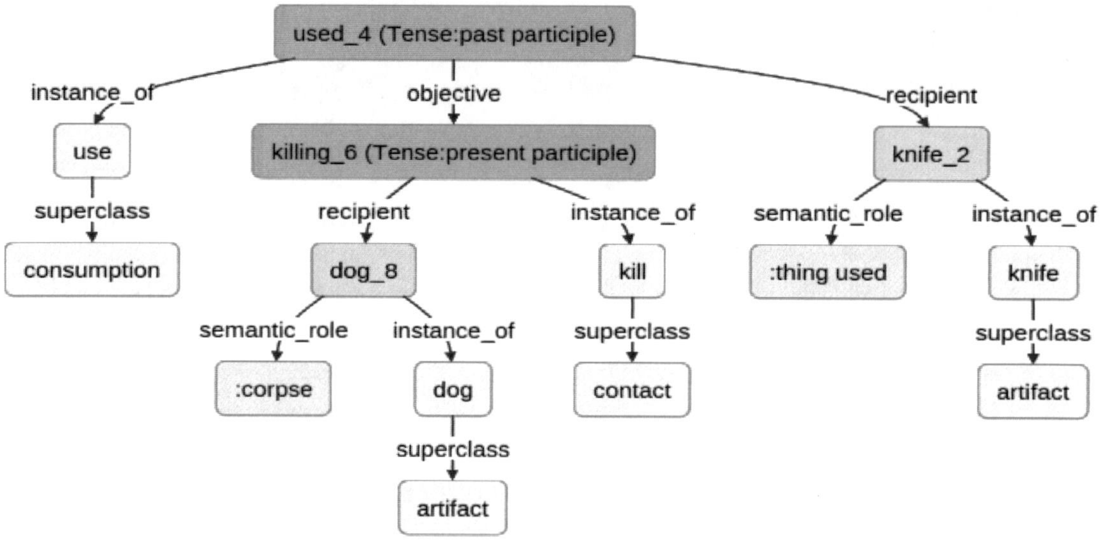

Figure 3: K-Parser output for *"The knife was used for killing the dog."*

lations in the text. The inclusion of the homonym-hypernym information and resolution of identical meaning words are important for downstream reasoning. Boxer system does not capture such ontological information about entities or similarities between connectives. Carbonell et al., (2014) presents another semantic parser that translates natural language strings into Abstract Meaning Representation (Banarescu et al., 2013). Similar to K-Parser, TRIPS (Allen et al., 2007) translates text into a semantic graph. The system encodes the features such as the conceptual classes of the words, quantification of entities and representation of the participants of an event. However, it does not have event-event relations in the text. These relations are required to specify the causality and dependency of events in a particular context. Another parser that participated in STEP 2008 shared task (Bos, 2008a) is the TEXTCAP semantic interpreter (Callaway, 2008). It translates the input text into a list of co-indexed semantic triples that represent the explicitly recoverable semantic content in the input text. Though it uses Word Sense Disambiguation on the WordNet data (like K-Parser) to extract the classes of events and entities, it does not label the specific relationship between events and their participants. For example in the sentence *My dog quickly chased rabbits yesterday.*(from TEXTCAP paper), the triple *(DOG492,CHASING141,RABBIT#n1)* represents the relation between two entities *the dog* and *the rabbits* in the form of the event *chasing*. In the output of K-Parser for the above sentence, there is an event node *chasing* which has an agent *dog* and the recipient *rabbits*. The other meaningful words in the sentence (such as quickly and yesterday) are also identified by K-Parser.

6 Conclusion

In this paper we showed how our parser i.e. K-Parser, is able to identify various kinds of events that are present in the input text. We also explained how the output of K-Parser can be further used to differentiate between the types of events (*processes, achievements, accomplishments* and *states*). Furthermore, we showed that the event mentions can be identified by extracting the verbs from the text and connecting the entities that participate in those verbs (using appropriate relations). This is an ongoing research and an on-line demo of our system is available at *www.kparser.org*.

Acknowledgements

We thank NSF for the DataNet Federation Consortium grant OCI-0940841 and ONR for their grant N00014-13-1-0334 for partially supporting this research.

References

James Allen, Mehdi Manshadi, Myroslava Dzikovska, and Mary Swift. 2007. Deep linguistic processing for spoken dialogue systems. In *Proceedings of the Workshop on Deep Linguistic Processing*, pages 49–56. Association for Computational Linguistics.

Laura Banarescu, Claire Bonial, Shu Cai, Madalina Georgescu, Kira Griffitt, Ulf Hermjakob, Kevin Knight, Philipp Koehn, Martha Palmer, and Nathan Schneider. 2013. Abstract meaning representation for sembanking.

Ken Barker, Bruce Porter, and Peter Clark. 2001. A library of generic concepts for composing knowledge bases. In *Proceedings of the 1st international conference on Knowledge capture*, pages 14–21. ACM.

Pierpaolo Basile, Marco Degemmis, Anna Lisa Gentile, Pasquale Lops, and Giovanni Semeraro. 2007. The jigsaw algorithm for word sense disambiguation and semantic indexing of documents. In *AI* IA 2007: Artificial Intelligence and Human-Oriented Computing*, pages 314–325. Springer.

Marzieh Bazrafshan and Daniel Gildea. 2013. Semantic roles for string to tree machine translation. In *ACL (2)*, pages 419–423.

Jonathan Berant and Percy Liang. 2014. Semantic parsing via paraphrasing. In *Proceedings of ACL*.

Jonathan Berant, Andrew Chou, Roy Frostig, and Percy Liang. 2013. Semantic parsing on freebase from question-answer pairs. In *EMNLP*, pages 1533–1544.

Claire Bonial, Jena Hwang, Julia Bonn, Kathryn Conger, Olga Babko-Malaya, and Martha Palmer. 2012. English propbank annotation guidelines. *Center for Computational Language and Education Research Institute of Cognitive Science University of Colorado at Boulder*.

Johan Bos. 2008a. Introduction to the shared task on comparing semantic representations. In *Proceedings of the 2008 Conference on Semantics in Text Processing*, pages 257–261. Association for Computational Linguistics.

Johan Bos. 2008b. Wide-coverage semantic analysis with boxer. In *Proceedings of the 2008 Conference on Semantics in Text Processing*, pages 277–286. Association for Computational Linguistics.

Charles B Callaway. 2008. The textcap semantic interpreter. In *Proceedings of the 2008 Conference on Semantics in Text Processing*, pages 327–342. Association for Computational Linguistics.

Jeffrey Flanigan Sam Thomson Jaime Carbonell and Chris Dyer Noah A Smith. 2014. A discriminative graph-based parser for the abstract meaning representation.

Peter Clark, Bruce Porter, and Boeing Phantom Works. 2004. Kmthe knowledge machine 2.0: Users manual. *Department of Computer Science, University of Texas at Austin*.

Dipanjan Das, Nathan Schneider, Desai Chen, and Noah A Smith. 2010. Semafor 1.0: A probabilistic frame-semantic parser. *Language Technologies Institute, School of Computer Science, Carnegie Mellon University*.

Marie-Catherine De Marneffe and Christopher D Manning. 2008. Stanford typed dependencies manual. *URL http://nlp. stanford. edu/software/dependencies manual. pdf*.

Marie-Catherine De Marneffe, Bill MacCartney, Christopher D Manning, et al. 2006. Generating typed dependency parses from phrase structure parses. In *Proceedings of LREC*, volume 6, pages 449–454.

Myroslava O Dzikovska, James F Allen, and Mary D Swift. 2003. Integrating linguistic and domain knowledge for spoken dialogue systems in multiple domains. In *Proc. of IJCAI-03 Workshop on Knowledge and Reasoning in Practical Dialogue Systems*.

Anthony Fader, Luke Zettlemoyer, and Oren Etzioni. 2014. Open question answering over curated and extracted knowledge bases.

Bevan Jones, Jacob Andreas, Daniel Bauer, Karl Moritz Hermann, and Kevin Knight. 2012. Semantics-based machine translation with hyperedge replacement grammars. In *COLING*, pages 1359–1376.

Tom Kwiatkowski, Eunsol Choi, Yoav Artzi, and Luke Zettlemoyer. 2013. Scaling semantic parsers with on-the-fly ontology matching.

Hector J Levesque, Ernest Davis, and Leora Morgenstern. 2011. The winograd schema challenge. In *AAAI Spring Symposium: Logical Formalizations of Commonsense Reasoning*.

Ken Litkowski. 2013. The preposition project corpora. Technical report, Technical Report 13-01. Damascus, MD: CL Research.

George A Miller. 1995. Wordnet: a lexical database for english. *Communications of the ACM*, 38(11):39–41.

Martha Palmer, Daniel Gildea, and Paul Kingsbury. 2005. The proposition bank: An annotated corpus of semantic roles. *Computational linguistics*, 31(1):71–106.

James Pustejovsky. 1991. The syntax of event structure. *Cognition*, 41(1):47–81.

Karthik Raghunathan, Heeyoung Lee, Sudarshan Rangarajan, Nathanael Chambers, Mihai Surdeanu, Dan Jurafsky, and Christopher Manning. 2010. A multi-pass sieve for coreference resolution. In *Proceedings of the 2010 Conference on Empirical Methods in Natural Language Processing*, pages 492–501. ACL.

Arpit Sharma, Nguyen H Vo, Shruti Gaur, and Chitta Baral. 2015. An approach to solve winograd schema challenge using automatically extracted commonsense knowledge. In *2015 AAAI Spring Symposium Series*.

Ian H Witten, Eibe Frank, Leonard E Trigg, Mark A Hall, Geoffrey Holmes, and Sally Jo Cunningham. 1999. Weka: Practical machine learning tools and techniques with java implementations.

Xuchen Yao and Benjamin Van Durme. 2014. Information extraction over structured data: Question answering with freebase. In *Proceedings of ACL*.

From Light to Rich ERE: Annotation of Entities, Relations, and Events

Zhiyi Song, Ann Bies, Stephanie Strassel, Tom Riese, Justin Mott, Joe Ellis, Jonathan Wright, Seth Kulick, Neville Ryant and Xiaoyi Ma

Linguistic Data Consortium, University of Pennsylvania
3600 Market Street, Suite 801
Philadelphia, PA, 19104, USA
{zhiyi,bies,strassel,riese,jmott,joellis,jdwright,skulick,nryant,xma}@ldc.upenn.edu

Abstract

We describe the evolution of the Entities, Relations and Events (ERE) annotation task, created to support research and technology development within the DARPA DEFT program. We begin by describing the specification for Light ERE annotation, including the motivation for the task within the context of DEFT. We discuss the transition from Light ERE to a more complex Rich ERE specification, enabling more comprehensive treatment of phenomena of interest to DEFT.

1 Introduction

DARPA's Deep Exploration and Filtering of Text (DEFT) program aims to improve state-of-the-art capabilities in automated deep natural language processing, with a particular focus on technologies dealing with inference, causal relationships, and anomaly detection (DARPA, 2012). Evaluations within the DEFT program focus on a variety of component technologies, united by a common focus on the problem of populating a knowledge base with information about entities and events and the relationships among them. Given the variety of approaches and evaluations within DEFT, we set out to define an annotation task that would be supportive of multiple research directions and evaluations, and that would provide a useful foundation for more specialized annotation tasks like inference and anomaly. The resulting Entities, Relations and Events (ERE) annotation task has evolved over the course of the program, from a fairly lightweight treatment of entities, relations and events in text, to a richer representation of phenomena of interest to the program.

While previous approaches such as ACE (Doddington et al., 2004), LCTL (Simpson et al., 2008), OntoNotes (Pradhan et al., 2007), Machine Reading (Strassel et al., 2010), TimeML (Boguraev and Ando, 2005), Penn Discourse Treebank (Prasad et al., 2014), and Rhetorical Structure Theory (Mann and Thompson, 1988) laid some of the groundwork for this type of resource, the DEFT program requires annotation of complex and hierarchical event structures that go beyond any of the existing (and partially-overlapping) task definitions. Recognizing the effort required to define such an annotation task for multiple languages and genres, we decided to adopt a multi-phased approach, starting with a fairly lightweight implementation and introducing additional complexity over time.

In the first phase of the program, we defined Light ERE as a simplified form of ACE annota-

Proceedings of the 3rd Workshop on EVENTS at the NAACL-HLT 2015, pages 89–98,
Denver, Colorado, June 4, 2015.

tion, with the goal of being able to rapidly produce consistently labeled data in multiple languages (Aguilar et al., 2014). In Phase 2, Rich ERE expands entity, relation and event ontologies and expands the notion of what is taggable. Rich ERE also introduces the notion of *Event Hopper* to address the pervasive challenge of event coreference, particularly with respect to event mention and event argument granularity variation within and across documents, thus paving the way for the important goal of creating (hierarchical or nested) cross-document event representations.

In the remaining sections we describe the Light ERE annotation specification and the resources produced under this spec. We discuss the motivation for transitioning from Light ERE to Rich ERE, and present the Rich ERE specification in detail, along with developments in smart data selection and annotation consistency analysis. We conclude with a discussion of annotation challenges and future directions.

2 Related Annotation Efforts

A number of previous and current event annotation tasks have influenced the development of Rich ERE, including ACE and several tasks with the TAC KBP Evaluation series. We describe each in turn in the sections that follow.

2.1 ACE and Light ERE

At the start of the DEFT program it was necessary to scale up quickly to produce resources for system training and development, and so we looked to existing annotation tasks that were compatible with our desired approach. One such task was ACE (Automatic Content Extraction), designed to benchmark research in information extraction, focusing on entity detection and tracking, relation detection and characterization, as well as event detection and characterization (Doddington et al., 2004; Walker et al., 2006). ACE annotation labels mentions of people, organizations, locations, geopolitical entities, weapons, and vehicles, as well as subtypes for each entity type. ACE also annotates a target set of relations and events between and among those constructs. Multiple mentions of the same entity, relation or event within a document are coreferenced.

Light ERE was designed as a lighter-weight version of ACE (LDC, 2005; Walker et al., 2006) and a simple approach to entity, relation, and event annotation, with the goal of making annotation easier and more consistent. Light ERE captures a reduced inventory of entity and relation types, with fewer attributes (for example, only specific entities and actual relations are taggable, and entity subtypes are not labeled). Events are labeled following approaches developed in ACE and Machine Reading (Strassel et al., 2010), but adapted for informal genres such as Discussion Forums (DF). The event ontology of Light ERE is similar to ACE, with slight modification and reduction, and events are coreferenced within documents (Aguilar et al., 2014). As in ACE, the annotation of each event mention includes the identification of a trigger, the labeling of the event type, subtype, and participating event argument entities. Simplifying from ACE, only attested actual events are annotated (no irrealis events or arguments).

Our Light ERE annotation effort also includes creating fully annotated resources in Chinese and Spanish in addition to English, with a portion of the annotation being cross-lingual. We developed a Chinese-English parallel Light ERE corpus which consists of approximately 100K words of Chinese data along with the corresponding English translation, both annotated in Light ERE. Portions of the parallel data have had other layers of annotation performed on it, particularly Chinese Treebank (CTB) on the Chinese side (Zhang and Xue, 2012) as well as English-Chinese Treebank (ECTB) on the English side (Bies et al., 2014). Light ERE annotation is in progress for Spanish on a dataset which is currently being annotated for Spanish Treebank as well. Multiple levels of annotation, such as ERE and treebank, that are keyed to the same dataset should together provide a resource that is expected to facilitate experimentation with machine learning methods that jointly manipulate the multiple levels.

2.2 TAC KBP Event Evaluations

The Text Analysis Conference (TAC) is a series of workshops organized by the National Institute of Standards and Technology (NIST) that was developed to encourage research in natural language processing (NLP) and related applications by providing a large test collection, common evaluation procedures, and a forum for researchers to share their results. Through its various evaluations, the Knowledge Base Population (KBP) track of TAC encourages the development of systems that can match entities mentioned in natural texts with those appearing in a knowledge base and extract novel information about entities from a document collection and add it to a new or existing knowledge base.

In 2014, TAC KBP moved into the events domain with the addition of the Event Argument Extraction (EAE) evaluation, in which systems were required to extract mentions of entities from unstructured text and indicate the roles they played in events as supported by text (Ellis et al., 2014). Additionally, TAC KBP 2014 also conducted a pilot evaluation on Event Nugget Detection (END), in which systems were required to detect event nugget tuples, consisting of an event trigger, the type and subtype classification, and the realis attribute (Mitamura et al., 2015).

TAC KBP 2015 EAE and END evaluations both plan to expand the tasks such that event tuples would be grouped together or linked to one another to show event identity, either by linking event arguments that participate in the same event (EAE) or by grouping event nuggets that refer to the same event (END). Such expansion in both evaluations would require identification of event coreference, which is a challenging issue in both ACE and Light ERE. The transition from Light ERE to Rich ERE tackles this challenge with the addition of event hoppers.

3 Transition from Light ERE to Rich ERE

The simplified annotation in Light ERE allowed the annotation effort to scale up quickly. As the DEFT program moves toward more sophisticated algorithms and evaluations, the transition to a richer representation of events within the ERE framework becomes necessary. The development of Rich ERE lays the groundwork for upcoming expansion into the realm of event-event relations, as well as cross-document and even cross lingual event representation. Transitioning to Rich ERE requires both developing annotation guidelines for the expanded annotation of events and event arguments and also developing a new annotation tool to handle the new annotation task.

3.1 Development of Annotation Guidelines for Rich ERE

3.1.1 Expanded Entity Annotation

Rich entity annotation expands many areas of Light annotation starting with a general increase in taggability. Instead of restricting annotation to specific, asserted entities, we have added what ACE called underspecified and generic entities to the scope for Rich ERE annotation. Under the umbrella term "non-specific" (NonSPC), we now capture both underspecified and generic entities, in addition to the specific (SPC) entities that Light ERE already captured. We encountered many discussion forum documents that contained generic language while annotating Light ERE data. Previously, we would deprioritize such documents, but with the inclusion of NonSPC entity tagging in Rich ERE, our range of annotatable documents is much larger.

Some other ACE features that we have revived are nominal head marking and distinguishing between Location and Facility entity types. Instead of marking heads for named and pronominal mentions as required in ACE, heads are manually marked only for nominal mentions in Rich ERE. Since named and pronominal heads are generally exactly the same string of text as the entity mention, their heads do not need to be manually marked separately. However, since the heads of nominal mentions are not trivially derivable, they are manually marked in Rich ERE. Furthermore, Light ERE lumped regions, landforms, buildings, and other structures into the Location entity type. Following ACE and to better align with TAC KBP evaluation tasks[1], Rich ERE separates the Light ERE Location entity type into Facility as well as Location types. Man-made structures and infrastructure are considered Facilities, while regions, landforms, and other non-descript sites fall under Locations. Examples include (note that the heads of nominal mentions are indicated by underscoring):

- [<u>Tourists</u>]$_{\text{PER.NOM.NonSPC}}$ always end up at [Love Park]$_{\text{FAC.NAM.SPC}}$
- [The last four <u>tourists</u> to show up]$_{\text{PER.NOM.SPC}}$ missed the bus

In addition, we created a new class called Argument Fillers, which are entity-like participants in

[1] NIST, 2015. http://www.nist.gov/tac/2015/KBP/

relations and events that are not annotated at the entity level. Argument fillers are annotated only when they fill argument roles in tagged relations or events. Examples of argument fillers are included in the discussion of relations and events below. Whereas ACE exhaustively tagged weapons and vehicles as entities, Rich ERE captures them as argument fillers. Rich ERE also adds the annotation of commodities as fillers.

Additionally, title entities from Light ERE have been reclassified as argument fillers, because they are only annotated when they can be connected to a named person entity in the relation phase. The full list of argument fillers is Title, Age, URL, Sentence, Crime, Money, Vehicle, Weapon, Commodity, and Time types. Each of these argument fillers corresponds to specific relation or event subtypes, meaning that they will only appear if the corresponding subtype lends itself to such information. For example, a person's age will only be annotated as an argument filler of a generalaffiliation-personage relation, and a weapon will be annotated only in a limited number of event subtypes, including Conflict.Attack, Manufacture.Artifact, and Life.Injure.

3.1.2 Expanded Relation Annotation

Rich ERE relations looked to the TAC KBP Slot Filling Evaluation for inspiration by doubling the ontology from ten subtypes in Light ERE to twenty subtypes in Rich ERE. The KBP Slot Filling task asks annotators to look for textual information that is very similar in scope to ERE annotation. For example, both ERE and KBP Slot Filling annotate material that is based on a person's employment or membership within an organization, familial relations, and nationality, as well as subsidiary-parent organization relationships and organization location. It was a natural step to expand the ERE relation ontology to incorporate more facets of KBP Slot Filling. Part of this cross-project sync up required the addition of brand new argument fillers for some relation types. Three new subtypes of relations use the argument fillers described above: personalsocial-role (Title), generalaffiliation-orgwebsite (URL) and generalaffiliation-personage (Age). Table 1 shows the newly added relation inventory in Rich ERE as compared with Light ERE.

Light		**Rich**	
Type	**Subtype**	**Subtype**	**Type**
physical	n/a	orgheadquarter	physical
	located	locatednear	
		resident	
	origin	orglocationorigin	
		member-origin-religion-ethnicity (more)	generalaffiliation
	n/a	personage	
	n/a	orgwebshite	
	n/a	org-political-religious-affiliation (opra)	
partwhole	subsidiary	subsidiary	partwhole
personalsocial	membership	membership	
	business	business	personalsocial
	family	family	
	unspecified	unspecified	
	role	role	
orgaffiliation	employment-membership	employmentmembership	orgaffiliation
	leadership	leadership	
	n/a	investshareholder	
	n/a	studentalum	
	n/a	ownership	
	n/a	founder	

Table 1: ERE Relation Taxonomy in Light and Rich

Finally, while Light ERE only annotated attested, asserted relations, Rich ERE annotates future, hypothetical, and conditional (but not negated) relations as well. All relations are assigned a realis attribute of "Asserted" vs. "Other" to mark this distinction. Examples of these additions and changes can be seen below:

- Now [53]$_{AGE.ARG}$, [Barack Obama]$_{PER.NAM.SPC}$ signed important documents this morning. (General-Affiliation.PER-Age, Realis: Asserted)
- [[Spanish]$_{GPE.NAM.SPC}$ students]$_{PER.NOM.SPC}$ gathered to protest the growing cost of tuition. (General-Affiliation.MORE, Realis: Asserted)

- [She]$_{\text{PER.PRO.SPC}}$ has been living in [California]$_{\text{GPE.NAM.SPC}}$ for three years now. (Physical.Resident, Realis: Asserted)
- [He]$_{\text{PER.PRO.SPC}}$ may end up in [New York]$_{\text{GPE.NAM.SPC}}$. (Physical.Located-Near, Realis: Other)

3.1.3 Expanded Event Annotation

For each event mention, Rich ERE labels the event type and subtype, its realis attribute, any of its arguments or participants that are present, and a required "trigger" string in the text.

Rich ERE event annotation includes increased taggability in several areas[2], compared to Light ERE Event annotation: a slightly expanded event ontology, the addition of generic and other (irrealis) event mentions, the addition of argumentless triggers for event mentions, additional attributes for contact and transaction events, double tagging of event mentions for multiple types/subtypes, and multiple tagging of event mentions for certain types of coordination.

A. Expansion of event ontology, and additional attributes for Contact and Transaction events

Rich ERE adds one new event type (Manufacture) to the Light ERE inventory of event types. The complete list of event types is as follows: Life, Movement, Business, Conflict, Contact, Personnel, Transaction, Justice, Manufacture. The Manufacture event type has only one subtype (Manufacture.Artifact), and can have the following arguments: agent, patient (weapon, facility, vehicle, commodity), time and location. For example,

- [China]$_{\text{AGENT}}$ is reportedly **constructing** [a second aircraft carrier]$_{\text{PATIENT.VEHICLE}}$
- [the Imboulou hydroelectric power station]$_{\text{PATIENT.FACILITY}}$, which was **constructed** by [Chinese technicians]$_{\text{AGENT}}$

In addition to the new event type, Rich ERE adds several new event subtypes to already existing event types: Movement.Transport-Artifact, Contact.Broadcast, Contact.Contact, Transaction.Transaction.

The Movement.Transport-Artifact subtype can take weapon, vehicle, facility, or commodity as the patient. For example,

- [122 kilos of heroin hidden in a truck]$_{\text{ARTIFACT.COMMODITY}}$ which was set to **cross** into [Greece]$_{\text{DESTINATION.GPE}}$
- [the cans of marijuana]$_{\text{ARTIFACT.COMMODITY}}$ were **launched** about 500 feet into the [U.S.]$_{\text{DESTINATION.GPE}}$ using [a pneumatic-powered cannon]$_{\text{INSTRUMENT.WEAPON}}$

Contact event mentions are now labeled with attributes to describe Formality (Formal, Informal, Can't Tell), Scheduling (Planned, Spontaneous, Can't Tell), Medium (In-person, Not-in-person, Can't Tell), and Audience (Two-way, One-way, Can't Tell). Contact event subtypes are determined (automatically) based on the annotated attributes:

- Contact.Meet: Medium attribute must be "In-person" and audience attribute must be "Two-way"
- Contact.Correspondence[3]: Medium attribute must be "Not-in-person" and audience attribute must be "Two-way"
- Contact.Broadcast: Any Contact event mention where the audience attribute is "One-way"
- Contact.Contact: Used when no more specific subtype is available, and occurs when either the medium or audience attribute is "Can't Tell"

Contact.Meet and Contact.Correspondence as subtypes are unchanged from Light ERE, but Contact.Broadcast and Contact.Contact are new subtypes in Rich ERE.

Note that that the Formality and Scheduling attributes are annotated for all Contact event mentions, but these attributes have no effect on the subtype determination.

Transaction.Transaction is a new subtype added to indicate cases where it is clear that a transaction event is mentioned, but it is not clear in context whether money or a commodity is being transferred. For example,

- I **received** a gift (Transaction.Transaction)

B. Addition of generic and other irrealis event mentions

In order to align ERE annotation more closely with the current EAE and END tasks, Rich ERE annotates a Realis attribute for each event mention.

[2] Changes to coreference in Rich ERE are discussed below, in section 3.1.4.

[3] The Contact.Correspondence subtype is simply the new name for the subtype called Contact.Communication in Light ERE.

This is in sync with both EAE and END and is also compatible with ACE annotation.

The realis attributes are Actual (asserted), Generic (generic, habitual), and Other (future, hypothetical, negated, uncertain, etc.). Previously Light ERE annotation was restricted to Actual event mentions only.

- Actual: He **emailed** her about their plans
- Other: Saudi Arabia is scheduled to begin **building** the world's tallest tower next week
- Generic: Turkey is a popular passageway for drug smugglers **trafficking** from south Asia to Europe

The realis of the relationship between each argument and the event mention will also be tagged, separately from the realis of the event mention itself. For example,

- [+irrealis] "Jon" as the agent for the asserted Conflict.Attack event: [Jon] denied [he] master-minded the **attack**

C. Addition of argumentless triggers for event mentions

Unlike Light ERE, Rich ERE will allow the annotation of event mention triggers even when there are no arguments or participants of the event present in the text. This additional annotation will allow Rich ERE to align more closely with END (Mitamura et al., 2015).

D. Double tagging of event mentions for multiple types/subtypes

Rich ERE will permit double tagging of event triggers to allow obligatory inferred events that are in the ERE event taxonomy to be tagged. For example, if both money and ownership are transferred in a Transaction event, then the event mention should be tagged twice, once for each subtype:

- I **paid** $7 for the book (tagged as both Transaction.TRANSFER-OWNERSHIP, and Transaction.TRANSFER-MONEY)

The triggers that can be annotated this way are restricted to triggers that clearly indicate more than one event type or subtype in context. For example,

- Conflict.Attack and either Life.Injure or Life.Die: murder, victim, decapitate, kill
- Transaction.Transfer-Money and Transaction.Transfer-Ownership (money being exchanged for an item): buy, purchase, pick up
- Legal language that might trigger multiple Justice Events or other Event Types: guilty plea, execution (Life.Die / Justice. Execute), death penalty, testimony (Justice.Trial-Hearing, Contact.Meet)

In a change from Light ERE, event triggers may be the same string of text as an entity or the same string of the head of a NOM entity mention. Event triggers that are nested within an entity mention are also acceptable.

- The situation escalated and the **[murderer]** fled the scene. (This is an event trigger, even though "murderer" would already be a nominal PER entity.)
- The mayor agreed to meet with [angry **<u>protestors</u>**]. (This is a trigger, even though "protesters" would already be the head of a nominal PER entity.)
- [The <u>one</u> who **divorced** me] only thinks of himself. (Here "divorce" can be a trigger for a Life.DIVORCE event, even though it is nested within a longer PER entity and it is not the head noun.)

E. Multiple tagging of event mentions for certain types of coordination

Rich ERE will also allow a single trigger to be tagged multiple times in cases where multiple events are indicated through coordination of arguments. The argument role that is coordinated determines whether a single event mention or multiple event mentions are tagged:

- If the TIME or PLACE role is coordinated or if there are separate times and places indicated, then multiple events are tagged.
- If any other argument role is coordinated, a single event is tagged. In this case, each of the coordinated arguments will be tagged separately as an argument of the event mention, and the result will be a single event with multiple arguments tagged for the coordinated argument role.

If the context or the language is too complicated to sort out the number of events, annotators are instructed to default to annotating a single event with multiple arguments.

In this example, there are two Conflict.Attack events, and two Life.Die events triggered by "murder", because the TIME argument is different:

- Cipriani was sentenced to life in prison for the **murder** of Renault chief George Besse in 1986 and the head of government arms sales Rene Audran a year earlier
  - Conflict.Attack: Trigger = murder, agent = Cipriani, victim = George Besse, time = 1986
  - Conflict.Attack: Trigger = murder, agent = Cipriani, victim = Rene Audran, time = a year earlier
  - Life.Die: Trigger = murder, argument = George Besse, agent = Cipriani, time = 1986
  - Life.Die: Trigger = murder, argument = Rene Audran, agent = Cipriani, time = a year earlier

In the following example, only one event is tagged, with multiple giver arguments and multiple recipient arguments:

- China and the US are the biggest **lenders** to Brazil and India
  - Transaction.Transfer-Money: Trigger = lenders, giver = China, giver = US, recipient = Brazil, recipient = India

3.1.4 Event Hoppers and Event Coreference

In Light ERE as well as ACE, event coreference was limited to strict event identity. Following component judgments, annotators marked two events as coreferential in Light ERE if they had the same agent(s), patient(s), time, and location. However, there are many event mentions that annotators intuitively feel are the same that do not meet the strict event identity standard and therefore would not be coreferential in Light ERE or ACE. Some events might have been inconsistently marked as coreferential because of the conflict between the annotators' intuitive judgment and the strict identity coreference standard.

In Rich ERE, we instead introduce the concept of *Event Hopper* as a more inclusive, less strict notion of event coreference. Event hoppers contain mentions of events that "feel" coreferential to the annotator even if they do not meet the earlier strict event identity requirement. More specifically, features of event mentions that go into the same hopper are

- They have the same event type and subtype (exceptions to this are Contact.Contact and Transaction.Transaction mentions, which can be added to any Contact or Transaction hopper, respectively)
- They have the same temporal and location scope, though not necessarily the same temporal expression or specifically the same date (*Attack in Baghdad on Thursday* vs. *Bombing in the Green Zone last week*)
- Trigger granularity can be different (*assaulting 32 people* vs. *wielded a knife*)
- Event arguments may be non-coreferential or conflicting (*18 killed* vs. *dozens killed*)
- Realis status may be different (*will travel [OTHER] to Europe next week* vs. *is on a 5-day trip [ACTUAL]*)

Every tagged event mention will be put into an event hopper in Rich ERE, and all tagged event mentions that refer to the same event occurrence will be grouped into the same event hopper.

Event hoppers will allow annotators to group together more event mentions and therefore also label more event arguments in Rich ERE. This richer annotation will lead to a more complete knowledge base and better support for the Event Argument Linking and END evaluations in 2015, when one of the goals is to evaluate event identity.

3.2 Development of an Annotation GUI for Rich ERE

The Rich ERE annotation tool was developed following the framework described in Wright et al. (2012), allowing for rapid development of a new interface for Rich ERE. Numerous features were included "for free" in that they were developed for previous interfaces, and therefore required no additional development time. One important example of this is the representation of annotated text extents with underlines that can overlap arbitrarily, be color coded based on other annotations (e.g., entity type), and allow the user to click to navigate among the annotations. An important feature developed specifically for the Rich ERE tool is a "reference annotation", which is essentially one widget pointing to another. Once a complete set of annotations for a mention or entity has been done, a single annotation can be used to plug them as a whole into relation or event arguments, but referentially, allowing the original annotations to be safely changed. In addition, annotation managers had an important role in development of the tool beyond specification, as there is an editor that grants direct access to the database where the interface is defined. Managers can add widgets, change them (e.g., add menu choices), and even specify logical constraints between the annotations (e.g., a "resident" relation must take a "person" argument).

4 Linguistic Resources Labeled for ERE

To date we have released approximately 570,000 words of English Light ERE data, including both NW and DF, plus 200,000 words of Chinese DF. Another 100,000 words of Spanish Light ERE data is currently in progress and is expected to be completed in the coming weeks. Rich ERE annotation in English is also currently underway, with 32,420 words (91 documents) completed to date. We expect to complete another 170,000 words of English and 100,000 words in each of Chinese and Spanish within the next several weeks. A portion of the Rich ERE data is new, while the remainder has previously been annotated for Light ERE. Details for each language, genre and task are provided in Table 2 below. The ERE data is currently available to DEFT and TAC KBP performers and will also be published in LDC's catalog in future, making it available to the research community at large.

	Genre	English	Chinese	Spanish
Light ERE	*NW*	220Kw	--	50Kw
	DF	350Kw	200Kw	50Kw
Rich ERE	*NW*	24Kw	--	50Kw
	DF	175Kw	100Kw	50Kw

Table 2: Existing and Planned ERE Resources

The overall target for this phase of DEFT is to complete 400Kw of Rich ERE annotation per language on English, Chinese and Spanish data. 100Kw each from Spanish and Chinese will be parallel to Rich ERE annotation on English translations of the same data. We expect the annotation goal to be met by the end of this year.

4.1 Smart Data Selection

In an attempt to minimize annotator effort on documents with insufficient content, documents were fed into the annotation pipeline in descending order of event trigger density, defined as the number of event triggers per 1,000 tokens. Triggers were automatically tagged using a deep neural network based tagger trained on the ACE 2005 annotations (Walker et al., 2006) with orthographic and word embedding features. The word embeddings were trained using word2vec (Mikolov et al., 2013) on several billion words of newswire and discussion forum data. Preliminary results using this selection process have been very encouraging, with annotators reporting much richer documents on average, compared to the prior approach in which no ranking was imposed.

4.2 Rich ERE Challenges and Next Steps

One of the challenges in event annotation is to determine the level of granularity that will be distinguished as sub-event vs. event hopper. We observed this issue in our pilot Rich ERE annotation, and the goal is to have sub-event annotation be a relationship between event hoppers in the future. In order to represent the relations between event hoppers, we are planning the addition of a notion such as Narrative Container (Pustejovsky and Stubbs, 2011) to capture non-identity event-event relations such as causality, part-whole, precedence, enablement, etc. Event hoppers will serve as a level between individual event mentions and Narrative Containers. Event hoppers will be grouped into Narrative Containers, and so relations will be between event hoppers, instead of between individual event mentions. More specific relations between individual event mentions can then be derived from the event-event relations between the event hoppers within narrative containers or from relations between narrative containers.

4.3 Inter-Annotator Agreement

Work on inter-annotator agreement (IAA) will be based on the method outlined in Kulick et al. (2014), which described a matching algorithm used at each level of the annotation hierarchy, from entity mentions to events. This work focused on the evaluation for entity, relation, and event mentions, as well as for entities overall. The algorithm for entity mention mapping is based on the span for an entity mention, while the mapping for relation and event mentions is more complex, based on the mapping of the arguments, which in turn depends on the entity mention mapping. IAA work will be conducted on dual annotation for Rich ERE. Analysis will be reported in the future.

5 Conclusion

Rich ERE annotation includes a more comprehensive annotation of entities, relations and events, including expanded taggability, expanded categories, annotation for realis and specificity, and expanded coreference with the event hopper level. The expansion and change will populate more information to a knowledge base. Looking to the future, the additions to Rich ERE, particularly expanded taggability and the looser coreference of the event hopper level, are expected to improve support of within-document event-event relations and eventually cross-document and cross-lingual annotation.

Event Hoppers group events according to a more inclusive coreference specification, which will allow a wider range of event mentions to be coreferential. This is closer to the real world situation in which the same event is often referred to in a variety of ways that cannot meet a strict identity standard as was used in ACE and Light ERE. This kind of more inclusive event coreference will be increasingly necessary as work on informal genres, cross-document, and cross-lingual data is desired. In addition, event hopper annotation will allow knowledge base population to draw from a broader grouping of coreferenced event mentions, allowing for a more complete representation of event slots.

Acknowledgments

This material is based on research sponsored by Air Force Research Laboratory and Defense Advanced Research Projects Agency under agreement number FA8750-13-2-0045. The U.S. Government is authorized to reproduce and distribute reprints for Governmental purposes notwithstanding any copyright notation thereon. The views and conclusions contained herein are those of the authors and should not be interpreted as necessarily representing the official policies or endorsements, either expressed or implied, of Air Force Research Laboratory and Defense Advanced Research Projects Agency or the U.S. Government.

References

Jacqueline Aguilar, Charley Beller, Paul McNamee, Benjamin Van Durme, Stephanie Strassel, Zhiyi Song, Joe Ellis. 2014. A Comparison of the Events and Relations Across ACE, ERE, TAC-KBP, and FrameNet Annotation Standards. ACL 2014: 52nd Annual Meeting of the Association for Computational Linguistics, Baltimore, June 22-27. *2nd Workshop on Events: Definition, Detection, Coreference, and Representation*.

Ann Bies, Justin Mott, Seth Kulick, Jennifer Garland, Colin Warner. 2014. Incorporating Alternate Translations into English Translation Treebank. In *Proceedings of the 9th Edition of the Language Resources and Evaluation Conference* (LREC 2014), Reykjavik, May 26-31.

Branimir Boguraev and Rie Kubota Ando. 2005. TimeML-Compliant Text Analysis for Temporal Reasoning. In *Proceedings of International Joint Conference on Artificial Intelligence* (IJCAI), pp. 997--1003.

DARPA. 2012. *Broad Agency Announcement: Deep Exploration and Filtering of Text (DEFT)*. Defense Advanced Research Projects Agency, DARPA-BAA-12-47.

George Doddington, Alexis Mitchell, Mark Przybocki, Lance Ramshaw, Stephanie Strassel, Ralph Weischedel. 2004. The Automatic Content Extraction (ACE) program- tasks, data, and evaluation. In *Proceedings of the Fourth International Conference on Language Resources and Evaluation* (LREC 2004), Lisbon, May 24-30.

Joe Ellis, Jeremy Getman, Stephanie M. Strassel. 2014. Overview of Linguistic Resources for the TAC KBP 2014 Evaluations: Planning, Execution, and Results. In *Proceedings of TAC KBP 2014 Workshop, National Institute of Standards and Technology*, Gaithersburg, Maryland, USA, November 17-18, 2014.

Seth Kulick, Ann Bies, Justin Mott. 2014. Inter-annotator Agreement for ERE Annotation. ACL 2014: 52nd Annual Meeting of the Association for Computational Linguistics, Baltimore, June 22-27. *2nd Workshop on EVENTS: Definition, Detection, Coreference, and Representation*.

Linguistic Data Consortium. 2005. *ACE (Automatic Content Extraction) English Annotation Guidelines for Events Version 5.4.3*.

William C. Mann and Sandra Thompson. 1988. Rhetorical Structure Theory: Toward a Functional Theory of Text Organization. *Text 8(3)* (243-281).

Tomas Mikolov, Kai Chen, Greg Corrado, Jeffrey Dean. 2013. Efficient estimation of word representations in vector space. In *ICLR*, 2013.

Teruko Mitamura, Yukari Yamakawa, Sue Holm, Zhiyi Song, Ann Bies, Seth Kulick, Stephanie Strassel. 2015. Event Nugget Annotation: Processes and Issues. The 2015 Conference of the North American Chapter of the Association for Computational Linguistics - Human Language Technologies (NAACL

HLT 2015). *3rd Workshop on EVENTS: Definition, Detection, Coreference, and Representation.*

Sameer S. Pradhan, Eduard Hovy, Mitch Marcus, Martha Palmer, Lance Ramshaw, Ralph Weischedel. 2007. OntoNotes: A Unified Relational Semantic Representation. In *Proceedings of the First IEEE International Conference on Semantic Computing* (ICSC-07). Irvine, CA.

Rashmi Prasad, Bonnie Webber, Aravind Joshi. 2014. Reflections on the Penn Discourse TreeBank, Comparable Corpora and Complementary Annotation. *Computational Linguistics, Vol. 40, No. 4*, pp. 921-950, doi:10.1162/COLI_a_00204.

James Pustejovsky, and Amber Stubbs. 2011. Increasing Informativeness in Temporal Annotation. *Linguistic Annotation Workshop V* (LAW-V), Portland, Oregon. ACL, June 2011.

Heather Simpson, Christopher Cieri, Kazuaki Maeda, Kathryn Baker, Boyan Onyshkevych. 2008. Human Language Technology Resources for Less Commonly Taught Languages: Lessons Learned Toward Creation of Basic Language Resources. In *Proceedings of SALTMIL Workshop: Free/Open-Source Language Resources for the Machine Translation of Less-Resourced Languages*, at LREC 2008: 7th International Conference on Language Resources and Evaluation, Marrakech, May 28-30.

Stephanie Strassel, Dan Adams, Henry Goldberg, Jonathan Herr, Ron Keesing, Daniel Oblinger, Heather Simpson, Robert Schrag, Jonathan Wright. 2010. The DARPA Machine Reading Program - Encouraging Linguistic and Reasoning Research with a Series of Reading Tasks. In *Proceedings of the 7th International Conference on Language Resources and Evaluation* (LREC 2010), Valletta, May 17-23.

Christopher Walker, Stephanie Strassel, Julie Medero, Kazuaki Maeda. 2006. *ACE 2005 Multilingual Training Corpus*. Linguistic Data Consortium, LDC Catalog No.: LDC2006T06.

Jonathan Wright, Kira Griffitt, Joe Ellis, Stephanie Strassel, Brendan Callahan. 2012. Annotation Trees: LDC's Customizable, Extensible, Scalable Annotation Infrastructure. In *Proceedings of the 8th International Conference on Language Resources and Evaluation* (LREC 2012), Istanbul, May 21-27.

Xiuhong Zhang and Nianwen Xue. 2012. Extending and Scaling up the Chinese Treebank Annotation. In *Proceedings of the 2nd CIPS-SIGHAN Joint Conference on Chinese Language Processing* (CLP-2012), Tianjin, China.

Classification and Acquisition of Contradictory Event Pairs using Crowdsourcing

Yu Takabatake[1] **Hajime Morita**[1,2] **Daisuke Kawahara**[1]
Sadao Kurohashi[1,2] **Ryuichiro Higashinaka**[3] **Yoshihiro Matsuo**[3]
[1] Kyoto University [2] CREST, Japan Science and Technology Agency
[3] NTT Media Intelligence Laboratories
takabatake@nlp.ist.i.kyoto-u.ac.jp, {hmorita, dk, kuro}@i.kyoto-u.ac.jp,
{higashinaka.ryuichiro, matsuo.yoshihiro}@lab.ntt.co.jp

Abstract

We propose a taxonomy of contradictory event pairs and a method for building a database of such pairs. When a dialog system participates in an open-domain conversation with a human, it is important to avoid the generation of utterances that conflict with the context of the dialog. Here, we refer to a pair of events that are not able to co-occur or that are not inconsistent with each other as a contradictory event pair. In this study, we collected contradictory event pairs using crowdsourcing and constructed a taxonomy of such pairs. We also built a large-scale database of Japanese contradictory event pairs for each class using crowdsourcing. This database will be used for consistent utterance generation in dialog systems.

1 Introduction

In recent years, speech dialog systems such as Siri have become widespread. A user of such systems can obtain weather and traffic information by speaking to his/her smartphone. Although such information-seeking applications are now used in our daily lives, natural open-domain conversations are also expected.

Current open-domain conversation functions not only repeat single isolated utterances, but can also maintain previous dialog logs and conduct multitern conversations. However, many technical problems must be solved to generate natural utterances in the context of conversations.

In open-domain conversations, it is necessary to talk about related things. Such relatedness can be automatically learned from a large corpus, but a simple strategy of saying related things can lead to a nonsensical utterance as follows:

U: I like traveling, but I've never been to Paris.

S: Have you ever climbed the Eiffel Tower?

In this conversation, the system utterance (S) was generated using the keyword "Eiffel Tower," which is related to "Paris" in the user utterance (U). However, because "having never been to Paris" and "having climbed the Eiffel Tower" are contradictory, this system utterance is totally unacceptable. To conduct natural conversations, it is necessary to cope with contradictory phenomena.

In the field of natural language processing, contradictions have been dealt with in recognizing textual entailment (RTE), but there have been no studies that classify contradictory phenomena, to the best of our knowledge. In this study, we collected contradictory event pairs using crowdsourcing and constructed a taxonomy of such pairs. Furthermore, based on the contradiction taxonomy, we built a large-scale database of Japanese contradictory event pairs using crowdsourcing.

2 Related Work

There are several studies related to this research, including recognition and acquisition of contradictory event pairs (Harabagiu et al., 2006; Hashimoto et al., 2012; Kloetzer et al., 2013), acquisition of world knowledge (Fujita et al., 2014; Inui et al., 2005), and quality control of crowdsourced products (Whitehill et al., 2009). In contrast, we construct a taxonomy of contradictory event pairs, and thus the aim is different. However, our taxonomy could assist

Proceedings of the 3rd Workshop on EVENTS at the NAACL-HLT 2015, pages 99–107,
Denver, Colorado, June 4, 2015.

the recognition and acquisition methods proposed in these studies.

2.1 Recognition of Contradictory Event Pairs

As mentioned above, the recognition of contradictory event pairs is related to RTE. In some RTE tasks, contradiction is one of the relations between text and hypothesis. For example, Harabagiu et al. (2006) proposed a method to recognize contradictions between texts using negation expressions, antonyms, and discourse analysis.

Recognition of contradictory event pairs plays an important role in the systems that detect contradictions between information extracted from web texts. For example, there are several systems that detect contradictory information, such as WISDOM (Akamine et al., 2009), Statement Map (Murakami et al., 2009), and Dispute Finder (Ennals et al., 2010).

2.2 Acquisition of Contradictory Event Pairs

Hashimoto et al. (2012) and Kloetzer et al. (2013) proposed methods for acquiring contradictory event pairs. Hashimoto et al. (2012) collected Japanese contradictory and consistent event pairs using templates of semantic polarities that indicate excitatory, inhibitory, and neutral properties. A template consists of a particle and a predicate, such as "を (particle) 破壊する (destroy)" and "を (particle) 進行させる (develop)." They collected one million contradictory event pairs, such as "ガンを破壊する (destroy cancer)" and "ガンを進行させる (develop cancer)," with a precision of 70% in their experiments. Most of the pairs were categorized as simultaneous contradiction, in particular, as continuous or binary contradiction in our taxonomy (described later). Kloetzer et al. (2013) refined this method and collected 75,000 contradictory event pairs with a precision of 80%.

2.3 Construction of World Knowledge

Fujita et al. (2014) and Inui et al. (2005) proposed a method for constructing world knowledge. Both methods focus on causal knowledge among world knowledge and automatically collected such knowledge for Japanese. Fujita et al. (2014) extracted text fragments preceding and following the conjunction "のに (but)," aiming to collect expressions indicating events that are unexpected by the author of the text. They finally extracted a small number of causal event pairs (approximately 1,400 pairs) from community question answering texts.

Inui et al. (2005) defined four types of causal relations between events based on whether the event is an action or a situation. They classified sentences that included the conjunction "ため (because)" into the four types of relations. They achieved a precision of over 95% with a recall of 80% for three types of relations ("cause," "precondition" and "means"), and achieved a precision of 90% and a recall of 30% for the fourth relation, "effect."

2.4 Quality Control of Crowdsourced Products

There are two common approaches to quality control of crowdsourced products. Whitehill et al. (2009) proposed a probabilistic method for combining the labels of multiple crowdworkers to acquire reliable labels. Their method outperforms the commonly-used majority voting. The second approach is to measure the reliability of crowdworkers using gold standard data. We used both approaches to build a large-scale database of contradictory event pairs via crowdsourcing.

3 Taxonomy of Contradictory Event Pairs

3.1 Collecting Contradictory Event Pairs

To construct a taxonomy of contradictory event pairs, we need to investigate real examples of such pairs. To obtain a large number and variety of contradictory event pairs, we employed crowdsourcing, which can employ a large number of people to perform micro-tasks inexpensively and over a short period of time. We used Yahoo! crowdsourcing[1] as a crowdsourcing service.

Considering future applications of the resulting taxonomy in open-domain dialog systems, we focused on two domains: "gourmet" and "traveling." We first prepared sentences referring to events specific to each domain. Presenting the domain and one of its specific sentences (hereafter, called a **target sentence**), we asked crowdworkers to write contradictory sentences. We asked crowdworkers to avoid writing self-contradictory sentences such as "The sun rises in the west." as well as sentences that are unrelated to the target sentence, such as "It's my

[1] http://crowdsourcing.yahoo.co.jp/

birthday today." for the target sentence "It's raining today."

We prepared 15 target sentences for each domain, and asked 20 crowdworkers to write five contradictory sentences for each target sentence. That is, we collected 100 contradictory sentences for each target sentence. For example, presenting the domain "gourmet" and the target sentence "I love Chinese cuisine," we obtained contradictory sentences such as "I don't like Chinese cuisine." and "I've eaten only Japanese cuisine."

3.2 Basic Idea

When classifying collected contradictory event pairs, the interpretation of these sentences can be a problem. For example, the event pair ⟨being in Tokyo, being in Kyoto⟩ is not contradictory if the events happen at different times, but is contradictory when they happen simultaneously. The event pair ⟨the pasta tastes delicious, he didn't eat the pasta⟩ is not contradictory if the subject knew that the pasta was delicious but did not eat it for some other reason. However, for the event pair ⟨he ate the pasta, and the pasta tasted delicious⟩, if the former event is "he didn't eat the pasta," such an event pair is contradictory because the subject cannot know that the pasta that he did not eat tasted delicious.

Therefore, we do not interpret the collected event pair sentences, but instead examine the possible variations of contradictory phenomena between these event pairs by only referring to the original sentences.

As discussed above, it is necessary to discriminate whether an event pair occurs simultaneously or has a temporal or order relation to judge if it is contradictory. We call the former type a **simultaneous contradiction**, such as ⟨being in Tokyo, being in Kyoto⟩. We call the latter type a **transitional contradiction**, such as ⟨he didn't eat the pasta, the pasta tasted delicious⟩. In this way, we first classify contradictory event pairs into simultaneous contradictions and transitional contradictions.

The rest of this section further classifies both simultaneous contradictions and transitional contradictions. Table 1 summarizes our taxonomy of contradictory event pairs and lists examples.

Simultaneous contradictions	
(1-a) binary	⟨a coin comes up heads, a coin comes up tails⟩ ⟨eating pasta, not eating pasta⟩
(1-b) discrete	⟨eating pasta, eating ramen⟩ ⟨being in Tokyo, being in Osaka⟩ ⟨this is my first time traveling overseas, this is my second time traveling overseas⟩
(1-c) continuous	⟨the dish is expensive, the dish is cheap⟩ ⟨the sky is clear, it is raining⟩ ⟨the cake is delicious, the cake is disgusting⟩
(1-d) sequential event	⟨getting on a bus, getting off a bus⟩ ⟨reserving it, canceling it⟩
(1-e) counterpart perspective	⟨I sell a cake, I buy a cake⟩ ⟨shooting a gun, being shot by a gun⟩
Transitional contradictions	
(2-a) former negation	⟨not standing for an election, being elected⟩ ⟨not eating pasta, the pasta tasted delicious⟩
(2-b) latter negation	⟨entering a ramen shop, not eating ramen⟩ ⟨entering an Italian restaurant, ordering buckwheat noodles⟩

Table 1: Our taxonomy of contradictory event pairs with examples. Examples are translated into English.

3.3 Simultaneous Contradictions

When a pair of two events occurs simultaneously, contradictions of such pairs have a strong relation with negation, such as ⟨having a meal, not having a meal⟩ and ⟨eating to excess, eating moderately⟩. There are also contradictory event pairs based on sibling relations, such as ⟨being in Tokyo, being in Kyoto⟩, where "Tokyo" and "Kyoto" have a sibling relation. We therefore classify negation and sibling relations into **binary** (e.g., "single" and "married"), **discrete** (e.g., "Tokyo" and "Kyoto"), and **continuous** (e.g., "expensive" and "cheap").

Furthermore, negation has the following two classes that can cause contradictions (Izumi et al., 2014): sequential event relations, such as "getting on" and "getting off," and counterpart perspective relations, such as "selling" and "buying." We added these classes to our taxonomy. The subclasses of simultaneous contradictions are detailed below.

1-a. binary When an event pair includes mutually exclusive antonyms (e.g., "single" and "married") or a predicate and its negation (e.g., "going" and "not going"), these events are contradictory. We call such contradictory event pairs **binary**.

1-b. discrete When an event pair consists of predicates or arguments that have sibling relations, such as ⟨being in Tokyo, being in Kyoto⟩ and

⟨eating pasta, eating ramen⟩, these events are contradictory.[2] We call such contradictory event pairs **discrete** pairs to discriminate them from the next class, "continuous." We also include contradictory event pairs caused by numerical values in the discrete class such as ⟨this is my first time traveling overseas, this is my second time traveling overseas⟩.

1-c. continuous When an event pair consists of antonym predicates that represent continuous states, such as "expensive" and "cheap," these events are contradictory. We call such contradictory event pairs **continuous**. In addition to ⟨being expensive, being cheap⟩, ⟨being expensive, not being expensive⟩ and ⟨being extremely expensive, being a little expensive⟩ are also contradictory event pairs. Since continuous states are not necessarily one-dimensional, various continuous event pairs can be contradictory, such as ⟨it's clear, it's raining⟩, ⟨it's clear, it's stormy⟩, and ⟨it's snowing, it's raining⟩.

1-d. sequential event relations Sequential event pairs, such as ⟨getting on a bus, (and then) getting off a bus⟩, are not contradictory if time goes by between the two events. However, when we consider ⟨getting on a bus, getting off a bus⟩ as a pair of simultaneous events, this event pair is contradictory.

1-e. counterpart perspective relations
Counterpart perspective events such as ⟨I sell a book to him, he buys a book from me⟩ are not contradictory if these event descriptions indicate the same event from a different view. However, when we consider ⟨I sell a book to him, I buy a book from him⟩ as a simultaneous event with the same participants, this event pair is contradictory.

For an event pair of simultaneous contradictions, event pairs where one of the events is replaced by its synonymous event are also regarded as simultaneous contradictions. For example, ⟨tasting delicious, not tasting delicious⟩ is a "simultaneous contradiction: continuous," and thus ⟨tasting nice, not tasting delicious⟩, where "tasting delicious" is synonymous with "tasting nice," is also classified as a "simultaneous contradiction: continuous."

3.4 Transitional Contradictions

Transitional contradictions are a relation between two events that have a temporal or order relation. We call the event that happens earlier the **former event** and the event that happens later the **latter event**, and represent this relation as $A \rightsquigarrow B$. When A and B have such a temporal or order relation, a pair of ⟨$\neg$A, B⟩ or ⟨A, $\neg$B⟩ is contradictory if one of the following conditions is satisfied.

2-a. former negation Under $A \rightsquigarrow B$, there is a case such that A is a precondition for B. For example, for the event pair ⟨having a passport, going overseas⟩, the precondition for "going overseas" is "having a passport." For such a relation, the negation of the precondition ($\neg$A) is contradictory to B. For the passport example, ⟨not having a passport, going overseas⟩ is contradictory.

2-b. latter negation Under $A \rightsquigarrow B$, when A generally leads B, the negation of B is contradictory to A. For example, the event "entering a restaurant" generally leads to the event "ordering something." Accordingly, ⟨entering a restaurant, not ordering something⟩, which is made by negating B, is contradictory.

The above classification for $A \rightsquigarrow B$ is based on a temporal or order relation between A and B. This can be also interpreted from another viewpoint as follows. For the former negation class of $A \rightsquigarrow B$, it generally holds that if B is true, A is true as a precondition (e.g., "if going overseas, a traveler has a passport"), and A is negated to be a contradictory event pair. For the latter negation class of $A \rightsquigarrow B$, it generally holds that if A is true, B is true, and negating B leads to be a contradictory event pair. That is to say, the above classes are the negation of the former event and the latter event, respectively, from the viewpoint of a temporal or order relation, but they are also the negation of consequences from the viewpoint of an if-then relation.

For transitional contradictions, it is difficult to define the extent of generally accepted common sense.

[2]Event pairs that have a sibling relation in their arguments are not always contradictory, as in ⟨I like Toyotas, I like Nissans⟩.

If we suppose real-world event pairs, it is very rare that if-then relations absolutely hold. That is, we can easily think of a counterexample that does not satisfy an if-then relation. Furthermore, if there are some cases that do not meet an if-then relation, we do not believe that its former negation or latter negation is contradictory. For example, we can easily think of counterexamples for "if going to a spa, he/she wears a summer kimono," and thus we do not believe that the event pair ⟨going to a spa, not wearing a summer kimono⟩ is contradictory.

3.5 Multistage Inference Contradictions

There are contradictory event pairs based on multistage inferences. For example, ⟨I made a supper using leftovers, I had a full course dinner⟩ is a contradictory event pair. First, we can generally accept the following event relations: ⟨I made a supper using leftovers, I ate a few dishes for supper⟩ and ⟨I had a full course dinner, I ate many dishes for dinner.⟩ Here, ⟨I ate a few dishes for supper, I ate many dishes for dinner⟩ is classified as a "simultaneous contradiction: continuous" (1-c), and thus ⟨I made a supper using leftovers, I had a full course dinner⟩ is a result of these inferences.

4 Data Construction by Crowdsourcing

We constructed domain-specific contradictory event pairs using crowdsourcing, exploiting their classifications explained in the previous section. Considering the application to open-domain conversational systems, we selected 12 domains: "gourmet," "travel," "weather," "sports," "life," "political and economic," "child-rearing," "learn," "health," "work," "baseball," and "shopping."

To construct the data, we presented a domain to crowdworkers and asked them to create domain-specific contradictory event pairs. However, it is actually difficult to make this a single complete task. In crowdsourcing, a task is supposed to be relatively simple so that it may be done in a short time by ordinary people. The task explanation is also ought to be simple and quickly understandable. A complex task that requires a long explanation increases the load on crowdworkers and makes it difficult for the task to be accurately completed.

In this study, the process of constructing contradictory event pairs was divided into two phases, the construction of a domain-specific sentence and construction of its contradictory sentence. Furthermore, each phase was completed using a task comprising two stages: construction and evaluation. That is, the process of constructing contradictory event pairs consisted of the following four crowdsourcing tasks:

- Phase 1: Construction of domain-specific sentences (target sentences).
- Phase 2: Evaluation of target sentences to determine if they are actually suitable for each domain.
- Phase 3: Construction of contradictory sentences for each target sentence.
- Phase 4: Evaluation of each pair of domain-specific and contradictory sentences to determine if they are really contradictory.

Here, by using the classifications of contradictory event pairs in Phase 3 and 4, we make the task clearer and more simple (Sections 4.3 and 4.4 explain the details).

4.1 Phase 1: Construction of Domain-specific Sentences (Target Sentences)

Crowdworkers were shown a domain and were asked to submit sentences that express domain-specific events. For the music domain, the following examples of domain-specific events were shown to crowdworkers: "a guitar is too noisy" and "I bought high-quality earphones." To make Phase 3 easier, types of inappropriate sentences and instructions for revising them were also presented to crowdworkers.

- Nominals: "performance of instruments" → "I play instruments"
- Pronouns: "It's fun to play it" → "It's fun to play a violin"
- Monologue: "It's jazz!" → "I listen to jazz"
- Call/Invitation: "Let's go to a concert" → "I would like to go to a concert"

For each domain (out of 12 domains), we asked 100 crowdworkers to submit five sentences, that is, we constructed 6,000 target sentences in total.

4.2 Phase 2: Evaluation of Target Sentences

We asked crowdworkers whether the target sentence constructed in Phase 1 was really domain-specific and met all the following criteria. Counter-examples (CE) for each criterion in the domain of music are shown below.

- It makes sense.
  CE: "a component of a band is necessity to sell a music."
- It is domain-specific.
  CE: "These noodles are delicious."
- It is a sentence (not just a noun or verb)
  CE: "chorus", "enjoy."
- It is not a noun phrase
  CE: "favorite guitar", "performance of instruments."
- Not including a pronoun
  CE: "it's fun to play it."
- It is not a remark
  CE: "it's a jazz!"
- It is a call/invitation
  CE: "let's go to a concert"
- It is a interrogative
  CE: "Do you like a classic music?"

We asked five crowdworkers to evaluate for each of the target sentences in 6,000 sentences obtained in Phase 1. For each domain, approximately 200 sentences received all positive evaluations. Based on this result, for each domain, we selected the top 200 target sentences to use in Phase 3. To select these top sentences, we used Whitehill's EM-based evaluation method (Whitehill et al., 2009), which is widely used for the evaluation of crowdsourcing results.

4.3 Phase 3: Construction of Contradictory Sentences

Our preliminary experiments found that it is difficult to collect transitional contradictions by just asking crowdworkers to write "some contradictory sentences." To solve this problem, we divided the task into three smaller tasks to create, simultaneous contradictions, former-negative transitional contradictions, and latter-negative transitional contradictions.

Simultaneous contradictions

We asked crowdworkers to write simultaneous contradictory sentences for a given target sentence. To help workers understand the concept of simultaneous contradiction, the following examples, based on the taxonomy described in Section 3, were shown.

- *Opposite meaning*: ⟨a coin comes up heads, a coin comes up tails⟩ or, ⟨eating pasta, not eating pasta⟩
- *Same category, but different*: ⟨eating pasta, eating ramen⟩ or, ⟨I'm in Tokyo, I'm in Osaka⟩
- *Difference in degree*: ⟨the cake is delicious, the cake is disgusting⟩ or, ⟨it's clear, it is raining⟩
- *Different role*: ⟨I sell a cake, I buy a cake⟩ or, ⟨he shot a gun, he was shot by a gun⟩
- *Simultaneous occurrence of naturally sequential events*: ⟨getting on a bus, getting off a bus⟩ or, ⟨enrolling in a school, graduating from a school⟩

The following example contradictory phrases for "saving money" were shown to crowdworders: "saving stamps" and "spending money." The following cautions were also given:

- Do not write a sentence that is impossible by itself, such as "The sun rises in the West"
- Do not write a sentence that is totally unrelated to a given target sentence, such as "It's my birthday today." for "It's raining."

For each domain (out of 12 domains), we prepared 200 target sentences. For each target sentence, we asked 10 crowdworkers to submit more than one contradictory sentence. As a result, after discarding inappropriate sentences (such as single word sentences) and merging identical sentences, we obtained 14 contradictory sentences for each target sentence on average.

Former-negative transitional contradictions

A former-negative transitional contradiction is the relation between an event and the negation of its precondition. For crowdworkers, however, it is easier to consider preconditions for a target sentence than, consider the precondition negations. Therefore, we asked crowdworkers to write preconditions to a given target sentence.

As example of preconditions for "being elected," "standing for election" and "being eligible for election" were shown to crowdworkers. The following cautions were also given to them.

- Do not write an unrelated or mostly un-related sentence for a given target sentence, such as "there is air." to "The candidate is elected."

For each domain (out of 12 domains), we prepared 200 target sentences. For each target sentence, we asked 10 crowdworkers to submit more than one contradictory sentence. As a result, we obtained 17 precondition sentences for each target sentence on average.

Latter-negative transitional contradictions

A latter-negative transitional contradiction is the relation between an event and the negation of the event that generally follows it. However, similarly to the case of former-negative transitional contradictions, it is easier for crowdworkers to consider generally-following events than their negations. Therefore, we asked crowdworkers to write sentences that generally follow a given target sentence. We modified target sentences to be past tense in order to emphasize that former events expressed by the target sentences had already happened, and that we were interested in the following events.

As example events that generally follow "I went to a hot spring.", "I wash one's body." and "I soak in a hot spring." were shown to crowdworkers. The following cautions were also given to them.

- Do not write a sentences that is unrelated or mostly unrelated to a given target sentence, such as "The next day comes" for "He stood as a candidate."

Similarly to the case of former-negative transitional contradictions, we obtained 17 generally-following sentences for each target sentence on average.

4.4 Phase 4: Evaluation of Contradictory Sentence Pairs

Evaluations using crowdsourcing were performed for each of the three categories.

Simultaneous contradictions

We asked crowdworkers if a pair of the target and contradictory sentences was really contradictory.

We asked five crowdworkers to evaluate for each of the 34,900 simultaneous contradiction pairs obtained in Phase 3. As a result, 77% of the pairs received more than two positive answers.

Former-negative transitional contradictions

We modified the preconditions collected in Phase 3 into a negative form automatically. We then asked crowdworkers if a pair of target sentence and its negated precondition was really contradictory.

We asked five crowdworkers to evaluate each pair in 41,300 former-negative transitional contradiction pairs. As a result, 49% of the pairs received more than two positive answers.

simultaneous contradiction	
binary	⟨going to Tokyo by plane, going to Tokyo, but not by plane⟩ ⟨making a plan, planning nothing⟩
discrete	⟨going to Las Vegas on vacation, going to Hawaii on vacation⟩ ⟨going to Tokyo by air, going to Tokyo by train⟩
continuous	⟨I find overseas travel hard, I find overseas travel easy⟩ ⟨the guide was very kind, the guide was unkind⟩
sequential event relations	⟨checking into a hotel, checking out of a hotel⟩ ⟨booking a tour abroad, canceling a tour abroad⟩
counterpart perspective relations	⟨staying at a hotel, accomodating a guest⟩
Transitional Contradictions	
former negation	⟨not buying flight ticket, going to Tokyo by plane⟩ ⟨not applying for a passport, going to Las Vegas on vacation⟩ ⟨not arriving at a hotel, checking into a hotel ⟩ ⟨I have never traveled abroad, I find hard overseas travel difficult⟩
latter negation	⟨booking a tour abroad, not applying for a passport⟩ ⟨going to Tokyo by plane, not landing at the airport⟩ ⟨going to Las Vegas to play, not taking a plane trip⟩ ⟨staying at a hotel, not receiving a room key⟩

Table 2: Examples of contradictory event pairs obtained by crowdsourcing. Examples have been translated into English.

Latter-negative transitional contradictions

We modified the generally-following sentences collected in Phase 3 into a negative form automatically. We then asked crowdworkers if a pair of the target sentence and its negated generally-following sentence is really contradictory.

We asked five crowdworkers to evaluate for each of the 42,080 latter-negative transitional contradiction pairs. As a result, 37% of the pairs received more than two positive answers.

4.5 Discussion

As a result of the series of crowdsourcing tasks, we constructed 118,380 contradictory event pairs, each of which has been evaluations by five crowdworkers.

To make the crowdsourcing tasks clearer, we divided the tasks into three categories according to our taxonomy. However, we sometimes obtained miss-classified contradictory pairs in each category. For example, we acquired ⟨I have no credit card, I buy something with my credit card⟩ as a simultaneous contradiction, but we classify it as a former-negative

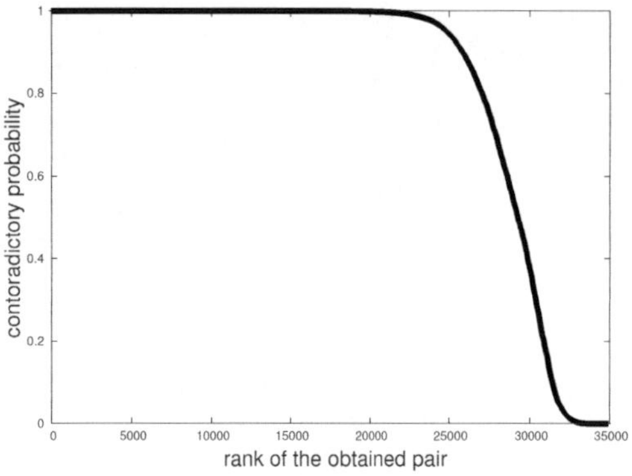

Figure 1: Contradictory probabilities distribution for simultaneous contradiction pairs.

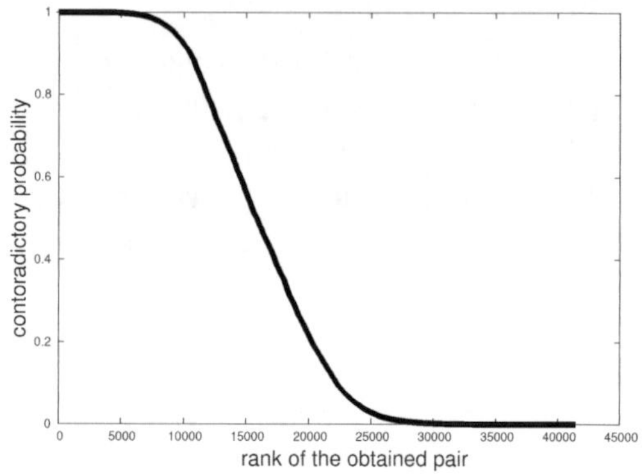

Figure 2: Contradictory probabilities distribution for former-negative transitional contradiction pairs.

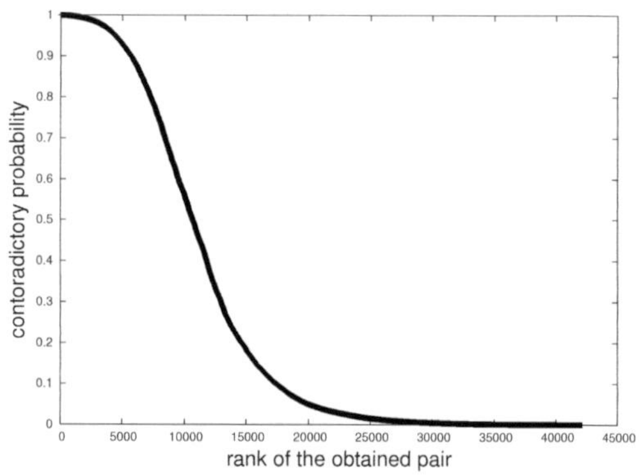

Figure 3: Contradictory probobility distribution for latter-negative transitional contradiction.

transitional contradiction.

The distributions of contradictory probabilities of the constructed pairs calculated by the Whitehill's EM-based method is shown in Figures 1, 2 and 3. Because negation, antonym and sibling relation are relatively clear, we were able to obtain high-quality data for simultaneous contradiction. However, the number of contradictory event pairs with a high probability became smaller for former-negative transitional contradictions, and much smaller for latter-negative ones.

In the case of latter-negative transitional contradictions, for example, ⟨the Japanese legislature was dissolved, there are no breaking news stories⟩ has a probability of 0.8, and it can be considered as a widely-acceptable contradictory event pair. However, ⟨I watched a baseball broadcast, I did not enjoy the baseball game⟩ has a probability of 0.5 and we feel that it is not necessarily a contradiction. Because the judgment of a transitional contradiction is based on common knowledge or the life-style of each person, its contradictory probabilitiy often decreases.

5 Conclusion

In this paper, we proposed a taxonomy of contradictory event pairs. We first discriminated between simultaneous contradictions and transitional contradictions, and then classified these further. The event pair ⟨having never been to Paris, having climbed the Eiffel Tower⟩, which was mentioned in Section 1, is classified as a "transitional contradiction: former negation" (2-a).

Based on our taxonomy, we built a large-scale database of Japanese contradictory event pairs for each class using crowdsourcing. As a result, we obtained more than 100,000 possible contradictory event pairs in total, and out of these, over 60,000 event pairs can be accepted as contradictory event pairs based on the evaluations of crowdworkers.

In the future, we intend to develop an open-domain conversational system that does not generate contradictory utterances on the basis of the acquired contradiction database.

References

Susumu Akamine, Daisuke Kawahara, Yoshikiyo Kato, Tetsuji Nakagawa, Kentaro Inui, Sadao Kurohashi, and Yutaka Kidawara. 2009. WISDOM: A web information credibility analysis system. In *Proceedings of ACL-IJCNLP2009 Software Demonstrations*, pages 1–4.

Rob Ennals, Beth Trushkowsky, and John Mark Agosta. 2010. Highlighting disputed claims on the web. In *Proceedings of the 19th international conference on World wide web*, pages 341–350. ACM.

Hiroshi Fujita, Akira Fujita, and Naoyoshi Tamura. 2014. Extracting implicit causal knowledge using the conjunctive marker noni (in Japanese). *IEICE technical report. Natural language understanding and models of communication*, 114(366):61–66, dec.

Sanda Harabagiu, Andrew Hickl, and Finley Lacatusu. 2006. Negation, contrast and contradiction in text processing. In *Proceedings of AAAI*, volume 6, pages 755–762.

Chikara Hashimoto, Kentaro Torisawa, Stijn De Saeger, Jong-Hoon Oh, and Jun'ichi Kazama. 2012. Excitatory or inhibitory: A new semantic orientation extracts contradiction and causality from the web. In *Proceedings of EMNLP2012*, pages 619–630.

Takashi Inui, Kentaro Inui, and Yuji Matsumoto. 2005. Acquiring causal knowledge from text using the connective marker tame. *ACM Transactions on Asian Language Information Processing (TALIP)*, 4(4):435–474.

Tomoko Izumi, Tomohide Shibata, Hisako Asano, Yoshihiro Matsuo, and Sadao Kurohashi. 2014. Constructing a corpus of Japanese predicate phrases for synonym/antonym relations. In Nicoletta Calzolari, Khalid Choukri, Thierry Declerck, Hrafn Loftsson, Bente Maegaard, Joseph Mariani, Asuncion Moreno, Jan Odijk, and Stelios Piperidis, editors, *Proceedings of the Ninth International Conference on Language Resources and Evaluation (LREC'14)*, pages 1394–1400, Reykjavik, Iceland, May. European Language Resources Association (ELRA). ACL Anthology Identifier: L14-1244.

Julien Kloetzer, Stijn De Saeger, Kentaro Torisawa, Chikara Hashimoto, Jong-Hoon Oh, Motoki Sano, and Kiyonori Ohtake. 2013. Two-stage method for large-scale acquisition of contradiction pattern pairs using entailment. In *Proceedings of EMNLP2013*, pages 693–703.

Koji Murakami, Eric Nichols, Suguru Matsuyoshi, Asuka Sumida, Shouko Masuda, Kentaro Inui, and Yuji Matumoto. 2009. Statement map: Assisting information credibility analysis by visualizing arguments. In *Proceedings of the 3rd Workshop on Information Credibility on the web*, pages 43–50. ACM.

Jacob Whitehill, Ting fan Wu, Jacob Bergsma, Javier R. Movellan, and Paul L. Ruvolo. 2009. Whose vote should count more: Optimal integration of labels from labelers of unknown expertise. In Y. Bengio, D. Schuurmans, J.D. Lafferty, C.K.I. Williams, and A. Culotta, editors, *Advances in Neural Information Processing Systems 22*, pages 2035–2043. Curran Associates, Inc.

Interoperability of cross-lingual and cross-document event detection

Piek Vossen
VU University Amsterdam
De Boelelaan 1105
Amsterdam, 1081HV, Netherlands
piek.vossen@vu.nl

Egoitz Laparra, Itziar Aldabe and German Rigau
The University of the Basque Country
Donostia-San Sebastián, Spain
egoitz.laparra@ehu.eus
itziar.aldabe@ehu.eus
german.rigau@ehu.eus

Abstract

We describe a system for event extraction across documents and languages. We developed a framework for the interoperable semantic interpretation of mentions of events, participants, locations and time, as well as the relations between them. Furthermore, we use a common RDF model to represent instances of events and normalised entities and dates. We convert multiple mentions of the same event in English, Spanish and Dutch to a single representation. We thus resolve cross-document event and entity coreference within a language but also across languages. We tested our system on a Wikinews corpus of 120 English articles that have been manually translated to Spanish and Dutch. We report on the cross-lingual cross-document event and entity extraction comparing the Spanish and Dutch output with respect to English.

1 Introduction

News reports on events in the world. Applying event extraction to many different news articles provides an interesting perspective on event-coreference, assuming that different sources in different languages report on the same events. These texts may partially provide the same and partly different information on these events. To deal with cross-document event coreference, it is necessary to make a formal difference between the mentions of an event in text and its representation as single event instance. Ideally, we want to be able to match event descriptions within a text, across texts and across languages into a single representation. The fact that different sources provide different information opens new perspectives to study the role of these sources in reporting on what happened in the world. When we consider news written in different languages this perspective becomes more complex but also more interesting.

For such a cross-document and cross-lingual perspective it is essential to define a semantically interoperable approach that can handle the large variation of event expressions within and across languages. In this paper, we report on a system to derive interoperable event representations across documents and across languages. In particular, we focus on English, Spanish and Dutch. Firstly, we developed Natural Language Processing (NLP) pipelines for interpreting mentions of events and event components in text in a uniform way and, secondly, we developed a method to derive instance representations for these interpretations in RDF that is agnostic for the linguistic forms of expression. We report on the evaluation of the systems on a publicly available corpus of English Wikinews articles that has been translated to Spanish and Dutch. We show the capability of our framework and system to perform cross-lingual event extraction from multiple documents, which is, to our knowledge, the first in its kind.

This paper is further structured as follows. In section 2, we describe relevant related work and in section 3, we describe our approach to aggregate event information across different mentions in RDF. In section 4, we explain the interoperability of the NLP pipelines in the three languages. The conversion of the NLP output to RDF is then explained in section 5. Finally, we present the evaluation results in section 6 and we conclude in section 7.

Proceedings of the 3rd Workshop on EVENTS at the NAACL-HLT 2015, pages 108–116,
Denver, Colorado, June 4, 2015.

2 Related work

In Unstructured Information Management Architecture (UIMA) (Ferrucci and Lally, 2004) interoperability is provided by platform independent data representations and interfaces. Information is represented in the Common Analysis Structure (CAS). In CAS, annotations are defined as typed objects. For each type, a set of features is defined and an is-a relation with its supertype from which features are inherited. The Subject of Analysis (Sofa) method is used to allow for multiple annotations of the same object. UIMA uses a layered stand-off representation for the annotations of text. A similar approach is followed in the OntoNotes project (Pradhan et al., 2007). In OntoNotes multiple layers of annotation defined in a relational database are combined to arrive at semantic interpretations. Both approaches focus on the generic annotation of text. Howewer, they do not specifically focus on the representation of events and they do not present events according to an RDF model independently of the text as a natural way of cross-document event representation.

The idea of using Linked Data and RDF to represent linguistic annotations for achieving interoperability among linguistic resources has been discussed previously (Chiarcos et al., 2012). Following Linked Data and RDF principles provides a way to address conceptual interoperability among resources, i.e. the ability of heterogeneous NLP resources and tools to talk and understand each other. (Ide et al., 2003) explicitly mention RDF as a possible format to provide semantic coherence in representations. The NLP2RDF initiative collects a number of efforts for representing NLP related information in RDF, including notable efforts such as Ontologies for Linguistic Annotation (OLiA) (Chiarcos, 2008). FRED (Presutti et al., 2012) also produces automatically RDF/OWL and linked data from natural language sentences, but its output is currently limited to English. Still, to our knowledge, there are relatively few implementations of RDF-compatible annotation formats that are actively used or produced by NLP modules. Notable exceptions are the NLP Interchange Format (NIF) (Hellmann et al., 2013), which is tightly linked to OLiA, UIMA Clerezza, and the conversion of GrAF to RDF by (Cassidy, 2010). NIF has the disadvantage that it is not easy to integrate its representations in NLP tools, as shown by user evaluations (Hellmann et al., 2013). Because linguistic annotations are linked to strings it is furthermore not practical for representing hierarchical structures. (Fokkens et al., 2014) presents a more detailed discussion of the formal representations of linguistic annotations.

Besides the formal representation of NLP output, our work relates to the representation of events and cross-document and cross-lingual event coreference. Cross-document event coreference so far has been addressed as a task, in which event markables are related to each other as coreference sets (Bejan and Harabagiu, 2010; Lee et al., 2012). For instance, the ECB corpus represents events and coreference relations using inline annotations in text and cross-document identifiers with offset references. Representation and evaluation of cross-document event-coreference is often done using scorers that use the CONLL-2011 format for expressing coreference (Pradhan et al., 2011). This format also exploits a simple token representation and identifiers. To the best of our knowledge, nobody really addressed the semantic representation of events as instances, exploiting interoperable semantic representations of event instances and entity instances according to Semantic Web practices.

3 The representation of event mentions and instances

Events can be defined as situations in the world in which certain entities participate, where this participation relation is bound in time and place. In text, we make reference to these events in many different ways. Each time we refer to an event in text, the expression through which we make reference can be seen as a mention of the event that we consider to be an instance of a mental representation or real-world event. Typically, there is a coreference relation between different mentions of the same event instance.

In many cases, mentions that refer to events are partial, i.e. not all the details about an event are given within a single sentence. For example, the next sentences from a Wikinews[1] article make reference to a single *flight* but the details are given in

[1] http://en.wikinews.org/wiki/A380_makes_maiden_flight_to_US

different expressions:

> A380 makes maiden flight to US. March 19, 2007. The Airbus A380, the world's largest passenger plane, was set to land in the United States of America on Monday after a test flight. One of the A380s is flying from Frankfurt to Chicago via New York; the airplane will be carrying about 500 people.

The main event is the *test flight* which is mentioned in the title, at the end of the first sentence and referred to again in the second sentence as *flying*. The *carrying* is a subevent of the main event, whereas one could argue whether *landing* is a subevent or a following event. The date of the event is given in the first sentence (*Monday*), which refers to *March 19, 2007*, the flight route is given in the second sentence and passengers are mentioned in the last clause: *500 people* through the implicit relation between *carrying* and *flying*.

Depending if *carrying* and *landing* are different events, we have in this example 5 mentions of 3 unique events. To aggregate the information for the *flight* event, we need to resolve coreference and combine the information from each coreferential mention into a single representation for the instance. To connect the mentions to the instance representation, we use the Grounded Annotation Framework (GAF) (Fokkens et al., 2013). Within GAF, instances are represented according to the Simple Event Model (SEM) (van Hage et al., 2011) using a unique URI and relations to actors, places and time. Furthermore, we use the *gaf:denotedBy* relation to point to the offset mentions of the event in the text. When applied to the above example, the event instance for the *flight* would be represented as follows, where we abstract from the specific roles of the actors and places:

```
:ev17Flight
rdfs:label "maiden flight", "test flight", "flying" ;
gaf:denotedBy
  wikinews:A380_makes_maiden_flight_to_US#char=19,25,
  wikinews:A380_makes_maiden_flight_to_US#char=174,180,
  wikinews:A380_makes_maiden_flight_to_US#char=202,208;
sem:hasTime wikinews:20070319;
sem:hasActor dbp:Airbus_A380, wikinews:500_people;
sem:hasPlace dbp:United_States, dbp:Frankfurt, dbp:Chicago,
 dbp:New_York.
```

Each of the actors, places and points in time is represented as an entity instance as well, with pointers to the mentions in the text. Below, we show the representation of *Airbus* as an example with 2 mentions in the same document:

```
dbp:Airbus
rdfs:label      "Airbus A380", "A380" ;
gaf:denotedBy
wikinews:A380_makes_maiden_flight_to_US#char=415,421,
wikinews:A380_makes_maiden_flight_to_US#char=1132,1138.
```

In this example, the actors, places and time points are aggregated from different mentions in a single representation. If another text is processed, we may detect more mentions of the same event and the same entities. In principle, this will lead to the same instance representation for the event where we only need to extend the *gaf:denotedBy* relations to the new mentions and if it happens aggregate more relations to other entities.

> A380 commercial route proving. 19-28 March 2007. Watch the A380 as it makes its first landings in the United States as part of a 12-day commercial route proving mission in 2007, performed in conjunction with Lufthansa. Follow the aircraft as it flies to New York, Chicago and Washington, D.C., as well as Hong Kong, Frankfurt and Munich.

This message partially overlaps with the previous one but also describes more stops on the route of the airplane. Establishing coreference across the two flights and the A380 results in a single event instance combining the data and pointing to different mentions across the two articles:

```
:ev17Flight
rdfs:label "maiden flight", "test flight", "flying", "flies" ;
gaf:denotedBy
  wikinews:A380_makes_maiden_flight_to_US#char=19,25,
  wikinews:A380_makes_maiden_flight_to_US#char=174,180,
  wikinews:A380_makes_maiden_flight_to_US#char=202,208,
  http://www.airbus.com/newsevents/events/mention#char=242,247;
sem:hasTime wikinews:20070319;
sem:hasActor dbp:Airbus_A380, wikinews:500_people;
sem:hasPlace dbp:United_States, dbp:Frankfurt,
   dbp:Chicago, dbp:New_York, dbp:Washington_D.C.,
   dbp:Hong_Kong; dbp:Munich.
```

Obviously, many similar events are reported which, however, do not refer to the same event instance. Consider the next news item[2] that reports on another *maiden flight* of the Airbus A380 in 2008:

> Qantas A380 arrives in LA after maiden flight. October 21, 2008. The first flight of an Airbus A380 by Qantas touched down in Los Angeles today, inaugurating the Australian carrier's service using the world's biggest commercial jet.

This flight involves a similar participant, *Airbus A380* and a different location: *Los Angeles*. The

[2] http://www.theage.com.au/articles/2008/10/21/1224351190665.html

main and only distinguishing feature is the date that makes it a different event from the previous example. Hence, it will get a different instance representation:

```
:ev18Flight
rdfs:label "maiden flight", "flight";
gaf:denotedBy
  http://www.theage.com.au/articles/2008/10/21/
 1224351190665.html#char=33,46,
  http://www.theage.com.au/articles/2008/10/21/
 1224351190665.html#char=72,78;
sem:hasTime wikinews:20081021;
sem:hasActor dbp:Airbus_A380;
sem:hasPlace dbp:United_States, dbp:Los_Angeles.
```

The above model allows us to combine the information across different mentions within and across documents of the same language. However, the model is also agnostic of the language in which the information is expressed. Likewise, we can use the same model to represent the information from texts in different languages. In order to achieve that, the processing of text across these languages needs to be semantically interoperable. Since we defined events as combinations of actions (or relations and properties), actors, places and time, we also need to achieve an interoperable interpretation of these elements across languages. This will be discussed in the next section.

4 The interoperable interpretation of event and entity mentions across languages

Detecting mentions of events, entities and time expressions in text in several languages requires the combination of various Natural Language Processing modules. Our framework and system obtains interoperable representations of the interpretation of events, the entities that play a role within these events as well as the time expressions associated to the events. The output of the language specific pipelines is represented in the Natural Language Processing Format (NAF) (Fokkens et al., 2014). NAF is a standoff layered format for many different annotations, such as tokens, entities, semantic role (SR) structures and time expressions, where the elements in the layers point to spans of terms. In the next examples, we show in NAF entities, a SR structure with a predicate and several of its roles, and a time expression for an English text. Each of the elements has a span element pointing to term identifiers that mark words and phrases in the text. We see in the first structure that the expression *United States* is detected as a named entity of the type LOCATION and is disambiguated to a DBpedia entry.[3] The SR element consists of a predicate and roles, where the predicate has references to various FrameNet frames (Baker et al., 1998) and WordNet synsets (Fellbaum, 1998) along with the predicate information included in the Predicate Matrix (Lacalle et al., 2014). The roles have a PropBank role (Palmer et al., 2005) and possibly one or more FrameNet elements.[4] Finally, the time expression *Monday* has been normalised by reference to a particular date.

```
<entity id="e3" type="LOCATION">
  <!--United States-->
   <span><target id="t28"/><target id="t29"/></span>
  <externalReferences>
     <externalRef confidence="0.94"
        reference="http://dbpedia.org/resource/United_States
        reftype="en" resource="spotlight_v1"/>
  </externalReferences>
</entity>

<predicate id="pr5"> <!--flying-->
  <externalReferences>
    <externalRef reference="fn:Bringing", "fn:Motion",
    "fn:Operate_vehicle", "fn:Ride_vehicle",
    "fn:Self_motion", "wn:ili-30-01451842-v",
    <externalRef reference="wn:ili-30-01847845-v",
    "wn:ili-30-01840238-v", "wn:ili-30-02140965-v"/>
  </externalReferences>
  <span><target id="t44"/></span>
  <role id="rl14" semRole="A1">
    <!--One of the A380s-->
    <externalReferences>
      <externalRef reference="fn:Bringing@Theme",
      "fn:Motion@Theme", "fn:Operate_vehicle@Vehicle",
      "fn:Ride_vehicle@Theme", "fn:Self_motion@Self_mover"/>
    </externalReferences>
    <span><target head="yes" id="t39"/><target id="t40"/>
              <target id="t41"/><target id="t42"/></span>
   </role>
   <role id="rl15" semRole="AM-DIR"> <!--from Frankfurt-->
    <span><target head="yes" id="t45"/><target id="t46"/></span>
   </role>
   <role id="rl16" semRole="AM-DIR"> <!--to Chicago-->
    <span><target head="yes" id="t47"/><target id="t48"/></span>
    </role>
    <role id="rl17" semRole="AM-MNR">  <!--via New York-->
     <span><target head="yes" id="t49"/><target id="t50"/>
     <target id="t51"/></span>
    </role>
</predicate>

<timex3 id="tmx2" type="DATE" value="2007-03-19">
  <!--Monday-->
  <span><target id="w33"/></span>
</timex3>
```

The English text from the first example above has been translated to Spanish and Dutch. The translations are shown in the next examples:

> El A380 hace su vuelo inaugural a los EEUU. 19 de marzo del 2007. El Airbus A380, el mayor avión de pasajeros del mundo, aterrizó el lunes en los Estados Unidos de América, tras un vuelo de prueba. Uno de los A380s volará de Francfort a Chicago pasando por Nueva York; el avión llevará unas 500 personas.

[3] We show here only the top-ranked DBpedia URI. The software also adds links to alternative DBpedia URIs

[4] We abbreviated the externelRef representation here and in the following examples by combining attribute values and separate them by commas for reasons of space

> Eerste vlucht van A380 naar V.S. 19-Mar-07. De Airbus A380, het grootste passagiersvliegtuig ter wereld, maakte zich maandag op om na een testvlucht te landen in de Verenigde Staten van Amerika . Een van de A380-machines vliegt van Frankfurt naar Chicago via New York en vervoert ongeveer 500 mensen.

Processing the translations through the Spanish and Dutch pipelines results in the following NAF elements, which are interoperable with the English output:

```
<entity id="e2" type="ORGANIZATION"> <!--EEUU-->
<span><target id="t9"/> </span>
<externalReferences>
  <externalRef confidence="0.99"
     reference="http://es.dbpedia.org/resource/Estados_Unidos"
     reftype="es" resource="spotlight_v1">
  <externalRef confidence="0.99"
     reference="http://dbpedia.org/resource/United_States"
     reftype="en" resource="wikipedia-db-esEn"/>
  </externalRef>
</externalReferences>
</entity>


<predicate id="pr3"><!--volará-->
<externalReferences>
 <externalRef reference="fn:Bringing,"fn:Motion",
   "fn:Operate_vehicle", "fn:Ride_vehicle", "fn:Self_motion"/>
 <externalRef reference="wn:ili-30-01451842-v",
   "wn:ili-30-01847845-v", "wn:ili-30-01840238-v",
   "wn:ili-30-02140965-v"/>
</externalReferences>
<span> <target id="t49"/> </span>
<role id="rl8" semRole="arg0"> <!--Uno de los A380s-->
<externalReferences>
 <externalRef reference="fn:Bringing@Agent", "fn:Motion@Theme",
   "fn:Operate_vehicle@Driver", "fn:Ride_vehicle@Theme",
   "fn:Self_motion@Source", "fn:Bringing@Theme",
   "fn:Operate_vehicle@Vehicle", "fn:Self_motion@Self_mover",
   "fn:Ride_vehicle@Vehicle", "fn:Operate_vehicle@Source"/>
</externalReferences>
<span> <target head="yes" id="t45"/> <target id="t46"/>
         <target id="t47"/> <target id="t48"/> </span>
</role>
<role id="rl9" semRole="arg3"> <!--de Francfort-->
<span><target head="yes" id="t50"/><target id="t51"/></span>
</role>
<role id="rl10" semRole="arg4"> <!--a Chicago-->
<span> <target head="yes" id="t52"/><target id="t53"/></span>
</role>
<role id="rl11" semRole="argM"> <!--pasando por Nueva York-->
<span> <target head="yes" id="t54"/>
<target id="t55"/><target id="t56"/><target id="t57"/></span>
</role>
</predicate>


<timex3 id="tx3" type="DATE" value="2007-03-19"> <!--el lunes-->
<span><target id="w30"/><target id="w31"/></span>
</timex3>


<entity id="e2" type="LOCATION">
<!--Verenigde Staten van Amerika-->
<span> <target id="t_29"/><target id="t_30"/>
   <target id="t_31"/><target id="t_32"/></span>
<externalReferences>
  <externalRef confidence="1.0"
    reference="http://nl.dbpedia.org/resource/Verenigde_Staten"
    reftype="nl" resource="spotlight_v1">
 <externalRef confidence="1.0"
    reference="http://dbpedia.org/resource/United_States"
    reftype="en" resource="wikipedia-db-nlEn"/>
 </externalRef>
</externalReferences>
</entity>


<predicate id="pr17"> <!--vliegt-->
<externalReferences>
        <externalRef confidence="0.95" reference="fn:Motion",
        "fn:Ride_vehicle", "fn:Self_motion",
        "fn:Operate_vehicle", "fn:Bringing"/>
        <externalRef reference="wn:ili-30-01451842-v"/>
</externalReferences>
<span><target id="t_38"/></span>
<role id="r26" semRole="AM-DIR"> <!--naar Chicago-->
 <span><target head="yes" id="t_41"/><target id="t_42"/></span>
</role>
<role id="r28" semRole="AM-DIR"> <!--via New York-->
 <span><target head="yes" id="t_43"/> <target id="t_44"/>
  <target id="t_45"/></span>
</role>
<role id="r54" semRole="A3"> <!--van Frankfurt-->
 <span><target head="yes" id="t_39"/><target id="t_40"/> </span>
</role>
<role id="r77" semRole="A0"> <!--Een van de A380-machines-->
<externalReferences>
 <externalRef reference="fn:Motion@Theme",
    "fn:Ride_vehicle@Theme", "fn:Ride_vehicle@Vehicle",
    "fn:Self_motion@Source", "fn:Operate_vehicle@Driver",
    "fn:Bringing@Agent"/>
</externalReferences>
 <span><target head="yes" id="t_34"/><target id="t_35"/>
  <target id="t_36"/><target id="t_37"/></span>
</role>
</predicate>

    <timex3 id="tmx5" type="DATE" value="2007-03-19">
      <!--maandag-->
      <span> <target id="w20"/> </span>
    </timex3>
```

First of all, note that the entity in Spanish and Dutch has been linked to the language-specific DBpedia URI but also to the cross-lingual and equivalent URI in English. In the SR layer, we see that predicates in Spanish and Dutch are matched with FrameNet frames and Wordnet synsets just as for the English SR structure. We can thus derive a similar SR structure across the three languages in the same way as we can map the DBpedia entity referenced to by the named entity expressions.[5] Finally, we can see that the time expressions detected have been normalised in the same way.

A similar output is generated for the all 120 news articles in the Wikinews corpus across different documents and languages.[6] In the next section, we explain how this output is converted into a unified RDF-SEM structure.

5 Event coreference across mentions

The NAF representations explained in the previous sections represent the cross-lingual and cross-document interoperable interpretation of entity, predicate and time mentions in text. In this section, we explain how we convert them to an RDF format using the SEM/GAF model. As explained in section

[5]Note that the English and Spanish predicate is aligned to multiple synsets, whereas the Dutch predicate only got a single synset assigned. This difference is the result of the different ways in which the SR modules have been implemented.

[6]On-line demos of the pipelines are available at `http://www.newsreader-project.eu/results/demos/`

3, different mentions of the same instance are represented only once. For entities and time expressions this is automatically achieved by the normalisation to DBpedia URIs and dates. When converting each mention of an entity or time expression to RDF, we create an URI on the basis of its normalised value. Within the RDF model, these data structures are automatically merged and the references to the mentions are combined, both for cross-document references and the cross-language references.

Obviously, for events this is more difficult. We follow an approach that takes the compositionally of events as a starting point (Quine, 1985). The compositionality principle dictates that events are not just defined by the action but also by the time, place and participants. For that, we use an algorithm that compares events for all these properties (Cybulska and Vossen, 2015). Currently, we compare first the events on the basis of the lemma of the predicates, the FrameNet frames and the Wordnet synsets.[7] From a cross-lingual perspective, it only makes sense to compare events according to language-neutral classes in FrameNet and WordNet.

The second important element is the time-reference. We relate all event mentions to time-expressions in the text, where we first consider the references in the same sentence, next the surrounding sentences (2 before, 1 after the current one) and finally the publication date of the news article. We then only compare events anchored to the same temporal reference.

Finally, note that the entity layer and the role layer are only indirectly aligned through their span references. Since the layers are generated by different software modules, we need to determine the expression in a role that is attributed to an entity in the entity layer. We match the output of the layers by intersecting the spans by calculating the Dice coefficient of the content words in each entity mention with the role mention. If the overlap is more than 75%, we assign the role to the entity. To be able to represent matching events through a shared URI across languages, we create an artificial URI from the set of WordNet synsets that were associated with the predicates in the SR from which they are derived. If predicates from different languages have been matched with intersecting synsets, we consider the actions to be similar. Note that this can be loosened to other similarity measures. In addition to event similarity, time and participants need to match in the same way as described for the cross-document case described before.

Below, we show the result of applying our cross-lingual and cross-document event extraction module to the Airbus A380 article in the three languages. Our current program creates two *flying* events from the first sentences. The first event is represented by a series of five WordNet synsets all related to *flying*. We see a series of RDF subclass relations for this event to various FrameNet frames. We also see labels in Spanish *volar*, English *fly* and Dutch: *verlopen* and *vliegen*.[8] Next, we see mentions from all three language texts and finally the aggregated relations. Some of these are detected as places and some as actors. Furthermore, we see some entities not matched to DBpedia for various reasons, such as *Chicago_via_New_York* and *Los_Angeles_LAX* coming from the Dutch processing. We can also observe that some places are detected as actors in the SR, with roles such as A3 or A4 instead of AM-DIR or AM-LOC. The same event was detected across the three languages and the relations have been merged in a single representation. The basis for the final merging is the fact that the events share WordNet references, all of them bound to the same point in time and also share at least one actor and place.

```
wn:ili-30-01451842-v;ili-30-01847845-v;ili-30-01840238-v;
ili-30-02140965-v;ili-30-01941093-v
   a  sem:Event, fn:Bringing, fn:Motion, fn:Operate_vehicle,
      fn:Ride_vehicle, fn:Self_motion;
   rdfs:label "volar", "fly", "verlopen", "vliegen" ;
   gaf:denotedBy
          wikinews:english_mention#char=202,208>,
          wikinews:english_mention##char=577,580>,
          wikinews:dutch_mention##char=1034,1042>,
          wikinews:dutch_mention#char=643,650>,
          wikinews:dutch_mention#char=499,505>,
          wikinews:dutch_mention#char=224,230>,
          wikinews:spanish_mention#char=218,224>,
          wikinews:spanish_mention#char=577,583> ;
   sem:hasTime nwrtime:20070391;
   sem:hasPlace
          dbp:Frankfurt_Airport, dbp:Chicago ,
          dbp:Los_Angeles_International_Airport,
          nwr:airbus/entities/Chicago_via_New_York;
   sem:hasActor
          dbp:Airbus_A380, nwr:airbus/entities/Los_Angeles_LAX ,
          dbp:Frankfurt,  nwr:airbus/entities/A380-machines.
```

The English pipeline generated an additional *flying* event that was not matched. Although there is a

[7] In fact, the Predicate Matrix provides many other mappings that could be used, such as PropBank, NomBank, VerbNet or SUMO

[8] *verlopen* is the result of an error by the word-sense disambiguation

match for the WordNet references and the time anchoring is the same, none of the actors and places match with the previous event.

```
wn:ili-30-01451842-v;ili-30-01847845-v;ili-30-01840238-v;
ili-30-02140965-v
 a sem:Event, fn:Bringing, fn:Motion, fn:Operate_vehicle,
    fn:Ride_vehicle, fn:Self_motion;
 rdfs:label "flight" ;
 gaf:denotedBy
          wikinews:english_mention##char=19,25,
            wikinews:english_mention##char=174,180,
            wikinews:english_mention##char=566,572;
 sem:hasTime nwrtime:20070391;
 sem:hasActor dbp:United_States_dollar, dbp:Qantas .
```

The complete system for processing text in English, Spanish and Dutch, as well the cross-document and cross-language coreference are available under an open source license and accessible through GitHub.[9] In the next section, we provide an initial evaluation of the cross-lingual processing.

6 Evaluation on the cross-lingual Wiki news corpus

We created an evaluation corpus from English Wikinews articles. We selected four different topics *Airbus*, *Apple*, *GM-Chrysler-Ford* and the *stock market*. For each topic, we selected 30 articles spread over a period of five years. The English corpus was manually annotated for various layers, including entities, events, time-expressions, event relations, and coreference relations. We translated the corpora also to Spanish and Dutch, where the sentences have been aligned.[10] The cross-lingual corpora allow for two types of evaluation: 1) we can evaluate the quality of the NLP modules in each language on each corpus, 2) we can apply the RDF-SEM extraction to the NAF output of each corpus independently and compare these structures. Currently, we report on the second evaluation. In the near future, we also plan to evaluate against the annotations in each language and across languages.

Since the corpora are manually translated, we expect that the same content is expressed in the three languages. Thus, if our cross-lingual NLP processing is fully interoperable and generates the same quality across the languages, we expect to obtain exactly the same events across the different languages. As such the translated corpus provides an excellent benchmark dataset for evaluating event extraction across languages. For the evaluation, we applied the pipelines for English, Spanish and Dutch to all 120 articles in each language. Next, we extracted the RDF representations from the NAF files in each topic. Since the final RDF representation is agnostic with respect to its textual realisation in the different languages, we can directly compare the extracted representations. In Table 1, we show the results averaged over the four different topics, where we compare the output from the Spanish and Dutch systems to the English output as a reference.[11]

	English		Spanish				Dutch			
	I	M	I	M	O	C	I	M	O	C
entities	318	4101	204	2209	1469	34.88	187	1313	1030	24.46
events	590	2402	323	1036	610	26.04	651	1545	281	11.88
triples	665	866	220	276	60	7.07	619	689	25	2.93

Table 1: Cross-lingual coverage of Spanish and Dutch RDF data compared to English.

Table 1 provides figures for the DBpedia entities, the events represented as WordNet synsets and triples where entities are related to the events either as actors or as places. For each language, we present the number of instances (*I*, unique URIs in the data) and the number of mentions (*M*) in triples. For Spanish and Dutch, we provide the overlap (*O*) and the micro-averaged coverage (*C*) of the English mentions. For entities, we can see that the mentions detected for Spanish is 34.88% of the English ones, while for Dutch this is 24.46%. We also see that detecting events and triples (which are combinations of events, entities and a SEM relation) is more difficult. Spanish coverage of the English events is 26.04% for events and only 7.07% coverage for full triples. In general, the Dutch system is performing less compared to Spanish. Obvious explanations for this behaviour are the different performance of the Spanish and Dutch pipelines, and the different coverage of the resources (both DBpedias and wordnets). As expected, the drop for the events and triples is bigger compared to entities. Detecting events correctly is more complex and challenging than disambiguating DBpedia references. Also recall that the comparison of events and triples is based on WordNet equivalences.

[9] http://github.com/newsreader

[10] Currently, the translated corpora is being annotated according to similar guidelines and cross-document coreference relations are added.

[11] Note that output that does not match with English is not necessarily incorrect. We are only measuring the coverage of one language with respect to the English data.

	English	Spanish	Dutch
Boeing	156	183	98
Airbus	107	81	37
European_Union	83	17	29
Indonesia	57	13	0
France	56	1	1
Boeing_Commercial_Airplanes	50	0	3
United_States_dollar	39	0	2
Government_Accountability_Office	36	0	0
Aer_Lingus	33	16	9
United_States_Air_Force	32	21	7
Boeing_747	30	0	0
Singapore	25	0	7
Airbus_A320_family	22	3	3
Toulouse	17	0	1
Northrop_Grumman	15	1	0
United_States_Armed_Forces	15	0	0
United_Kingdom	14	2	0
EADS	13	3	0
Sydney_Airport	12	0	0
United_States	11	7	23

Table 2: Entities most frequent in English data

We also inspected the results for the Airbus corpus by looking at the entities and events that are most frequently mentioned in the English output. Table 2 shows the top-frequent entities with the corresponding counts for Spanish and Dutch. We inspected obvious entities such as *Indonesia*, *France* and *Toulouse*. It turns out that the NLP modules did detect these entities: *Indonesia* (8 Spanish and 9 Dutch mentions), *France* (13 Spanish and 11 Dutch mentions), *Toulouse* (6 Spanish and 4 Dutch mentions) but that they were not linked to events and therefore not represented. This points to a difference and probably lower coverage of the semantic role module to connect entities to events in a uniform way. Another case is represented by *United_States*, *United_States_Air_Force(s)*, and *United_States_dollar*. The latter have high frequencies in English but none in Spanish and Dutch, while the former has even higher frequencies in Dutch. In this case, the English system makes a systematic mistake by not always resolving expressions such as *US* to the right URI but to the dollar, while the other systems do not make this mistake because their expressions are very distinct: *Estados Unidos de América* and *de Verenigde Staten van Amerika*. A final type of difference is illustrated by *Boeing* versus *Boeing_747*. Where the English module tends to prefer more specific entities, the other fall back to the more generic ones. Such metonymic mismatches are less of a problem.

Regarding events, the Dutch events are often linked to other meanings in WordNet that may also apply (e.g. *fly* 72 English, 34 Spanish and 8 Dutch but also *buy* 10 English, 17 Spanish and 16 Dutch). Furthermore whereas the English and Spanish module often provide more than one synset, the Dutch system only gives one, lowering the chances to intersect. In a future version, sets of closely related synsets will be generated for Dutch as well to solve the fine-grained sense matching problem. Another option is to fall back on more general event classes in the PredicateMatrix (e.g. VerbNet, FrameNet, etc.). Most of the other differences relate to small differences acorss systems and poor coverage of semantic resources in Spanish and Dutch.

7 Conclusions

We described a system for the cross-document and cross-lingual event and entity extraction that is unique in its kind. We use GAF to make a clear distinction between mentions and instances, where mentions of events and entities are interpreted according to an interoperable RDF framework that uses URIs, WordNet and FrameNet concepts, normalised time expressions and normalised relations between entities and events. We developed NLP pipelines in English, Spanish and Dutch that process text according to the shared framework. In addition, we developed software to convert the output of the NLP modules to the RDF representation of instances. We showed that we can represent the accumulated information from different articles and even across languages. We described the first evaluation results for our system.

The current system leaves room for improvement. The matching of entities across mentions and languages can be harmonised and the matching of events through WordNet concepts is not precise enough. In many cases, the background resources (DBpedia in different languages and wordnets in different languages) lack the proper mapping. Finally, the quality of the SR module needs to be improved to capture more expressions and harmonise the interpretations of these expressions. Nevertheless, the current work forms an excellent basis to flesh out these problems without the need to change the fundamental cross-lingual architecture. When the translated corpora are fully annotated, we will be able to further benchmark the NLP processing in the different languages and compare the results in terms of precision and recall independently of English.

Acknowledgements

We thank the anonymous reviewers for the feedback. This work was supported by the European Union's 7th Framework Programme via the News-Reader (ICT-316404) project and by the SKATER Spanish project (TIN2012-38584-C06-02) with European Regional Development Fund support.

References

Collin F. Baker, Charles J. Fillmore, and John B. Lowe. 1998. The Berkeley FrameNet project. In *Proceedings of COLING-ACL'98*, pages 86–90, Montreal, Canada.

Cosmin Adrian Bejan and Sanda Harabagiu. 2010. Unsupervised event coreference resolution with rich linguistic features. In *Proceedings of the ACL'2010*, Uppsala, Sweden.

Steve Cassidy. 2010. An RDF realisation of LAF in the DADA annotation server. In *Proceedings of ISA-5*, Hong Kong.

Christian Chiarcos, Sebastian Nordhoff, and Sebastian Hellmann. 2012. *Linked Data in Linguistics. Representing and Connecting Language Data and Language Metadata*. Springer, Heidelberg.

Christian Chiarcos. 2008. An ontology of linguistic annotations. *LDV Forum*, 23(1):1–16.

Agata Cybulska and Piek Vossen. 2015. "Bag of Events" Approach to Event Coreference Resolution. Supervised Classification of Event Templates. In *International Journal of Computational Linguistics and Applications (IJCLA)*. (to appear).

Christiane Fellbaum, editor. 1998. *WordNet: An Electronic Lexical Database*. Cambridge, MA: MIT Press.

David Ferrucci and Adam Lally. 2004. UIMA: an architectural approach to unstructured information processing in the corporate research environment. *Natural Language Engineering*, 10(3-4):327–348.

Antske Fokkens, Marieke van Erp, Piek Vossen, Sara Tonelli, Willem Robert van Hage, Luciano Serafini, Rachele Sprugnoli, and Jesper Hoeksema. 2013. GAF: A grounded annotation framework for events. In *Proceedings of the first Workshop on Events: Definition, Dectection, Coreference and Representation*, Atlanta, USA.

Antske Fokkens, Aitor Soroa, Zuhaitz Beloki, Niels Ockeloen, German Rigau, Willem Robert van Hage, and Piek Vossen. 2014. NAF and GAF: Linking linguistic annotations. In *Proceedings 10th Joint ISO-ACL SIGSEM Workshop on Interoperable Semantic Annotation*, pages 9–16.

Sebastian Hellmann, Jens Lehmann, Sören Auer, and Martin Brümmer. 2013. Integrating NLP using Linked Data. In *Proceedings of the ISWC'2013*.

Nancy Ide, Laurent Romary, and Eric Villemonte de La Clergerie. 2003. International standard for a linguistic annotation framework. In *Proceedings of the HLT-NAACL 2003 Workshop on Software Engineering and Architecture of Language Technology Systems (SEALTS)*. Association for Computational Linguistics.

Maddalen Lopez De Lacalle, Egoitz Laparra, and German Rigau. 2014. Predicate matrix: extending semlink through wordnet mappings. In *Proceedings of LREC'2014*, pages 26–31, Reykjavik, Iceland.

Heeyoung Lee, Marta Recasens, Angel Chang, Mihai Surdeanu, and Dan Jurafsky. 2012. Joint entity and event coreference resolution across documents. In *Proceedings of EMNLP-CoNLL'2012*.

Martha Palmer, Dan Gildea, and Paul Kingsbury. 2005. The proposition bank: A corpus annotated with semantic roles. *Computational Linguistics*, 31(1).

Sameer Pradhan, Eduard Hovy, Mitchell Marcus, Martha Palmer, Lance Ramshaw, and Ralph Weischedel. 2007. Ontonotes: A unified relational semantic representation. *International Journal of Semantic Computing*, 1(4):405–419.

Sameer Pradhan, Lance Ramshaw, Mitchell Marcus, Martha Palmer, Ralph Weischedel, and Nianwen Xue. 2011. Conll-2011 shared task: Modeling unrestricted coreference in ontonotes. In *Proceedings of CoNLL'2011*, pages 1–27.

Valentina Presutti, Francesco Draicchio, and Aldo Gangemi. 2012. Knowledge extraction based on discourse representation theory and linguistic frames. In *Knowledge Engineering and Knowledge Management*, pages 114–129. Springer.

Willard V. Quine. 1985. Events and reification. In *Actions and Events: Perspectives on the Philosophy of Davidson*, pages 162–171. Blackwell.

Willem Robert van Hage, Véronique Malaisé, Roxane Segers, Laura Hollink, and Guus Schreiber. 2011. Design and use of the Simple Event Model (SEM). *Journal of Web Semantics*, 9(2):128–136.

Modeling and Characterizing Social Media Topics Using the Gamma Distribution

Connie Yee, Nathan Keane, Liang Zhou
Text Analytics and Machine Learning
Thomson Reuters
New York, NY 10036, USA
{connie.yee,nathan.keane,l.zhou}@thomsonreuters.com

Abstract

We present a novel technique to identify emerging or important topics mentioned on social media. A sudden increase in related posts can indicate an occurrence of an external event. Assuming that the sequence of posts is a homogeneous Poisson process, this sudden change can be modeled using the Gamma distribution. Our Gamma curve fitter is used to return a set of emerging topics. We demonstrate our algorithm on Twitter data and evaluate empirically using the Reuters News Archive and manual inspection. Our experimental results show that our algorithm provides a good picture of the emerging topics discussed on Twitter.

1 Introduction

Over the past decade, microblogging sites, such as Twitter, have emerged as an important source of real-time news updates, with each microblogger acting as an information source. In contrast with news writing and reporting, microbloggers post content that is brief and uses colloquial language.

Some posts are reactions to events that have already broken out to the public. For content that originated in standard media outlets, such as newswire, the social medium can act as a filter and amplifier (Asur et al., 2011). Other posts serve as originators of events. For example, Twitter has been observed to lead newswire in reporting on sporting events and natural disasters (Petrovic et al., 2013). For sporting events, such as the FIFA World Cup, millions of users turn to microblogs to comment on what they just witnessed at a stadium or watched on television.

We are interested in discovering events related to both content from news outlets and content that originates on social media. An event occurrence can be detected by the volume and sudden change in volume of posts. After examining the distributions of the volumes of topics in Twitter, we observe two main categories of topics:

- Long-lasting topics that Twitter users frequently discuss in their daily lives, such as the foods they ate and the activities they are currently doing
- Emerging topics[1], or topics of importance to the general public, such as sporting events and natural disasters

Long-lasting topics tend to have a uniform distribution of volume over time, while emerging topics usually contain spikes in volume.

In this paper, we aim to detect the emerging topics by modeling a topic's frequency distribution with the Gamma distribution. It is a suitable function for modeling if we assume that the posts responding to an event arrive as a homogeneous Poisson process.

We begin with an initial set of event candidates by taking a topic modeling approach and assume that the words in a topic cluster represent one event. The event candidates are the inputs to the curve fitting algorithm, which returns the events that have valid model parameter values. We consider the outputs of our algorithm to be the emerging topics.

This paper is organized as follows: Section 2 introduces related work in event detection in Twitter.

[1] We view an emerging topic as an event so we use the words "topic" and "event" interchangeably in this paper.

Proceedings of the 3rd Workshop on EVENTS at the NAACL-HLT 2015, pages 117–122,
Denver, Colorado, June 4, 2015.

Section 3 explains our modeling algorithm and the theory behind it. Section 4 reports our experimental results, which are evaluated in Section 5. We conclude and discuss future work in Section 6.

2 Related Work

Event detection in Twitter has been well-researched in recent years. Some focus on a keyword-based approach, such as through hashtags or term n-grams, to track trends. Shamma et al. (2011) investigated using a normalized term frequency to identify peaky and persistent topics. A challenge with a bursty term analysis is the difficulty in capturing an event with just a single string of words. Furthermore, the ability to identify an event requires that at least one term has a burst of relative frequency.

Other research has leveraged topic models as a means of learning clusters of events that are associated with an event. Topic models express a distribution over terms and thus are more descriptive than single keywords. Of the research that is based on topic modeling, much has been in the form of retrospective event detection models (Ramage et al., 2010). Recently, more work has been performed in the area of on-line processing of documents as they arrive (Lau et al., 2012), temporal topic models (Hong et al., 2011), and user-temporal mixture models (Yin et al., 2013).

There has been some prior work to incorporate the above-mentioned types of event detection methods with the properties of the topics or events. Zubiaga et al. (2014) aimed to classify trending topics by running a classifier using 15 features that consider the way a topic spreads.

Much of the focus of unsupervised methods has been on particular types of tweets or terms. Yang and Leskovec (2011) examined patterns of temporal behavior for hashtags. They presented the K-spectral centroid clustering algorithm to determine six classes of common temporal patterns that tweets containing hashtags follow. Further research by (Matsubara et al., 2012) proposed a general model for the rise and fall patterns of influence propagation. Zhao et al. (2012) studied a global bursty pattern derived from multiple types of tweets (posts, retweets, URL-embedded tweets) and modeled the smoothness of the state context. Their model was solely tested on keywords.

Shapes are a concise way of describing temporal variable behaviors. Each shape can be assessed by attributes, such as the rate a spike increases (Gregory and Shneiderman, 2012). There is evidence in data from the digital web site `digg.com` that the novelty of a topic determines how it decays over time (Wu and Huberman, 2007). Asur et al. (2011) observed that the number of tweets across trending topics can be characterized by a log-normal distribution and a linear decay. The trending topics were provided by the Twitter Search API and mostly consisted of two to three word expressions.

3 Modeling Topic Frequency Distributions

3.1 Topic Modeling and Segment Selection

This section describes how we form our initial set of event candidates and then select the segment of the frequency distribution for the next step of our algorithm.

Topics can be extracted from textual corpora through probabilistic topic models. Latent Dirichlet Allocation (LDA) is a widely adopted generative model for topic modeling (Blei et al., 2003). For each document, there is a multinomial distribution over topics. For each topic, there is another multinomial distribution over words. A popular algorithm for LDA model parameter estimation and inference is Gibbs sampling (Griffiths and Steyvers, 2004).

We used an LDA algorithm, similar to the MALLET topic model package (McCallum, 2002), with an efficient Gibbs sampling to identify 50 topics per day as event candidates. Each tweet was treated as one document. The resulting topics were then analyzed as follows:

1. Count the number of tweets that contain at least 30% of the topic in 15-minute intervals.

2. Determine the most relevant portion of the time series to model. Identify the highest peak and the points immediately preceding and following it, whose volumes are at least x% of the peak volume. We experimented with x ranging from 10–90% in increments of 10% and selected $x = 30$ based on manual inspection.

3.2 Modeling Tweet Frequency

In this section, we explain how we model the number of tweets regarding a particular event.

We envisage the arrival of tweets as a Poisson process. A Poisson process is a widely-used stochastic process for modeling the times at which arrivals enter a system. The sequence of interarrival times $X_1, X_2, ...$ in the Poisson process is a sequence of independent and identically distributed (IID) random variables, each having a probability density of an exponential, $f_X(x) = \lambda e^{-\lambda x}$, for some rate $\lambda > 0$ and $x > 0$. A unique property of the Poisson process is the memoryless quality. This means that the distribution of the remaining arrivals is the same as the original arrival time distribution, i.e. the remaining arrival time has no "memory" of previous arrivals.

Using the Poisson distribution, we model a poster tweeting after an event as an IID random variable with an exponential density function $f_X(x)$. Assuming a homogeneous Poisson process, where the posting rate λ for this event is constant, a second poster independently tweeting after the same event also has an exponential density function $f_X(x)$.

The interarrival times of tweets after an event then become the sum of n IID random variables, each with the density function $f_X(x) = \lambda e^{-\lambda x}$. Given that the density of the sum of two independent random variables can be found by convolving their densities, the convolution of multiple exponential distributions is called the Gamma density (Akkouchi, 2005). Thus, the time of the nth post, T_n, follows a Gamma distribution.

If we let N_t be the number of posts in time interval $[0, t]$, it can be shown that $\{N_t \geq n\}$ and $\{T_n \leq t\}$ represent the same event. Using this duality, we can fix the time interval and model the frequencies of the tweets.

3.3 Curve Fitting and Parameter Estimation

The Gamma distribution has three different types, one of which is the two-parameter gamma distribution, given by (1).

$$f(x; \alpha, \beta) = \frac{1}{\Gamma(\alpha)\beta^{\alpha}} x^{\alpha-1} e^{-x/\beta}, \quad 0 < x < \infty; \alpha, \beta > 0 \tag{1}$$

The parameter α is known as the shape parameter, since it most influences the peakedness of the distribution, while the parameter β is called the scale parameter, which mostly influences the spread of the distribution.

Since there is no closed-form solution for the Gamma distribution, we used a heuristic search method to estimate the parameters of the distribution. A commonly used nonlinear optimization technique called the Nelder-Mead simplex algorithm (Lagarias et al., 1998) was employed for this purpose.

To avoid the need to normalize the time series, we fit the time series segments to the three-parameter probability density function. It can be obtained from (1) by adding a scaling factor A_0 and replacing x by $x - \mu$, where μ is the location parameter, as in (2).

$$f(x; \alpha, \beta, \mu) = \frac{A_0}{\Gamma(\alpha)\beta^{\alpha}} (x - \mu)^{\alpha-1} e^{-(x-\mu)/\beta}, \quad x \geq \mu; \alpha, \beta > 0 \tag{2}$$

The estimated values for α and β, as well as the sum of squared errors, or χ^2, were further analyzed. A threshold on A_0 can be optionally set so that only tweets that meet a minimum volume level are considered.

4 Experimental Results

Our experiments were conducted in a retrospective fashion, whereby we assumed the full document collection was given as input.

4.1 Data Cleaning and Topic Modeling

First, we gathered approximately 127 million tweets spanning 2014-06-14 0:00 GMT to 2014-06-27 11:59 GMT from Twitter Decahose, which is a feed of 10% of all tweets. We then conducted preprocessing by removing stopwords, URLs, and non-ASCII characters.

Following the data cleaning, we ran LDA on each of the 14 days of tweets to obtain 700 topics. Out of the 700 raw topics, we achieved convergence with defined χ^2 for 36 topics. Table 1 lists four topics that were randomly selected for further examination.

Date	Topic	Top Words
2014-06-14	Stanley Cup	game kings cup win hockey
2014-06-15	Wonder Goal	goal messi argentina france #worldcup
2014-06-19	Biting	england rooney suarez goal uruguay
2014-06-27	Player Contract	money pay million shaw united

Table 1: Selected topics.

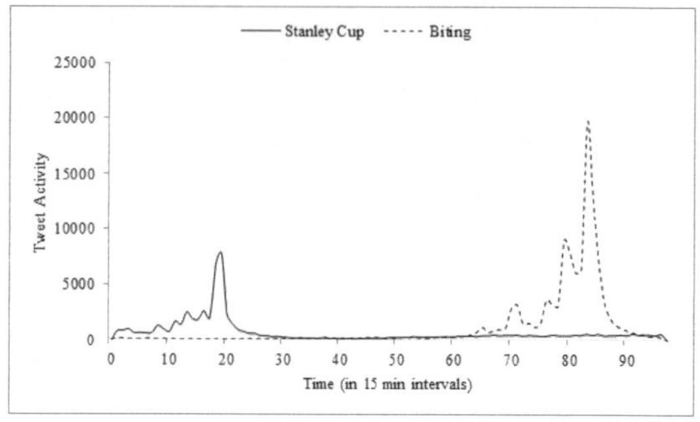

Figure 2: Distributions of two topics with $\beta = 0.08$ and different αs.

4.2 Curve Fitting

The frequency distribution of the "Stanley Cup" topic over a 24-hour window is shown in Fig. 1. The curve segment between the two labeled points served as the input to the curve fitter, which estimated α and β to be 48.55 and 0.08, respectively.

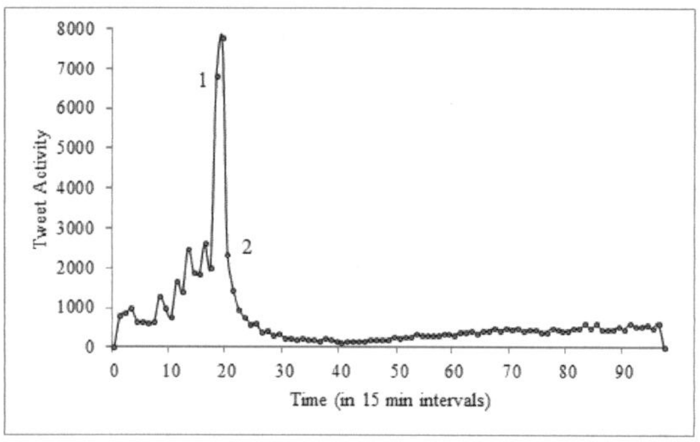

Figure 1: Frequency distribution of the "Stanley Cup" topic.

To better understand these estimated parameter values, we can compare it to another topic with the same β value. Fig. 2 shows the distributions of the "Stanley Cup" (solid line) and the "Biting" (dotted line) topics. The "Biting" topic, which refers to a shocking biting incident during the World Cup, has a sharper peak, thereby translating to a higher α value of 129.25. On the other hand, the "Stanley Cup" topic denotes an expected or planned event whose outcome happened to be predictable.

We can analyze the effect of the β parameter by keeping α constant. Fig. 3 shows two topics with the same α value. The solid line represents the "Player Contract" topic, while the dotted line is the "Wonder Goal" topic. The latter topic refers to one of the greatest soccer goals made by a player. While this event is impressive enough to make it on social media, it appears to dissipate quickly and is likely soon replaced by the next great play in the World Cup. Its α value is a mere 1.69. In contrast, the "Player Contract" topic with α of 8.03 is discussed over the course of ten hours, as the signing of a well-known player to a new team can have great implications for the coming season.

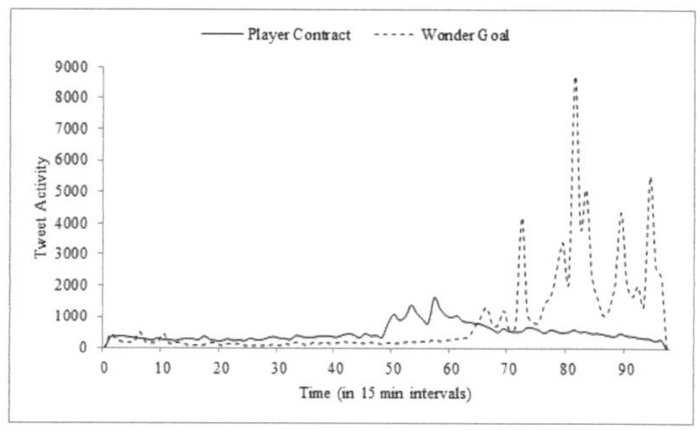

Figure 3: Distributions of two topics with $\alpha = 1.74$ and different βs.

5 Evaluation

We evaluated empirically all the events discovered from the curve fitting algorithm. For purposes of evaluation, we considered an event to be an actual event if it falls in one of two categories:

- *news*, if it reached the standard media outlets
- *social*, if it was solely discussed on social media

By determining the number of news and social events, and dividing it by the total number of events discovered, we calculated precision, as defined in (3). Our algorithm achieved 77.8% precision.

$$Precision = \frac{|news| + |social|}{total} \quad (3)$$

5.1 News Events

We leveraged the news domain to identify news events. Traditional news media, such as Reuters, typically span a wide range of categories, from fashion to finance. Although its distribution over the categories differs from that in Twitter, it is safe to assume that if an event is mentioned in newswire, it carries some importance.

We performed a query-based search in the Reuters News Archive to collect documents written within one day of the event date. By querying stories both before and after the event, we analyzed events that originated either in newswire or on social media. A news story was counted if it contained at least five of the top ten words. 15 of the 36 topics had at least one corresponding story in Reuters News, and concentrated on major sporting events.

5.2 Social Events

There are events that fail to reach the standard media outlets but are significant in the social media context. We inspected the remaining 21 topics which lacked a corresponding news story and categorized them into three main areas, as shown in Table 2.

Entertainment	#shawntotop shawn buy follow
	follow sos love luke
Daily Life	happy birthday day love hope
	day happy fathers dad
Twitter Related	tweet cool funny haha post
	follow ya follback yo click

Table 2: Examples of events not mentioned in newswire.

After examining some representative tweets, we concluded that the "Entertainment" events were largely based on the Twitter users' interests, such as a new music album release. They were labeled as social events. The "Daily Life" and "Twitter Related" topics are examples of long-lasting topics that do not carry much news nor social significance.

6 Conclusion and Future Work

Our novel technique based on the Gamma distribution offers a useful starting point for using the shapes of the frequencies to determine whether a topic is an emerging topic. Although some long-lasting topics were also detected, the algorithm is able to provide a good picture of the news and social events discussed on social media. Some advantages of our method are that it is unsupervised and independent of how the initial set of event candidates are formed, which means that LDA can be replaced with a different topic model.

While we made simplifications and assumptions in our algorithm, there are several directions for future research. One area is to relax the assumption of modeling the sequence of posts as a homogeneous Poisson process. Since the posting rate λ for an event likely changes over time, we can divide the entire sequence into smaller segments and model each separately. In addition, removing cyclical or seasonal topics before curve fitting may help eliminate false positives.

References

Mohamed Akkouchi. 2005. On the convolution of exponential distributions. *Soochow Journal of Mathematics*, 31(2):205-211.

Sitaram Asur, Bernardo A. Huberman, Gabor Szabo, and Chunyan Wang. 2011. Trends in social media: persistence and decay. In *Proceedings of the 5th International AAAI conference on Weblogs and Social Media*.

David M. Blei, Andrew Y. Ng, and Michael I. Jordan. 2003. Latent dirichlet allocation. *The Journal of Machine Learning Research*, 3:993–1022.

Machon B. Gregory and Ben Shneiderman. 2012. Shape identification in temporal data sets. In *Expanding the Frontiers of Visual Analytics and Visualization*, pages 305–321. Springer London.

Thomas L. Griffiths and Mark Steyvers. 2004. Finding scientific topics. In *Proceedings of the National Academy of Science*, 101: 5228-5235.

Liangjie Hong, Dawei Yin, Jian Guo, and Brian D. Davison. 2011. Tracking trends: incorporating term volume into temporal topic models. In *Proceedings of the 17th ACM SIGKDD International Conference on Knowledge Discovery and Data Mining*, pages 484–492.

Jeffrey C. Lagarias, James A. Reeds, Margaret H. Wright, and Paul E. Wright. 1998. Convergence properties of the Nelder–Mead simplex method in low dimensions. *SIAM Journal on optimization*, 9(1):112–147.

JeyHan Lau, Nigel Collier, and Timothy Baldwin. 2012. On–line trend analysis with topic models: #twitter trends detection topic model online. In *Proceedings of COLING 2012*, pages 1519–1534.

Yasuko Matsubara, Yasushi Sakurai, B. Aditya Prakash, Lei Li, and Christos Faloutsos. 2012. Rise and fall patterns of information diffusion: model and implications. In *Proceedings of the 18th ACM SIGKDD International Conference on Knowledge Discovery and Data Mining*, pages 6–14. ACM.

Andrew K. McCallum. 2002. MALLET: A machine learning for language toolkit. `http://mallet.cs.umass.edu`.

Sasa Petrovic, Miles Osborne, Richard McCreadie, Craig Macdonald, Iadh Ounis, and Luke Shrimpton. 2013. Can Twitter replace Newswire for breaking news? In *Proceedings of the 7th International AAAI Conference on Weblogs and Social Media*.

Daniel Ramage, Susan Dumais, and Dan Liebling. 2010. Characterizing microblogs with topic models. In *Proceedings of the Fourth International AAAI Conference on Weblogs and Social Media*, pages 130–137.

Daniel M. Romero, Wojciech Galuba, Sitaram Asur, and Bernardo A. Huberman. 2011. Influence and passivity in social media. In *Machine Learning and Knowledge Discovery in Databases*, pages 18–33. Springer Berlin Heidelberg.

David A. Shamma, Lyndon Kennedy, Elizabeth F. Churchill. 2011. Peaks and persistence: modeling the shape of microblog conversations. In *Proceedings of the ACM 2011 Conference on Computer Supported Cooperative Work*, pages 355–358. ACM.

Fang Wu and Bernardo A. Huberman. 2007. Novelty and collective attention. *Proceedings of the National Academy of Sciences*, 104(45):17599–17601.

Jaewon Yang and Jure Leskovec. 2011. Patterns of temporal variation in online media. In *Proceedings of the Fourth ACM International Conference on Web Search and Data Mining*, pages 177–186. ACM.

Hongzhi Yin, Bin Cui, Hua Lu, Yuxin Huang, and Junjie Yao. 2013. A unified model for stable and temporal topic detection from social media data. In *Data Engineering (ICDE)*, pages 661–672. IEEE.

Wayne X. Zhao, Baihan Shu, Jing Jiang, Yang Song, Hongfei Yan, and Xiaoming Li. 2012. Identifying event–related bursts via social media activities. In *Proceedings of the 2012 Joint Conference on Empirical Methods in Natural Language Processing and Computational Natural Language Learning*, pages 1466–1477. Association for Computational Linguistics.

Arkaitz Zubiaga, Damiano Spina, Raquel Martinez, and Victor Fresno. 2014. Real–time classification of Twitter trends. *Journal of the Association for Information Science and Technology*.

Author Index